PRAISE FOR *THE GREEN GHETTO*

"Reading Vern Smith is to be reminded that urban America is more than the sum of its con jobs; it is a texture built of rips and stitches, a circus tent under which some of its wackiest animators hold forth—from Phyllis Diller to Carl Stalling, from Erich Sokol to Ishmael Reed. *The Green Ghetto* is electric, eccentric, extracellular madness."

– Michael Turner, author of *Hard Core Logo*

"*The Green Ghetto* is quite a ride . . . fasten your literary seatbelt because the twists and turns can be jarring. *The Green Ghetto* is a story with pulp fiction themes and snappy urban dialogue . . . Vern Smith is running right up front with the heavy hitters of American fiction."

– Roland S. Jefferson, author of *The School on 103rd Street*

"A beautiful mix of genre and literary fiction. The dialogue and prose snaps, crackles and flows down the page at a breakneck pace. Smith has put together a wild, comedic romp with literary overtones."

– Tony Nesca, author of *Junkyard Lucy*

"It's easy to forget that Detroit is a border town, but it is. The setting after 9/11 was a good choice and added to the sense of danger. I thought the book was well paced, funny and surprising (in a good way). Pynchon meets Elmore Leonard and they nip on over to Canada."

– John L. Sheppard, author of *Small Town Punk*

THE GREEN GHETTO

A NOVEL

BY

ARTHUR ELLIS AWARD FINALIST

VERN SMITH

ISBN: 978-1-7327097-0-6
Run Amok Books, 2019
First Edition

RunAmok

Printed in the U.S.A.

THE
GREEN
GHETTO

For Bobcat James

Fowler Stevens scanned page one of today's *Detroit Free Press* fluttering in the sewer steam, TERROR ALERT ELEVATED TO RED. Thinking he couldn't remember a time over the last 12 months when the meter wasn't at red, or at least orange, he gathered his undone peacoat in one hand, stepping back to read the green neon overhead—THE GENTLEMEN'S CHOICE BURLESQUE REVUE AND SHOW BAR—changeable black letters below.

FEATURING

CASSIDY WILDER: BEAST MISTRESS

CATHERINE D'LISH, ELYCE ECSTACY

WITH HOST SADAO SAFFRON

"And we know the host is selling how?"

Enid Bruckner booted a pebble with one of her black shitkickers, said, "Cassidy Wilder."

"The one performs with an anaconda started as a garter snake?" Fowler pointed at the glassed-in poster of a lanky peroxide blonde draped in a serpent. "Beast Mistress?"

"That's right." Enid nodded. "She's the one said Sadao was dealing out of here, his dressing room. That she, Beast Mistress, scored from him."

"Reliable source." Fowler nodded back in jerks. "Tamer of *Eunectes murinus* provides *primo* narc intel."

Prick, she thought, adjusting a mountain-climbing clip, her key-chain, attached to her first belt-loop on the right, keys tucked into her pocket. "You ready?"

Distracted by the soot-stained high-rise across Woodward, Fowler figured the rusty sign meant $99 a week, but then what the shit did he know from Detroit? Aside from the burlesque, it seemed that the only other establishment around here that hadn't been boarded up was Zane's Chinese, the smell of Peking roasted duck wafting.

"Zane's," Fowler said. "What the shit kind of name is that for a—"

Enid cut him off. "I told you and I said, are you ready?"

Fowler puffed his cheeks, said, "I guess," following Enid through the swinging doors. Across burgundy carpet stained with gum, ashes, and shoes, she badged a skinhead girl holding a cigarette in a peace sign behind the glass.

Through more swinging doors—this set upholstered with red leopard—Sadao Saffron was up there on stage, speaking into the mic, saying he'd taken a mistress. "And wow, does she ever do this neat thing during sex." Sadao looked high, caressing the buttons on his trademark saffron Arnold Palmer shirt. "She moves." Holding his hands more than a steering wheel apart now, wide load. "I'm saying hey, what are you doing down there, hey—hey."

A third-row regular stood, smoothing his spearmint leisure suit. He shouted that it was funny the first three times. And yet, Sadao said, he kept coming back, wearing the same suit, too.

Other end, same aisle, the man in one-piece garage overalls, Kirk embroidered on his chest, made a megaphone of his hands. "Try again, slant."

Slant? Sadao said he didn't think you could whisper shit like that in 2002, let alone stand and shout it, proud, like you're still mad about Pearl Harbor.

That was the thing Sadao both loved and hated about the Gentlemen's Choice Burlesque Revue and Show Bar—it wasn't from this day and age, no table dancing, nothing like that. Yet it hadn't descended into the icky politics of what they were calling neo-burlesque, either, girls with hairy armpits saying no hitting, biting the heads off silicone dildos.

But man, looking out now, anything but gentlemen, it was clear the place had seen better days, empty seats everywhere. And what was that smell, dirty socks? No, it was dirty socks meets stress sweat. Near the back, just settling in, Sadao didn't recognize the May-December couple: Disenchanted keener, very London Fog in his navy peacoat, with an older broad. Swingers, Sadao thought, pulling a laser keychain out of his hip pocket, pointing it at them.

"So, are you and your son in from out of town?"

Sadao figured he'd blown that one, too, that he should have kept the red laser dot dancing on lady's forehead for a few more seconds, asked some questions, then started in on her. But it was only a delayed reaction, everyone in the house, all 35 or so, taking a gander, busting up, having a good laugh at the couple's expense.

It was mean, maybe even small, but Sadao would take any edge he could, if the material was fresh. What had that Kirk called him again—slant. Fuck that. There were no sacred cows around here, not even Sadao. Like, the minute he gave anyone an inch, they'd find his Achilles and take his job, pretty much. Nobody was looking to cut Sadao slack, so why should he cut any? He shouldn't.

Tipping a pork-pie hat, also the color of saffron, Sadao said thank you, then just thanks. He pulled the mic close, nose kissing it, opening his left hand, holding it back. "And now, for your pleasure, I have for you, the Interesting Elyce Ecstasy."

Leisure suit, followed by Kirk, perved up to the front as Sadao ducked behind the satin curtain, nicotine staining the lace trim a rare oxblood. Backstage, Elyce sat on the third step up to their roomette, a two-slit black dress riding high on her thighs, gloved-hands on bare knees.

"I said you're on." Sadao threw an open hand out to the empty stage. "What?"

Through bangs of a popsicle-blue retro bob, she trained matching lenses on him, standing, über-tire heels giving her leverage as she slapped his face. "Interesting?"

Sadao let out a sigh, rubbed his cheek. "Look, we've been here a long time, Elyce." Pointing vaguely over his shoulder, booing. "It's just a lot of adjectives I have to come up with, nine years now, and I'm tired, honey. I'm tired."

She looked up to the rafters, gold paint peeling. "Remember when you used to call me the Exemplary Elyce Ecstasy?" Placing her hands on her hips, feathered elbows sticking out. "The Exquisite Elyce Ecstasy?"

"Yeah." Sadao said. "And hey, you sure were something in *Weekend at Bernie's II.*"

Slap. "And I don't move?"

"It's just a gag." Sadao, rubbed his cheek again, Elyce hitting him in the same spot, making him feel it. "A routine, ours."

"Yeah, well count me out of the routine, now on."

"Honey," Sadao said, "I don't think there are going to be many more routines. There's like nine dedicated burlesque houses left in America. Ten if you count Chris Owens' club in New Orleans, which I don't. It's more a nightclub dabbling in burlesque."

"Well then, let's not go out on a low note, okay Sadao?"

Someone was demanding a refund by the time Elyce started off, walking. No, she was doing that booty shuffle, shaking her can. Shutting them up as soon as she split the curtain, hips rolling surf-a-billy fast with the first licks of "Pipeline." Dick Dale, king of surf guitar, was covering with more fuel than all five of The Ventures. And that was before Stevie Ray Vaughan kicked in with the greasiest six-string slide run Sadao ever did hear. It was the way he could feel Dick Dale play, the reverb in his belly.

Up the steps, inside the roomette he shared with Elyce, Sadao locked the door, plopped his ass on a cracked orange vinyl chair. On the wall, stockings, capes, boas, gowns, and G-strings hung from framed shots of tease queens passing through—Gypsy Rose Lee, Bambi Lane, Tempest Storm, Sir Lady Java, local girl Lottie the Body. A signed poster of current queen Dita Von Teese doing her malnourished Bettie Page thing was mounted near a cinema card of Elyce from the movies, then a frame of Sadao coming up through the open-mic circuit.

Pending approvals, the Coleman Young Community Center would rise in place of this, the last of the old-style Detroit burlesques. For now, the neighborhood committee had issues with city bureaucrats, namely control issues, and sundry red tape.

Wondering how much time said issues were buying, Sadao pulled his buckskin car coat over his shoulders, unzipping a pocket within an inside seam, removing a baggie, four joints. Sparking the skinniest one up, inhaling, replacing the rest, he re-zipped, exhaling, thinking he'd better replenish, make another call to the cowboy before they lost customers. Sadao, he could only put them off for so long.

He looked up at the *Weekend at Bernie's II* cinema card—a studio shot, the dead guy inadvertently snatching Elyce's bikini top. Beautiful, Sadao thought, funny too. Flinching when four knocks peppered the door. "Who is it?"

"The folks from out of town, now how about an autograph for my son here?"

Shit, Sadao dashed the heater, said, "Spectators are not allowed."

Seeing the knob jiggle, he put the roach in his mouth, chewing, swallowing as they kicked through the door, splinters flying. And yes, it was the disenchanted keener, mousy hair gelled and combed back, a bit spiky, his heavy black glasses very Tokyo. Up close, Sadao said he seen him somewhere, but where? The movies? Maybe that was it. Was he the guy who videotaped himself getting it on with Andie MacDowell in that Steven Soderbergh flick? Like, it was an honor for Sadao to have such a celebrity in his midst.

Then he kept going, pushing it, pushing it too far. No sacred cows, remember? Eyes on the lady now, Sadao thought her smile was tight, too tight, all the way to her earlobes. She'd had some work done. "And check you out," he said. "You must be from the movies as well." Waiting a beat. "Tell me, who did your face? Oscar Mayer?"

Dick Dale and Stevie Ray Vaughan were picking fast now, really going, laying down the soundtrack to Sadao Saffron's life. This was the part where The Gentlemen's Choice Burlesque Revue and Show Bar was supposed to be packed, everyone laughing at what Sadao had to say. It was all he ever wanted.

CHAPTER TWO

Mitchell Hosowich was pleased as a puppy with two tails, and he didn't think he had the right. Ever since he started growing this here wacky-tobaccy shit, he'd been thinking maybe it was time to show a speck of maturity, go legit. Same time, touring his leaning barn—new raw boards mixed with original red—he couldn't help but stroke his horseshoe moustache with satisfaction. Breathing deeply through his nose, so musky it burned, he thought, no sir, not even that so-called comedian was going to slip a cow patty in today's fair-trade coffee tin.

All week, Sadao Saffron had been peskier than a real job, phoning, saying, bring more, Mitchell . . . I can only put them off so long, Mitchell—Mitchell, Mitchell, Mitchell . . .

Then last night's message said some swingers yonder downtown at the Gentlemen's Choice Burlesque done beat him like a leased jackass after Sadao asks the cougar, is that your son? And to the stud, are you the guy videoed himself rodeoing your best friend's wife in the movies? Apparently, Sadao'd also made some sort of remark about Oscar Mayer performing the lady's rhinoplasty, so Mitchell reckoned the comedian had it coming. No matter what Sadao thought, some cows had to be sacred, and Mitchell didn't see as how speaking poorly of a lady's beauty was ever a particularly smart strategy.

The rest of Sadao's message was mostly static, but they did what to his butt?

Mitchell figured Sadao must have been talking metaphorical on account of he was sorrier than a two-dollar watch about something. He was yapping about the Taliban when the cab went into the tunnel, Canada. Mitchell never could wrap his head around the fact that Windsor was south of Detroit. He figured Sadao was on his way to a gig over there, trying to be funny.

"The hell's my bible?" Mitchell said, feeling his back pockets, fronts.

6

Locating a pack of plain Top papers in his faded mustard shirt with snap-on buttons, he removed a tan sheet, pinching a sticky bud from a dried plant he named after that actress played the Bionic Woman—Lindsay Wagner, fine, wholesome—rolling a nice fatty, lighting, inhaling, thinking of the way things used to be.

Way back when, Mitchell didn't know dope from a donkey's dong, only that he was a young man bent on being the lone hand on his own land, his own man.

After getting a little cash together, maybe he'd figure out how to put the land to use, legally. Maybe, but whenever Mitchell started coming around to that way of thinking, he'd invariably ask himself, what came first, grants or farmers?

Regulations, stipulations, connotations—just like Glen Campbell sang in "Rhinestone Cowboy," there'd be a load of compromisin' if Mitchell went legit. Forms to fill, conditions to meet, bureaucrat booty to buss, and that wasn't farming, either. Asides, if there'd been a good thing about the great American rust-out, it was that this part of Detroit had gone rural again, wild. As one scribe so eloquently wrote in the *City Journal*, it had long ago reverted to prairie so lush that Natural Resources was exporting pheasants to improve the local gene pool. Yes, it had been written, and to Mitchell, that was poetry, for pockets of wild turkeys and wilder dogs roamed amid rabbits, Canucklehead geese, a bunch of snakes, and the odd coyote. More recently, there'd been rumors that Natural Resources was trying to tag its first white-tailed deer.

A deer, huh? What the hell was this now? Even if true, Mitchell sort of liked it this way. Only how the hell was a deer going to make it here? Poor thing, sooner or later it was going to trot into a Pinto's ass out on Joy Road, boom, then what?

Poor things one and all—Mitchell couldn't reckon how all the wild animals found their way to Detroit. In fact, if this deer thing was true, Mitchell figured some slicker had been being a bit of a devil all along, running critters in here from his cottage, like when folks started releasing their aquarium piranhas into the Detroit River in the '70s.

But a deer? Sure, it was possible. Mitchell had to shoot a poor silver fox—foaming, disoriented—no more than a month back outside the chicken den. There were raccoons, too, but even the slickers had them now on account of fewer garbage pick-ups, cutbacks all around.

Out here, the key difference was, that, aside from a small Hispanic community sprinkled in a few empty blocks over, the people were largely gone, just gone. Left to its own devices, most everything was overgrown with trees, vines with berries, grasses, and all sorts of wild blossoms, most notably gray-headed coneflowers, wild daisies, and violet thistle. So much so bureaucrats even came up with a high-fallutin' name for it over cheese sandwiches.

"The green ghetto," Mitchell said quietly, taking another hit, holding the smoke.

It wasn't any Petrified Forest, no. But, in Mitchell's case anyway, there was civic pride. Better, harvest and everything that built up to it was the part that kept him here, interested. It was the lingering, the sampling, the marveling at how old sticky sweet cannabis sativa survived tomato disease, the wilts, drought, and even those creepy crawlies done did a number on his nasturtiums a couple months back. Suet, Mitchell was aiming to eat those, the petals making for a succulent, colorful salad garnish. But when it came to his cash crop, Mother Nature would do this here weed no harm, other than the locusts in '88.

Damn grasshoppers'd eat anything, Mitchell told himself. Pruning as he smoked, putting some baggies together, he recalled the archives left in the basement—claims that rock formations near the southeast corner of his land were part of a fort, the site of some skirmish with the Canuckleheads, circa 1812. Or was it 1813?

Didn't matter. Mitchell didn't bother verifying that. To him, it was just a safe place to grow some fairly good Detroit dope—a Midwest Stonehenge dismissed as insignificant.

Moseying on in from the Polish suburb of Hamtramck, Mitchell struck his claim back in '74, the year Coleman Young became mayor. Same year 714 slickers went to the boneyard, murdered.

Got so bad at one point Coleman told criminals to hit the white side of 8 Mile Road as some sort of equal-opportunity deal. So yeah, pale face was on the run, Coleman left behind to sell off the badlands for overdue taxes, or a portion thereof. By now, they'd stopped leveling the burnt houses, or even boarding them up.

Last farmer to work the land, name of Fryer, sold out to speculators in the '50s, who lost their Levi's after the riots wiped out the real-estate market like a bad case of mad cow in '67.

Mitchell, in turn, snapped up his three dozen acres for $3,600 and change. As part of the package, he also had himself some key zoning exemptions to go with a couple barns, a farmhouse, and a pasture—all salvageable with a bit of elbow oil.

Every summer, he paid some kids to set up shop for a few weeks on the Livernois exit on I-94, selling tomatoes and corn that served as camouflage. Leftovers went to food co-ops, so right there he had himself a downright respectable front. It also helped that he took a few freelance gigs for appearance sakes, working on people's homes every winter in order to be seen as a contractor supplementing his modest farm income, wall-papering, painting, shit like that.

But yonder downtown on Woodward Avenue—no more than a mile or two from the burlesque—a new ballpark was named after a bank, the football field a car company. Folks were patronizing the new casinos, along with handfuls of little boutiques and eateries that had been springing up. Slowly, it was said, the people were coming back, and Mitchell, he couldn't reckon how much longer he'd be allowed to go on like this.

Catori Jacobs chose a stars-and-stripes bikini for the first anniversary of September 11, figuring gynecology row would see it as patriotic. Kind of like Jewel singing "God Bless America" during the seventh-inning stretch, tits half out of something between a flag and a tank top. For sure, Kate Smith would have been down with that.

Pulling up hemmed denim short-shorts, doing the button fly, she reached for thigh-high stretch-leathers with tie-dyed stitching, working her nines in, kneeling on the bed to get a look at herself in the mirror. The lopsided part in her coarse hair framed caramel freckles in an upside-down V. On her hips, a belt with jade details rode too high, so she loosened it a notch. Sliding into the buckskin car coat, feeling for the last few baggies along the zipper seams— she didn't like taking her stash downstairs into The Motown Hoedown any more than she liked leaving it here in her roomette above the place.

It's just that girls here could get competitive, and there'd been stories, most notably about that young stripper with the Brazilian —Danny Zalev, the owner, called it a Mohawk pussy—dousing Tabasco on the electric bull back in May. Freakin' strip joint with an electric bull. What part of Detroit had Mitchell Hosowich said this was? Farmer's ghetto, something like that? No, the Hoedown was on the outskirts of the green ghetto, that was it. The ghetto here was green.

Whatever, back in May, while two girls were off on a scare to the free clinic after unknowingly sitting in the asskick sauce, Cartori heard that someone broke into their roomettes upstairs, lockers. Of course, the one with the Mohawk pussy denied all, but Catori was thinking someone ransacked something when her one o'clock knocked a few minutes late. Voice on the other side of the door said, "It's Ronnie."

Catori removed two eighths from the zippered seam, undid the lock on her roomette door. Ronnie—Veronica Cake, she called herself—walked in, locked the door, reaching into a tiny purse, extending two twenties, a five.

Catori took the money, checking out what Veronica did to those poor Wranglers she was wearing. Six inches of material cut from the thighs, save the seams—wallah, denim garters. And yes, she was wearing a red-and-silver paisley handkerchief as a halter, classy.

"Also," Veronica said, "I want to buy for a friend, can we catch up again in a few hours?"

Catori said, "If I still have some."

"No—first time you're short, in what, four, five weeks? Everyone's going dry." Veronica brushed her curled bang, revealing a second eye—she did have two—white liner. "May as well be back in Wichita. It's hard to score in Wichita. That's where I'm from, by the way, you?"

Catori adjusted a natural suede five-gallon in the mirror, careful not to do that thing. But dammit she was biting her freakin' lip anyway, nervous habit. "Death Valley."

"C'mon."

"Better than here, warm, plus we have a national park. Detroit have a national park? I don't think so."

Veronica thought Death Valley was simply a park, nothing more, but didn't mention it on the way out.

Feeling for the last baggy in her car coat, Catori thought it odd that Ronnie was buying now and that she also wanted to score later. Why wouldn't Ronnie just buy everything at once? Did she need to make some money down on the floor? And did she want Catori to hold that last little bit? Ronnie didn't say.

Catori grabbed the bullwhip coiled on her inside door knob and left during the last leg of Dwight Yoakam's song, cutting it close now. Locking up, tilting her head down the stairs, she sang along with "Suspicious Minds," thinking how she preferred the Fine Young Cannibals' take. Preferred it? It was the best freakin' cover in the history of covers. The video didn't hurt either, Roland Gift glittering tangerine, shaming Elvis.

Dwight faded as she opened the gunmetal door, seeing the one with the Mohawk pussy down on one knee near the stage pole, pushing herself up. Good timing; RJ the DJ reminding all five patrons present she's available, two-for-one dances until four. Now put your hands together for Gina the Ballerina.

Gina the freakin' Ballerina—that Mitchell Hosowich swore Catori was Italian, too. Close enough to olive anyway, and no offence but it was probably best to take herself a stage name of Gina in a bucket of blood like this.

And bucket of blood—Catori had lived in ratfuck Ontario for 37 years and couldn't remember a Polack cowboy yet. Now here she's working for one saying something about white-tailed deer around here, trying to be so damn PC after he says make like you're Italian. And what did he call her for real? Oh yeah, Mitchell said Catori was a First Person of Canada, like she was the narrator of a CBC documentary.

Moving to the stage, Catori caught a scene on the TV over the bar. The sound was off, but she could see Bing Crosby wearing a tall hat, chatting up a redhead, big hair.

The drum intro to Cher's "Half-Breed" played on the speakers, inside joke to keep Catori sane, as she walked onstage. Dropping the bullwhip near the front where she could pick it up during song three, she heard that elder in her head saying maybe she had too much cream in her coffee for a card, white by law; preacher Wayne arguing, advocating for status on her behalf. Then, from the front row, she heard the one called Cooley.

"If there's a good thing came out of all this trouble, it's that everyone—and I mean everyone—is a comin' together. Look at her." Cooley pointed at Catori, her stars and stripes top. "She knows what day it is."

"An American girl," said Mickey Joseph, owner and operator of the nearby Mickey Joseph's Service Station. "One with a whiskey -stained soul, but an American girl nonetheless—you can tell."

Placing a folded towel on the electronic bull, mounting, Catori rocked slowly in first gear, watching Veronica through ferns near the back—hooking thumbs into belt loops, working the Wrangler garters down for some tight-faced swinger lady. Apparently, there was a roving club for that sort of thing around here. Clove and Butternut, the lifestyle people called it. And how would she feel about a trio? That's what they'd say. As soon as couples told you they were into swinging, next they'd be talking *ménage*.

Mitchell reached into the stall to stroke his horse's two-tone snout. When the otherwise all-white filly twitched, took a nip, neigh, he pulled back saying how he'd saved her, cared for her even though she wouldn't be mounted.

"And goddammit, Hasty Kiss. That's why I got you in the first place, to ride you."

The hell did Mitchell expect anyway? Poor thing had been so hopped up on go-go juice in her prime she'd run a 1:59 as a harness racer. Besides, she was good now, mostly, doing her job. Like the tomatoes and corn, Hasty just being out there grazing made it look a little more like a half-assed working farm. And ever since people started crashing airplanes into buildings a year ago today, Mitchell needed her to be out there, normalizing the place with her presence.

"Now more than ever," he told her, "what with the Federales running spots on CNN—locally on 2, 4, and 7. Some teenager looking into the camera, saying, 'This here's the dime bag Mitchell Hosowich sold me, messed me up bad. This here's the dime bag Mitchell Hosowich sold me done financed every martyr, tyrant, and rabble-rouser from bin Laden all the way back to Little Dick West.' How do I do that even a little, Hasty?"

Hasty Kiss twitched, took another nip, neigh. Mitchell said to hell with it, figuring, if he hustled, he might catch that First Person of Canada girl's early act yonder at the Hoedown, replenish her supplies. Watch her do that thing with the tattoo on her caboose, one word at a time. Make sure everything was keno with Danny Zalev, too. The hell'd Danny been anyway?

Zipping a dozen baggies into inside seams, he slid into his own buckskin coat, part of his system.

"Take care of your people, they'll take care of you," he always said.

Sadao, seven strippers, and a drag queen bingo caller were his newly minted Sandinistas—every one of them in buckskin this fall. Mitchell had swung a bulk deal with a nice Polish sweatshop, name of Nowokowski's, back home in Hamtramck that had been stuck on an order by the aforementioned and now disbanded gangbangers, saved some money. Whatever their demise, Mitchell couldn't see what a Nicaraguan political party tossed out by the CIA had to do with local drive-bys. Mrs. Nowokowski didn't want to discuss it. Still, Mitchell sort of liked the label, the way it said *bandito* without quite saying it.

Outside of the barn, he stumbled on the oval sinkhole worn at the door. Making a mental yellow-sticky to fill it in proper before winter, dragging his spurs up the gravel walkway—yeah, he liked his diggers as much as he liked saving—he brought Hasty Kiss to the pasture to join his cow Simmi, fencing them in. He heard the chickens squawking as he headed for the driveway, made another mental yellow-sticky to buy meal worm for the weekend.

Climbing into his Dodge Ram van, he noticed his homemade green-black tint job peeling at the far upper corner of the windshield, so he wetted his thumb, working some spit behind the filmy material, smoothing it out, there. Then he hit the ignition, 99.5 WYCD on the music box.

"Detroit's best country station," the DJ said, bringing up Johnny Cash, "The Beast in Me."

"Also Detroit's only country station," Mitchell shot back, reading the dashboard clock, 1:18 P.M., following the curves of his long driveway.

With Johnny, Christian as all get-up, lamenting the bad things he'd done, Mitchell turned right, north on what used to be Medland, passing a sign that said Unassumed Road. Careful to drive no more than 40, he figured Mickey Joseph's Service Station to be a half-mile from home. On the way by, he saw no one minding the shop, reckoned Mickey was having his liquid lunch at the Hoedown. A mile away, Mitchell's marker was a boarded-up bodega, Smeetons.

Another half-mile or so, something that looked kind of like creeping Charlie—they said don't eat the berries, even if the purple-grape-looking thingies did appear downright succulent, this time of year—ran in an angry weave over a box of a building. ZAKOR'S PRODUCE was still faintly stenciled out front, a crooked pine sprouting from the sidewalk, mellow-yellow dandelions leading up to that cardboard sign on the side of the road again.

IF YOU THINK IT'S DRY NOW
WAIT TIL NOVEMBER

Mitchell slowed, eyeballing the rearview. Getting his NESW visuals, he figured some sort of law officer or another must have put that sign there, just for him. Paranoid or not, he'd passed it a few times and didn't care for it. Hubris—that's what it was, hubris.

Satisfied he was alone, Mitchell veered onto the sidewalk, gave the gas a nudge.

"Wait 'til November." He blinked at himself in the mirror, noticing his gray-blue eyes pink on the edges, a little dilated, as he slowly rolled over the declaration. "We'll just see if it's dry then. We'll just see about this whole deal."

CHAPTER THREE

From the side of the Motown Hoedown's stage, Catori Jacobs rode the electric bull in low gear as Cher faded out. She watched an aging frat boy—and yes, he did look a little like James Spader, the actor—join Veronica and that Mrs. Robinson swinger lady in the shrubs. Then Catori heard The Clash, RJ the DJ playing the correct song from her cassette, "The Guns of Brixton." Bassist Paul Simonon was singing, almost talking, asking, when they kick down your door, how you gonna' come?

Sliding the buckskin halfway down her back, Catori closed her eyes, thinking at least there was one good thing about Michigan. By law, girls could not take their panties off, and who wanted to shave every day? Razor burn, she was saying inwardly when the bullwhip bit her throat. It coiled around her neck, tight. One hand at her windpipe, the other hanging onto the saddle, wide-eyed, she saw the blurry image of scuffling in the DJ booth, someone punching her bull into overdrive.

"Got it in fifth already," Cooley observed. "Look at her, fighting like a silver bass."

"Been around animals," added Mickey Joseph. "You can tell."

They groaned when she was tossed, her five-gallon rolling sideways, nipples peeking over the stars and stripes. Paul Simonon was repeating his refrain, you can crush us, you can bruise us, then the music stopped abruptly.

Looking up, Catori saw the swinger lady up close, her tight face smiling as she pulled hand over hand.

"DEA," Enid Bruckner said, reeling Catori to the edge of the stage. "Now let's see if we're holding any D on our person." Yanking her over the side.

Catori awkwardly landed on her boots, stumbling, standing upright. "You're going to strip search a stripper?"

Enid placed one hand on her mountain-climbing clip keychain attached to her front belt-loop, pointing at the floor with the other. "Pants down."

"You couldn't just wait a freakin' song?"

"Your pants. I told you and I said, down."

Catori scrunched her face to one side, undoing buttons with her thumb, shaking her short-shorts down to her boots. Looking at Enid, Catori said, "Ever wish you did more experimenting back at the academy?" One foot stepped out of the denim, then the other. Enid was still pointing, down. Catori looked at herself, patriotic panties. "Supposed to have at least this much on at all times, state law."

"Then how come you're wearing tearaways?" Enid turned sideways. "Fowler, a little help, please."

Fowler was watching the movie at the bar, Slim Pickens walking in. "What?"

Enid nodded at the girl. "Subdue the suspect."

Fowler looked at Enid, then Catori, back to Enid. "Why?"

"To intimidate her." Enid was impatient, like it should have been obvious, even if Fowler was new. "So that we might extract what we need. Can you do that? Intimidate the suspect?"

Holding his hands up like he didn't quite know what to do, awkward, Fowler took Catori's shoulders, turning her, pushing her up against the short stage wall, pulling the buckskin coat all the way off. Enid grabbed the back of Catori's hair, jack-knifing her over the stage. Saying stay, she reached for Catori's waistband, pulling the bottoms below her buttocks. Stepping back to read the tattoo—one word on the left cheek, another on the right—Enid leaned in, breathing Drambuie. "Comedian downtown at the burlesque tells a funny joke how you're selling." Sliding her hand down, pinching one of the words. "In the Hoedown."

Catori looked straight ahead into a mirror, seeing herself bent over, nice. Really nice. "Only thing I'm selling you're holding, my ass."

Enid looked to Fowler, rifling through Catori's buckskin. "Find anything?"

"This coat is clean as a gated community, same as her room."

"Take it anyway, evidence."

"Evidence of what?"

"Evidence of the comic sent us here, Sadao, had the same coat, custom job, same label, Sandinistas. Has eyes like Robert Downey Jr.'s mugshot, yet somehow he's also clean, maybe hidden pockets." Enid looked at Mickey Joseph, three other patrons. "Fowler's going take you to the pool room for drinks, tell you what's happening, official unofficial briefing, peace of mind."

Fowler looked concerned, money.

"Agency plastic." Enid looked back at the one with the Mohawk Pussy—tan vest open, silver dollar nipples. And hey, why wasn't she wearing pants? "Take the help with, and ask for gloves. We're out."

Passing a run-over prairie dog, poor thing, Mitchell sparked up at the top of the news break—suet, he was running late—Linda Lau reporting a bust on gangs of marijuana bandits using fishing boats to ship Canadian pot into Detroit, possible links to al-Qaeda, the Taliban, or both.

Mitchell pondered the key differences between al-Qaeda and the Taliban, counter-clockwising the volume when Linda Lau got to the weather, a dense air mass moving in. Yeah, Mitchell always allowed for the possibility that paranoia was in the mix. Just the same he'd cut back to 59 plants this year, down 20. Worst case, even one more had started to seem like too damn many. Like at 60, he was definitely financing some sort of religious Commies gonna blow up the Detroit-Windsor Tunnel.

Luckily, the African Violet Mix made up the difference per plant and then some, meaning he could grow more marijuana with fewer plants, less exposure.

Retailing at Gall's Hardware for $2.45 a bag, he'd started a dozen plants on the mix after reading a *High Times* article in July. Seeing instant results, all his Marys got a helping, another in August. Mitchell couldn't believe what the concoction was doing for his blooming herbs, either, the legal kind. Lavender more purple than a one-eyed people eater, soothingly fragrant flower bunches as thick as his wrist. And man, if some horticultural slicker could have seen the nutmeg thyme doubling as his lawn, a sea of tiny yellow flowers threatening a third bloom when Mitchell was only entitled to two, this far north.

He would have given everything another shot. But last time he stocked up, the kid at Gall's Hardware—Tyler's young son, name of Ivan—was working the cash. Pointing at one of the 20 bags, Ivan asked, did Mitchell have African Violets?

No, Mitchell had said, referring to the part on the bag about "other flowering plants." He had portulacas, young man, plus blooming herbs. Then Ivan rings it all up, saying that's a lot of portulacas, mister, and what kind of blooming herbs are you talking?

"Whole thing's getting to be more trouble than it's worth," Mitchell told himself, making a conscious decision to think about something else, anything.

That First Person of Canada girl he was on his way to see, for instance, came over to work The Motown Hoedown for Mitchell as a personal favor to Phil Legace, Mitchell's pseudo Mennonite drug buddy who ran a similar, but increasingly larger, operation yonder in Dresden, Ontario near Catori's reservation. What was it? Tadpole? No, it was Walpole—Walpole Island.

Mitchell had looked her name up, and point of fact: The name Catori was not Italian, a First Person website saying the name means she's happiest expressing herself creatively.

Phil said she had trouble—something about hogtying a young RCMP narc copping free feels—which was why she was here, hiding. Important thing was that she was clearing a good two-grand a week, and business was still business no matter what her tattoo said.

"Lucky You." Enid read the girl's double butt stamp aloud. "Still say you're not selling?"

Catori, bent over the foot of the stage, said, "My ass is so clean you can eat off it, lady."

Enid snapped on a yellow glove. "All you need to do is take me to your dealer, your source." Catori laughed when the latex touched her, Enid asking, "Something funny, Gina?"

"I'm just wondering if you have anything bigger." Catori, looked over her shoulder, waiting for a reaction, a response. The old broad smiled, sides of her face pulling tighter, what was left of her features fading into auburn highlights.

Whatever they were playing now on 99.5 WYCD, it wasn't country music, not hardly, not the way Mitchell knew country music. Even with the volume low, the song was making him ornery, agitated. He held the roach between his lips, reaching into the glove compartment for his own special stash of mental floss, a CD single of Neil Young doing "Home on the Range." Mitchell carefully removed the disc from the jewel case and dropped the platter in the player, cranking the volume, hearing the distorted guitar intro, then Neil's voice, and only his voice, humbly requesting a home where the buffalo roam.

Thinking how this year's batch was indeed a slow creeper, sort of sneaks up on you, Mitchell tossed the roach. He felt a bit warm —that Mal Sillars on News 4, supposed to be a meteorologist, said Indian Summer was done, the devil—so he fought out of his buckskin as he turned right on Joy Road, taking another right into the first driveway.

Out back, behind the Hoedown, Mitchell found the lot almost empty. Then a woman, someone he hadn't seen before, took the back door out, walking in front of him, purposefully.

Too old for a dancer, Mitchell thought, reaching to the sunflap for his aviators. Looking back at her through mirrored frames, he licked his lips, thinking, nice, this distance anyway. Yeah, this one had fine child-bearing hips flaring that tight ankle skirt, clay stitching. Plus, she must have been five-ten in her shitkickers, substantial, and Mitchell liked big girls on account of they tended to work harder. Those wispy side-bits hanging next to her ears like girl sideburns were cute, too. But, closing in on him now, what was with her face? It was tight, so tight. A girl that age had to moisturize. And whoa Nelly, what kind of badge was she flashing?

Enid Bruckner, DEA

Special Agent, Michigan

Mitchell read it two times, looked up, waiting for the law lady to say something. When she didn't, Mitchell said, "Can I help you?" Feeling his voice drowned out by the stereo, he said it louder, compensating. "Can I help you?"

"I hope Neil Young will remember Southern man don't need him around."

Mitchell was stunned, didn't know what she could mean quoting Skynyrd like that.

"The volume," Enid said, "off."

Mitchell reached out, killed the song just as Neil sang the last part about how the skies are not cloudy. Looking back, Mitchell said, "All apologies, ma'am. I'm just courting to the Hoedown here for some bark juice."

"Yeah, well, no courting just yet, Little Dick West."

Mitchell pushed his hat back, shucks. "You flirtin' with me?"

"Crime scene," Enid said, looking at his white straw Stetson, blue feather. Who was this guy, some kind of prairie pimp? She liked him already. "Maybe drug activities funding terror."

Mitchell stroked his moustache, said, "Pardon?"

"Sick new form of lashing out at perceived Yankee decadence." Enid pointed at Mitchell, back at the Hoedown. "Lots of chatter, FBI says, electronic, then zap—a Taliban-looking guy lands in the shrubs weekly with the same peeler. No lap dancing, mind you, just talking, likely replenishing her supply, and so, it would appear to be drug pushing for terrorism."

Mitchell couldn't reckon who the lady was trying to convince of what. Maybe he could see where this was going. "Drug pushing for terrorism, here?"

"It would appear," Enid said, "drug pushing for terrorism, here."

As it would also appear, she told Mitchell, this stripper sells it, gives the money to the Taliban-looking guy, who presumably gives it to the Taliban, and then the Taliban presumably uses the money to train people to fly planes into buildings, and other nefarious activities.

"Taliban-looking guy uses a dancer wears the flag as beach undies to sell their drugs to our people on the anniversary of 9/11, and that's about as anti-American as a Commie parade on Veterans Day." Enid glanced at the two-story building, red aluminum siding sun-bleached a dull pink. "This kind of place, also looks like drug involvement at the local level, so I'm asking you, cowboy, do you know any guys go by Muhammad?"

Muhammad? No, Mitchell didn't know any guys who went by Muhammad.

Seeing the younger detective walk outside carrying Catori's coat and bullwhip, Mitchell resisted the urge to look down at his own buckskin gathered about his hips, chatting up the DEA lady instead. "You telling me al-Qaeda done targeted the Hoedown?"

"Taliban, close enough."

Mitchell looked at the building, back to the lady DEA. "Are you sure somebody's not stringing you a whizzer?"

"You saying I'm being pissed on?"

"Whoa, Nelly." Mitchell held his hands high as he could in the van. "Would never speak to a lady in such a way, especially a law lady. What I'm saying is, are you sure somebody wasn't feeding you something the least bit mendacious?"

Enid squinted. "Men-what?"

"Mendacious," Mitchell said. He thought about defining the word, but didn't want to condescend, so he just left it there.

"Mendacious." Enid clicked her jaw, said she'd never heard of it, asked if it was some kind of Taliban cuisine. And how was it that he came to know so much about Taliban cuisine?

CHAPTER FOUR

Sadao Saffron gazed at the tiled ceiling, water stains, for several minutes before realizing he was awake. Turning over, getting a whiff of himself, same smell as The Gentlemen's Choice Burlesque, he looked at the GE clock radio on the bedside table, 1:44 P.M. By Sadao's calculations, he didn't get to sleep until around nine this morning, shortly after going to the front desk to pay for another day and putting the ixnay on room service. Told the guy he was tired, no disturbances, and that he, Sadao, could make his own bed, thanks.

Whatever happened last night—like, it was DE-fucking-A, serious shit—Sadao probably shouldn't have just smoked one of those last few joints he smuggled over. There was a time to smoke and a time to refrain, and he probably should learn to refrain from now on when he's already paranoid. From now on—what was he thinking smuggling anything into Canada? If Sadao kept pulling stunts like that, there wasn't going to be any from now on.

All of a sudden, after running the same drill for nine years—hosting the burlesque, selling for Mitchell on the side—the whole thing had been cranked up about a dozen notches.

It was the way that lady DEA got so mad when she couldn't find anything on him, breaking out the gloves. And what was that about a Taliban-looking guy? Sadao was Japanese-American, born here. He didn't know a Taliban guy. Why should he know a Taliban guy?

Like, Sadao was just lucky they didn't have a lookout waiting for him at all border crossings in the vicinity. Whatever Mitchell had gotten him into, this was a federal case.

Peeling back the tan coversheet, he got out of bed to crack the drapes. Sunny, no cops, and where was he again? That's right, The Travellers Choice Motel, Windsor, Ontario, Canada, less than a mile from the Ambassador Bridge. Uh huh, yeah, this actually a good thing, circumstances considered.

Back to bed, feverish, he reached for his cellphone and hit the power button, no juice. Damn battery was dead, spare back in

Detroit at his apartment, and Sadao didn't happen to have the charger handy. Sitting on the edge of the mattress, he checked his wallet for cash, a few hundred American plus littles. That would go further here, what with the exchange, so he went ahead and followed the directions decaled on the motel phone, dialing zero, plus one, plus the area-code, 313, plus the number. On the other end, it rang a half-dozen times or more, probably to give Hosowich time to run in from the field, clicking over to the answering machine again.

"Hello, you've reached Mitchell P. Hosowich at Mitchell P. Hosowich Farms. I'm tending to either critters or corn, so kindly leave a message, plus your number, plus the subject matter, so as I can be better prepared to lasso you later. Much obliged."

Sadao thought about it, deciding that he didn't want to leave anything else on tape. That anything he said could and would be used against him. Hanging up, he thought if Mitchell wasn't answering, maybe his shit was monitored. And if his shit was monitored, who knew why all that happened back at The Gentlemen's Choice Burlesque last night?

Reminding himself it couldn't be about anything good, especially with the questions about a Taliban guy, Sadao looked to the bedside table for the now creased cinema card from *Weekend at Bernie's II*, the dead guy snatching Elyce's top. Sadao had taken it out of its frame on the dressing room wall last night, folded it in his pocket before he fled. Elyce had to have more copies, right? Even if she didn't, in the mad rush Sadao had to have something to take with him, something personal, something from home until this thing blew over. He was looking at her picture again as soon as he was done dialing their apartment, hearing her answer on the first ring.

"Sadao?"

"Yeah, me."

"The hell did you do to the roomette?" Elyce said. "It's trashed."

"Me." Sadao shifted his weight, that pain again. "I didn't do anything. You should have seen what they did to me."

"Look, I come off stage last night, the roomette door's broken, lock's broken, panties everywhere. One of my G-strings is missing, the one with the emeralds."

Sadao blinked. "You mean fake emeralds?"

"Yeah, you got it?"

"No."

"Then how do you know that's the one missing."

"Because you don't have one with real emeralds." Sadao rubbed his eyes. "Jeez."

"Fine," Elyce said. "Someone else did it, right. Now what gives? I mean, my picture's gone, too, why?"

"That I did take."

"So you took my picture but not my panties?"

"Look." Sadao sighed. "I'm in some trouble, Elyce."

There was a pause, Elyce saying, "What kind?"

"I don't entirely know, and I don't want to get into it now, over the phone." Sadao held his head in his free hand. "Just called to say something."

"What's that?"

He picked up the cinema card, looking at Elyce again. Goddamn, she was finer than a third-rate Japanese-American comedian at the end of the line could rightfully expect.

"Sadao?"

He snapped out of it, yeah?

"You said you phoned to tell me something."

"Right." Sadao was still looking at her picture, breasts so full you wanted to stick your head between them and hide from the world. And her eyes, Sadao couldn't remember what color they really were ever since she started wearing matching lenses with her wigs. But they were just as beautiful in black-and-white. Dark, soft around the edges, something that told you her bitch pose was a mask. "I just wanted to say that you sure were something in *Weekend at Bernie's II*."

"Bastard." She banged the phone a couple times, hung up.

Sadao put the phone on the cradle and shook his head, wondering why that still got to her. Oh, he'd tried to explain. Told her he would've been happy to get interviewed by one of the bar rags, *The Metro Times*. Maybe they'd come around to do a retrospective once word came that they were closing the Gentlemen's Choice for sure, set a date. Until then, Sadao hadn't made his high-school paper. And Elyce, she actually had been in a movie. Even if it wasn't particularly good, Sadao would always say, name one good Elvis picture. She couldn't.

Like, whatever Elyce thought of the screenwriters, the director, the reviews, or Andrew McCarthy, the point was she had been reviewed, had been to Hollywood, had acted alongside Andrew McCarthy. Even if he never escaped his awkward '80s pigeonhole, how many girls could say they'd been there, acted with Andrew? Not a lot.

That being the case, Sadao felt that he ought to tease her, that it was his duty. He was genuinely trying to make her see that she'd accomplished all that. And ashamed? Are you kidding? Sadao didn't know if she was his for-always girl, but he was so damn proud of her for getting as far as she did.

Thinking she'd learn appreciate it one day, he stood the cinema card up against the clock radio and grabbed the phone. Again, he followed the long-distance directions, gave the cowboy another try. Getting no answer at the farm, Sadao was pissed. What was this, the third time? Had to be, he told himself, listening to that message, stupid cowboy saying he'd lasso you later.

Hearing the beep, finally, Sadao found himself shouting. Goddammit, he knew Mitchell was there, just knew it, so pick it up. P-I-C-K I-T U-P. C'mon, pick it the fuck up. He was about to say where he was staying, you call me, but he pulled back in time, disclosing only that they had to talk. That he'd call back tonight, collect because Sadao had to pay for each one of these calls, that he was hemorrhaging dough, and for Mitchell to be around, bye.

Hanging up, Sadao reached for his buckskin coat, thankful that Hosowich had done one thing right. No matter how many times those DEAs looked, they couldn't find the secret pockets, the seams. Then again, that's what made the chief of rhinoplasty so angry. Checking Sadao for keister stash, the DEA lady said, the sicky. It was like she enjoyed the ritual of pulling the rubber gloves on, dragging it out, telling Sadao exactly what she was going to do next before she did it, asking if he was ready. Like, what was Sadao going to say? No?

CHAPTER FIVE

Parked at the side of Unassumed Road, Fowler watched a color-ful bird, about three-feet tall, strut across the Jeep Cherokee's path. Leaning out the window, he said, "You're telling me we're still in Detroit proper?"

"That's right." Enid stood in the dandelion patch with her homemade sign propped up against her thigh, mending the frac-tured wooden legs with duct tape.

Fowler pointed at the bird. "Then what the shit is that?"

Enid looked, said, "Pheasant, proud male."

"I know the species. I mean, what's it doing in Detroit?"

"This's what they call a green ghetto. Urban ecosystem is fucked." Enid fished the hammer out of her toolbox, gently tapping the sign's legs back in the ground. "You know everyone left after the riots, half anyway. Here in particular, save for a few Latins and whatnot, it's a ghost town. Land was developed, supposed to be a big subdivision. But all they ended up doing was leveling some old homes. Over time, everything got overgrown. Animals came back —pheasants, Canadian geese, wild turkeys, all kinds of animals, even coyotes. Anyway, it's fucked up, is what it means to be a green ghetto. Nature takes over."

Fowler looked both ways on Unassumed Road, no humans. "It's a little more complicated than fucked up."

"You want to know more, academic, ask the assistant deputy director. Olin's a local history buff. Has a card says so, vice something of the historical society of something. Has a book breaks ghettos down into three types: One's race, two's economic, three's green. This one's the third. No people, just plants, animals. Hence the green ghetto."

"So, Unassumed Road," Fowler pointed at the street marker. "That supposed to be funny, an inside joke?"

Enid opened the driver-side door, looked at him oddly. "Means the city doesn't service it, doesn't assume responsibility, drive at your own risk. It's a city sign, Fowler."

"Huh," Fowler said. As Enid dumped her toolbox over her shoulder on the backseat floor, he read the homemade sign she had been repairing. "'If you think it's dry now wait 'til November.'" Turning to her. "You did this?"

"Intimidation purposes." Enid sat down, hit the ignition. "Something to get the natives running scared, rattled."

Fowler put his ring finger in his ear, scraped out some wax, flicked it out the window. "It's the goddamn prairie, said so yourself. Who the hell's going read it out here?"

"Drug people." Enid punched the transmission into drive. "Someone's rattled." Hitting the gas, tires crunching on gravel. "Who else would run my sign over but drug people mad at it? Who else would care enough? It's bait. You find the guy knocks down the sign, bang, you find a drug person who leads to another drug person who leads to terror funding." Tapping her temple. "Hip bone is connected to the leg bone. It's never just about the drugs."

Fowler watched Enid wipe her mouth with a red-and-silver paisley hanky, guiding the stardust-gray Jeep Cherokee south, en route to the I-94.

Alright, he thought, Enid was supposed to break him in. Fine, he was in fresh from the Baltimore drug squad. How long had he been in Detroit, three weeks? What the shit was he supposed to know about the urban prairie? Nobody mentioned the hinterlands during the interview process. And Fowler had to come down, what, six times? You'd think someone would've said something, the way they vetted him.

Didn't matter. Enid wasn't supposed to use dish gloves to check for keister stash. That much about DEA work Fowler already knew. He was going to document it, along with everything else he was already making a note of on his PC back at the office. For now, he was just a very junior man, so what the shit was he supposed to say, except, "Where to?"

"Menjo's. Girly-man bar Madonna made famous on West McNichols. Be there in 10."

Fowler leaned against his window, looking up at the clear blue sky. "Early to be bar hoping. Who's there?"

"Drag queen calls afternoon bingo," Enid said, passing a boarded-up, fire-burnt, tar-paper home. Nailed to the front door, a black-on-white sign with a pair of eyes read, THIS HOUSE IS BEING WATCHED, STOP HALLOWEEN ARSON. "Also selling."

"And we know this how?"

"Kendra."

"Kendra?" Fowler said.

"Kendra Mann, runner-up Miss Empress Michigan."

Fowler nodded, satisfied. "Another reliable source."

There it was, that smug attitude. Enid ignored it. "Winner runs bingo like a territory."

"Mind if we play a few cards?"

"No time." Enid glanced at him, back to the road. "Look, I'm telling you it's the same as the comedian at the burlesque, the peeler at the Hoedown—common thread being that they deal while doing gigs that don't pay, at least not enough. Gig's a front for dope selling."

"Due respect, common thread seems to be none of them are holding a girl named Mary."

"Doesn't matter." Enid approached the weather-beaten Medland Estates sign, which read backwards from this angle. She took a series of quick lefts and rights, finally another right onto Warren. "Soon as we find one holding off that list the comedian gave us, we have something to scare them with, get the supplier—the grail."

"The grail?" Now what was she talking about?

"The link, Fowler, between terror and drugs in Michigan. You're going to see how some shitbirds in Detroit lead right to the Taliban in Afghanistan."

"Link—what'd that cowboy say again? Sure someone's not stringing you a whizzer?"

Enid hung another right, this one onto Livernois. "I'm telling you, these people call themselves the Sandinistas. Says so inside their coats, behind the collar, Sandinistas."

"I thought we were Taliban hunting." Fowler wrinkled his nose, showed teeth. "So now you mean to say we're on the lookout for thought-provoking Nicaraguans?"

"Sandinistas means it's political, is what I'm saying." Enid pulled a pad of paper from the visor, handing it to Fowler, motioning to the Microsoft laptop between them. "And something makes me like that cowboy. Run his plates."

"I didn't see he had a coat, why him?"

"Found navy paint on my sign," Enid said, merging onto I-94. "Same as his van, also navy. And if he hit my sign, it's because it affected him. Made him mad."

Fowler watched as she went for the red-and-silver paisley hanky, wiping her mouth again. "Hey, may I ask, did you get that from Veronica Cake?"

Enid looked down at the hanky, back to the road, said, "No."

"Yes, you did." Fowler pointed at the hanky. "That's her top." Shaking his head. "That's appropriate in the workplace? To be wiping your mouth with a CI's top? I don't think so."

Upstairs at The Motown Hoedown, Catori was packing her things into grocery bags from Mitchell's glove box. Mitchell, he sat at the bar downstairs, and he could not believe what Mickey Joseph just said. The music had been off since Fowler commandeered the DJ booth. TV over the bar was still on that western, the sound on now. Mitchell reckoned it was *Stagecoach*, the 1966 version, watching Bing Crosby fire a handgun from his horse buggy. Mickey Joseph was explaining, again, what the DEA told him, when Channel 4 cut to that public service announcement. Instinctively, Mitchell shushed Mickey, focusing on the screen as the government spot cut from young person to young person.

The first said he helped murder families. He was followed by another who said it was innocent fun. A third helped kidnap people's dads. A girl said it was harmless. Next guy taught kids to kill, then the first young man piped in, having fun. Faces and voices were coming fast now, a kid who helped kill cops, more fun. The first young man said he helped a bomber get a fake passport, a girl adding that all the kids do it. She helped kill a judge. Yet another helped blow up buildings, to which a woman stated, "My life, my body." The screen flashed:

DRUG MONEY
SUPPORTS TERROR.
IF YOU BUY DRUGS,
YOU MIGHT TOO.

Finally, there was a woman. No face, just her voice saying, "It's not like I hurt anybody."

It was a brilliant piece of propaganda. Mitchell was objective enough to see that. He was also subjective enough to see that it was aimed at people like him. To get people looking at him, hating on him, calling the cops on him, and generally acting as a distraction to George W. Bush's secret agenda. To a certain extent, Mitchell blamed his predicament on this very ad. Same time, he blamed himself. What was he doing burning one on the way over? C'mon, man.

As the following Little Caesars spot played out, Channel 4 cut back to *Stagecoach*, an actor Mitchell didn't recognize beating back an Indian brandishing a tomahawk. Looking at Mickey Joseph, Mitchell was going to try, one last time, to get this whole thing straight.

"Now, even though your prices are a few cents higher, I've been buying gas from you going on 28 years, right?"

"Yeah," Mickey said. "Not another drop 14 minutes either way."

"Point of fact." Mitchell held his hands out, conceding. "That's why your prices are higher, and that's a reasonable stance. You offer a service. Service costs. But I've been a loyal customer all that time, right?"

Mickey thought on it, said yeah, okay. Mitchell had been loyal.

Mitchell looked over Mickey's shoulder at the poster on the wall, a red-haired cowgirl holding a bottle of shine riding a giant video camera rodeo-style: HARD LIQUOR AND PORN FESTIVAL, September 28. Yeah, Mitchell thought that was a good idea, mixing the two like that. Refocusing on Mickey, he said, "Then I want you to look me in the eye, tell me that girl done got bullwhipped on account of she's conspiring with the Taliban."

Mickey did like he was told, again, except Mickey said it was an A-rab the girl was working with, Mitchell noting the hard A. Also, Mickey said it was a different kind of A-rab, from what they called a bogue sleeper cell. Mitchell said Mickey must've meant rogue. No, Mickey meant bogue, adding that bogue A-rabs were al-Qaeda.

Mitchell brought his open hand down on the bar, slap. "That does it."

"What?"

"Goddammit, Mickey, if I find out you're stringing me a whizzer, I'll hold my nose, go to town, and patronize BP for all my oil and gas needs."

"That don't phase me a bit," Mickey said. "You're not a franchise man."

"Yeah, well I can be if my independent is lying to me about Taliban in my backyard."

"It's al-Qaeda."

Catori approached from behind with a knapsack and four over-filled Farmer Jack bags, telling Mickey that was so much bullshit, that al-Qaeda had nothing to do with it. Mitchell took two of the Jack's sacks, said c'mon.

He held the door. Catori stepped into the daylight first, walking out in jeans tucked into her boots. Up top, her torso was draped in a blue poncho with a crested horse. Mitchell passed her, opening the passenger side. Rounding the van, he scanned the lot, clear, dropping the bags behind the seat, jumping in, keying the ignition. "Now, I am sorry." Throwing it into reverse, backing out. "But Mickey Joseph looked me square in the eye, said you're working with Arabs, saying it wrong with the hard A. He says it's al-Qaeda. DEA lady says it's a Taliban-looking guy. Somebody's stringing me a whizzer."

"There was no Arab," Catori said. "Mickey was only told to say that. They all were."

Shifting into drive, Mitchell took a left on Joy, then another, south on Unassumed Road, saying he'd see that Catori got out of

Dodge with some greenbacks, but was she sure?

"The one with the tight face talks crazy shit." Catori massaged her temples. "What would al-Qaeda want with a honky tonk titty bar?"

"Law lady said it's a sick new form of lashing out against Yankee decadence."

Catori swatted that away. "All I know is that I'd just sold almost the last of it to—Veronica Cake, she calls herself."

"Wears so much powder she can't blush?"

"You're thinking of the one with the Mohawk pussy. Veronica Cake's supposed to look like Veronica Lake, actress with the peek-a-boo bangs."

"You can only see one of her eyes." Mitchell held a hand over half his face. "Girl with the one-eyed hairdo, that's who were talking?"

"Right." Catori managed a smile, a nod. "Ever since Kim Basinger played her in *L.A. Confidential*, every club has to have one. Anyway, Veronica's dancing in the shrubs for the DEAs, I'm on the bull. I close my eyes. It's the second song, brooding, then I hear a snap, whip around my neck like a lasso. Bitch uses my own whip to drag me off stage. Young one, Fowler, she calls him—looks like the guy from *Sex, Lies, and Videotape*—he holds me down while she says take me to your dealer, you. When I don't, she checks me for—she called it keister stash."

That seemed to interest Mitchell, his moustache stirring. "Sadao said something about his butt, but it was static." Putting a hand over his mouth when it occurred to him. "Said he was sorry about something. Mentioned the Taliban, too. Then he was going into the tunnel, Canada, more static."

"DEA woman said she did the same thing to him last night, that he was stoned, but clean. Said he had the same coat, that he told them where to find me. You know him, Sadao?"

Mitchell steered high, trying to smile, natural, duck the question. "Federales must have Danny Zalev's dingle berries on a skillet. He's set it so I could have a girl selling out of the Hoedown going on 14 of 16 years. Only exceptions being '88, locusts, and

'94, the first chopper program. Had to harvest a tad premature that year, dumped it on our mutual man in Canada, Phil. Very next week, some slicker in Inkster done shoots the chopper down with his varmint gun."

"Varmint gun? What about Danny? He say anything?"

"No." Mitchell said. "But then he didn't check in either."

"Danny's MIA, a dealer's gloved, he's sorry, everybody's talking about the Taliban, and you don't think to say anything to me? A little heads-up?"

"I told you, static on Sadao's message."

"Static." Her golden-brown eyes narrowed. "You told Phil I'd be safer than an ox on a hobby farm."

"Okay," Mitchell said, "okay."

"You talk about taking care of your people—you left me twisting in the wind, white man, exposed me to the DEA."

"Alright already, I said."

"Don't you alright already me." She looked at him hard, squinting. "Phil will slit your throat, he hears this. I'll slit your—"

"Look." Mitchell briefly took his hands off the wheel, framing a gap between his front teeth, a single gold chopper below. "First off, I come today specifically to make sure Danny's keno, so I was already on that. Second, I thought Sadao got it over something he said about a lady's rhinoplasty. He was also talking about some guy gets caught taping sex he has with his best friend's wife in the movies. What's that supposed to mean to me?"

"The one she calls Fowler, I told you." Catori reached back, raised her ass, pulled a cassette from her pocket. "Looks like James Spader—he gets it on with Andie MacDowell, an unfulfilled housewife taking vengeance on her husband, also cheating. That's who he meant."

"I know that now." Mitchell slid his aviator glasses down his nose, watching his eyes, quick in the sideview, still pink at the edges. "Danny, he been around?"

"Haven't seen him from Thursday," she said, checking out the console. "You have a tape player or just CDs?"

"Both formats." Mitchell pointed to two mounted components then to the glove box. "Some of each in there."

"I have something." She slid the tape into the player, hit play, Paul Simonon singing how some London outlaw feels like Ivan, born under the Brixton sun.

"Okay, okay," Mitchell said. Thinking of that kid hassling him over the African Violet Mix at Gall's Hardware, also name of Ivan, cutting the music. "Okay."

"Okay, what?"

"Sounds an itty-bit negatory just now. Also sounds like we got a hair in the butter." He slowed at the dandelion patch when he saw that the sign had already been resurrected. She leaned across his lap, smelling the oil of sage, putting an arm around him for balance, reading.

IF YOU THINK IT'S DRY NOW
WAIT TIL NOVEMBER.

"The hell?" Catori said. "You mean to tell me there's a freakin' sign in the road and you still didn't say anything? 'If you think it's dry now . . .' The hell does that mean?"

"Means we got to belly through the bush."

"Oh, no." She crossed her arms. "You're not bellying through my bush, old-timer."

Mitchell accelerated, clenching teeth. "Means it's time to make ourselves scarce. Federales involved, dirty one, right off her mental reservation."

"Hey."

Mitchell breathed slowly, speaking at the same pace. "Let's just say it, political correct." Lowering his voice so as there was less bite to it. "We got to go."

"Where?"

"Depends. All I know is I've got a lot of dope to unload, no time."

"You willing to cross the border?"

"Same thing I was thinking."

Then they both said it—Phil.

Sitting four tables back from Menjo's stage, Fowler Stevens looked over the back of some guy's head, a swirling salt-and-pepper cowlick, watching Empress Envy casually click her compact open. Touching up her lips while the machine in front of her made a sucking sound, a ping-pong ball with a number came to her through a caged canister chute. Fowler figured this was part of the act, primping, fussing for a few seconds, making them wait. He'd noticed the comedian last night do roughly the same thing. It wasn't so much what they were doing as how they were doing it, setting up their delivery.

"Twenty-one under the J," she said into the mic, plucking the ball from the hole. "J as in J-string."

Confused, Fowler looked at his card, red-ink dauber poised. "You mean G?" he said, raising his voice to be heard up at the front. "G as in G-string?"

Enid kicked him under the table. Up on stage, Envy shielded her eyes, looking through the glare at the direction of his voice. "J'es, under the J, I said. J as in J-string." By then, the machine was making that sucking sound, producing another ball. She reached for it, looking out to the audience, saying 33 under the O, her favorite letter. O as in Binjo was his name-O.

"Then it's BINGO!" a young black man shouted from the second row of tables.

Envy waved him up, her corkscrew hair changing from blue to red as she moved around in different lights. Checking out the guy's natural, then his outfit, off-white cords and a matching turtleneck, she reminded him it was *inapropos* to wear white after Labor Day. He said his threads were off-white, meaning it was totally *apropos* to wear them whenever he damn well wanted.

By the time he was saying, besides, this is a turtleneck, Envy wasn't listening. Concentrating instead, verifying his daubed numbers, she decided enough jived, throwing her hands behind her head, saying, "J'es, boom-boom, j'ou are the winner of a hundred-dollar credit at downtown Detroit's MGM Grand Casino." Thrusting her hips, gyrating. "Boom-boom." Nodding. "Boom-boom, j'es."

Most of the afternoon crowd was standing up with her, already a little tipsy, doing their own little dances, thrusting their hips, too, boom-boom.

Empress Envy, speaking over them now, reminded all that today's proceeds would be donated to the Greater Detroit PWA Alliance. So play early and often, because the next prize up would be a George Foreman Grill, boom-boom, j'es, courtesy of Target, valued at $49.99. Also, all winners would have their names entered in a draw to win a free hot-tub courtesy of Sundance Spas, water jets shooting up your whoopsie-daisy. Now she'd be right back for another game after a quick meeting with a friendly stranger, boom-boom.

Watching her nod to some young, tanned blond guy—about 21 or 22, dressed in an old-style Adidas suit, pastel blue with gold details—near the stage, Fowler and Enid looked at each other, then back to the side of the stage as Envy and her companion disappeared behind it. Enid stood and said, "Empress says she's meeting a friendly stranger. Dope for she's going to get high, probable cause for our involvement, so let's get involved."

"Sounded more like she's doing some sailor at the glory hole." Fowler held up his card. "How's about just one more game?"

Enid pointed to the side of the stage then at herself. "I'm going back there to do my job, catch the bitch in the act, find the dope, then her source, the cowboy. Cowboy's the grail to the Sandinistas, which, of course, leads right back to the poppy fields in Afghanistan."

Fowler made a sniffing sound, looking at the card and dauber in his hands, placing them on the table. He'd never heard of anything linking the Sandinistas to the Taliban, but he was standing up anyway, going through the motions and following Enid through the crowd. A waiter dressed in black Levi's and matching shirt, tarnished brass buttons, pulled up in front of them at the mouth of the hallway, saying the back area was for employees only.

"DEA," Enid said.

That, she could see, made the guy less sure of his cock and balls. He was blinking, eyes jumpy like maybe he was holding. "Is this the part where you're supposed to show me ID?"

Fowler went for his badge. Enid put an arm up, holding him off. She smiled at the guy asks the DEA for ID, running her left hand over her mouth, distracting him before she brought her right up from the hip, open as it shot up, the heel of her hand connecting with his nose. "There's your ID, son." Enid looked at him on his back now, holding his face, looking though his fingers, a bit of blood. Still looking at him, she spoke to Fowler, saying c'mon. Fowler followed her through the doorway, past the kitchen. When they came to a supply room, Enid drew her Les Baer Prowler III, checking the eight-round magazine, looking at Fowler. "Well?"

Well, what?"

"Are you going to arm yourself?"

"It's maybe a drag queen bingo caller in there with her dude." Fowler held a hand out. "Hardly what I'd call a gun situation."

Enid looked at him. "This is Detroit, and I told you and I said, arm yourself."

Reluctantly, Fowler complied, reaching inside his peacoat for the Glock 17 clipped to his belt, watching Enid go for the knob, throwing the supply door open. Fowler produced a yellow Bic, flicked it, lighting the space, nothing except a bucket, mops, sundry cleaning supplies, and industrial-sized rolls of toilet paper.

"I think Al Capone was here," Fowler said. "Want I should call Geraldo? I'll make it look like you're not after the attention."

Enid reached inside the bucket, retrieving some used yellow dish gloves, pocketing the pair, shutting the door, leading Fowler down to the end of the hall, the EXIT. Nodding once, she threw the door open, catching the jogging suit guy passing a roach clip attached to a keychain to the drag queen. Enid saw it right away. Now she had one of those buckskin car-coats, same as the others, thrown over her shoulders. Seeing the guns, jogging-suit pretty boy took off, leaving Envy standing next to a garbage container holding the jay.

"Empress Envy?" Enid said, taking a step closer.

Mirroring the move, still holding the roach clip, Envy said, "J'es?"

Enid produced ID this time. "DEA, now turn around, hands on that garbage bin."

Envy looked at the cobalt-blue container. Holding out her perfectly manicured hands, red-and-navy nails, she said, "I don't think so, lady." By then, Enid was breaking out the gloves, Envy looking back and forth at the two of them. "J'ou gonna look up my whoopsie-daisy?"

Enid rubbed her hands together, the material squeaking. "J'es."

CHAPTER SIX

Mitchell reached over Catori's legs into his glove box, grabbed a new CD, *When The Man Comes Around*, Johnny Cash. Tearing the wrap as he drove, he put the platter in the player. First, Johnny spoke of a beast saying come see this white horse. Catori didn't know what to make of it, Johnny all fire and brimstone. And was he singing about virgins trimming wigs? Wicks, Mitchell said he thought the virgins were trimming their wicks. The CD would be out in November. Maybe he'd know for sure once the reviews started. Catori wanted to know how he had the album if it wasn't out. Mitchell said he'd been gifted an advance copy from a DJ at WDET, one of his direct customers. Whatever, Catori had never heard Johnny this way, and she didn't like it.

At the end, Johnny stopped singing and went back to speaking of the pale horse, that the name of set upon it was death, and hell followed with him.

"Hell followed?" Catori hit the stop button. "That's not negatory?"

Mitchell thought about arguing how Johnny was talking all metaphorical until she put a thumbnail to a bubble in the windshield tinting. Slapping her hand, he said don't pick. Catori wasn't picking, just smoothing it. Well, the do-it-yourself kit cost Mitchell $29.99 at People's Auto Parts, so whatever she was doing, could she please stop. She crossed her arms, fine.

He nodded as they drove by his pasture, his Australian Shepherds, Wolfie and Lou, play-fighting on a bale of hay. Simmi was chewing something, giving the familiar van a lazy moo.

"Okay, now what is that?" Catori said.

"Simmi." Mitchell said. "Simmental-Hereford cross."

She looked up and down the road. "You got power lines? Bad water?"

"No, why?"

"Why?" Catori said, her voice rising as she faced Mitchell's profile. "Something's growing out of that cow's freakin' head."

"Third horn," Mitchell said proudly. "Ten inches, almost. I measured."

Catori sighed, looking at the two-tone cow. "Same kind of things where I'm from, downstream from chemical valley, birth defects."

"Simmi's natural. Uncommon, like the cow patty on John Boy's face, but natural nonetheless. Like, she's okay."

"Why didn't you cut it off? That's what you're supposed to do with girl cows anyway—cut off their horns."

Mitchell blinked, wistful. "She's beautiful, as God intended."

Now here we go with the God squad, Catori thought, checking out the premises. Huge clumps of lavender, hearty nutmeg thyme for his lawn, gray-headed coneflowers. It looked like a dope man's place, rock-a-billy paisley the way colors blended when she let her eyes out of focus. She saw cacti of various breeds and sizes in clay pots on the front porch, likely the cowboy's way of saying don't even think about knocking here, come around back.

Motioning to the outhouse covered in whitewashed tar-paper, she asked, did Mitchell rent? He shook his head, uh-uh, no, turning into his drive lined with thousands of sundial-white portulacas, tiny yellow centers, passing a sign drenched in ivy.

MITCHELL P. HOSOWICH FARMS

"I'm the big sugar here." He put the van into park. "And that honey pot, what you call an outhouse, is for show, historical purposes. Running water's inside, plumbing."

Plumbing—Catori thought she should be impressed.

Soon as Mitchell got out, Lou, the smaller of the two Australian Shepherds, was jumping all around. Mitchell bent down to meet her at eye level. "Licking, licking, licking—all she does," Mitchell said, standing upright, scratching the dog behind the ears, wincing at a half-dozen bald spots on her red and white fur. "Been getting her cortisone shots for years."

Catori looked the animal over, bare welts. "Seems to be working."

Mitchell waved the sarcasm off, impatient. "Problem is, it's not working for very long anymore. Dr. Mallard, what I call the vet, says next step is to give Lou this experimental drug, Ovaban, a hormone. Might make her worse. If it doesn't work, might even give her diabetes."

"Think maybe it's time, to you know."

Mitchell bent down again as Wolfie made some noise, jogging over, Mitchell smoothing out his fur. "Don't say that."

Catori said, "Now what's wrong with this one?"

"Nothing." Mitchell covered his animal's ears. "He just has two different colored eyes, gray-white, burnt orange. David Bowie has the same condition, heterochromia."

Big word, Catori thought. "I'm not talking about that. He has a cough."

"That's his bark," Mitchell said, walking away, the animal making that sound again.

"Sure sounds like a cough." Catori followed him up the walk, checking out his land. "You ever thought of being a real farmer, legit?"

"No."

"Why not?"

Mitchell sucked his lips in. "Because, what came first, young lady, grants or farmers?"

Grants or farmers—was he some psycho civil libertarian out of a Steve Earle song, his grand pappi putting the gover'ment man down? It was just so freakin' American she didn't bother, nodding to the far side of the pasture, his pale horse. "Mind if I take her for a spin?"

"A spin." He rounded a hammock hanging near the porch, keying his door. "She's just to look at, Hasty Kiss. Bent on wearing no man's saddle." Whirling an index around his temple. "Loco if you even think about stepping up. She knows if you want to ride her, senses it."

"You some mail-order cowboy, can't break a pale horse, bad, like Johnny says?"

Mitchell let that go, taking his boots off at the landing. Catori did likewise, looking at a snapshot on the washstand. It seemed to be Mitchell but she had to ask: "Why would you bother getting a picture framed with your eyes closed?"

"That's not me. That there's the last known photo of Little Dick West, and he's dead."

"He the one who died in shame after a botched train job?" She looked at the picture, back at Mitchell. "Got 50 dollars?"

"Common misconception. Time came when a lucky law man just plain caught up with Little Dick, shot him. No shame. And it was more like 300 dollars, big money in 1898."

Saying they had the same moustache, understandable mistake, she followed him into the living room. Signs of the new century consisted of a Dell computer on a small white Formica desk, a stack of CDs from the library next to a package of blank discs, Fugi, and a portable Sony to play the bootleg discs. An antique scale sat on a shelf over the fireplace along with Little Dick West display plates and Red Rose Tea animals.

On a raw pine bookshelf she noticed a row of cassettes, *Yoga for Rodeo Riders*, volumes 1 through 13, between old books on the civil war, a surgery manual among them. Did he do his own operatin' too, his own doctorin'? The freak.

Another shelf held vintage Larry McMurtry paperbacks wrapped in plastic, a tattered copy of *Animal Farm*, and neat stacks of magazines, *High Times* and *Horse & Rider*. Original western landscapes hung on the walls among three numbered prints by Mexican artist Diego Rivera. On the floor, Catori saw old jeans strewn about—two pairs on the *faux* cowhide loveseat, another on the Singer. "You sew?"

"Buy my range clothes used, mend them," Mitchell said, hitching his jeans, off-color patch above the left knee. "These here're Tommy's. I get most everything by the pound." Taking off his Stetson, showing her the inside rim, gold lettering, CALGARY CONVENTION & VISTOR'S BUREAU. "Found this in mint condition—mint."

She had to admit he had a sweet smile when he got to talking about saving. Plus, he was decent, good with animals. But his hair was a freakin' fire hazard, everywhere, and nice 'stache. Was Little Dick West his dude or something?

Watching him walk to the phone, she asked why did he have

an answering machine? He said to take messages, young lady. No, she meant why didn't he use voicemail, reliable? He pointed at the tan button phone, saying she knew what he did for a living, right? Well, he didn't want Michigan Bell to have his business messages. This way, Mitchell had control, old school.

And about what she was saying before—mail-order cowboy, huh? Point of Fact: Did she know how many times men out-numbered women on the prairie? Eight to one, she said, why? Drawing his chin to his chest, he said it was more like ten to one, recalling a time when a cowboy had to sew—stitches, patches, tents, sleeping bags, hems, whatever.

Point made, he hit the answering machine's play button, hearing a hang-up. Then the second message, Sadao's voice: "Goddammit Mitchell, I know you're there, so pick it up. P-I-C-K I-T U-P. C'mon, pick it the fuck up, man. Listen, I'm staying—I'm not even telling you, but we have to talk. I'll call tonight, collect because, like, I have to pay for each of these calls and I'm hemorrhaging dough. Be around, bye."

Hearing the click, Mitchell watched the machine play the next message. From the tinny speaker, his dancer at the Booby Trap on Michigan Avenue, name of Wyndi, spoke of two DEAs, the Taliban, and gloves. For now, she was out of town, at a friend's, see ya.

Next, Champagne from the Black Orchid Cabaret on Livernois said her buckskin had been seized. And what was she supposed to do, Mitchell?

He hit erase as the phone rang again. "Envy," he said, reading call display.

"Another stripper?" Catori said.

"Lovely drag queen calls bingo, sells on the side." Picking up, speaking into the phone, Mitchell answered, saying, "Hail the empress." Hearing another string of words from another freaked-out Sandinista.

It just happened, and Stryker took off in his stupid little tracksuit because he probably did have something up his ass, Envy's diamond. What kind of man was that? Leaving her alone while they looked up her whoopsie-daisy . . .

Mitchell waited until it was over, said, "Did they find anything in your coat?"

Envy said, "She don't see the secret compartments, no. But she take my buckskin, seize it, she said. Going to find some baggies. J'ou got trouble, Hosowich?"

"Never mind about me. You got a stage out?"

"Stage—I run from the stage, you idiot. That is where tight face finds me, the stage."

"Stagecoach," Mitchell said. "I mean, do you have transportation out of town?"

Envy paused, said, "I have Stryker's keys, his Firefly. His keychain was attached to his roach clip. He leaves me holding his roach clip, his keys."

Mitchell pictured all six-two of her in that little car, big, multicolored corkscrew hair. "Then get in and drive."

When Mitchell finally said bye, hung up, he looked into Catori's glare. She said, "Now I don't feel so bad."

"Why?"

"Looks like you left all of us twisting."

Mitchell said no, there were three more.

Catori looked at him, said, "Well?"

"Well what?"

"Aren't you going to call them?"

Fowler sat dutifully on the Jeep Cherokee's passenger side, watching Enid drive east on McNichols toward Hill Street, passing a brownstone industrial building with a cross on the front, the Explosion Ministry of Deliverance, Pastor Leon Montgomery.

Okay, all these people they were shaking down were on the edge, marginalized, even by Detroit standards. But dealers or not, Fowler didn't see how any of them had a part in sending anthrax to Dan Rather. And the Taliban would have stoned that Envy soon as they figured out she was a dude dressed like a lady. They were against that sort of thing, right? Besides, she wasn't wearing a headscarf. So, if they didn't kill her for a being a dude dressed like a lady, they'd stone her for showing her hair. Maybe they'd do it just for the gambling. Wasn't that against being Taliban, too? Gambling?

If Enid wanted to take Fowler to bars all day under the guise of rooting out something more sinister than the odd jay, hey man, he was just going to go with the flow and document her into the ground. Even the gay bingo was alright. Fowler didn't judge. In fact, he had a hunch that he had a pretty good card up next, maybe good enough to win that George Foreman grill, a $49.99 value, if only they'd stuck it out another few minutes.

Main thing was work was getting to be fun. It wasn't that Fowler was warming to Enid. He wasn't, and he couldn't figure why she seemed to enjoy putting her hand in people's whoopsie-daisies, either. Yeah, Fowler was making a mental note to document this stuff for sure, add it to his computer files back at the shop. It's just that pissing Enid off was getting to be good sport, finding new buttons to push, and she was so affected by the little things Fowler said, like, "So when do I get to drive?"

"When you're the senior partner," Enid said, merging the Jeep Cherokee onto I-75. "Senior agent drives here. That's the way."

"Okay, alright, personal question, let me ask you something."

Enid made a pistol of her right hand, aiming at a Honda. "Fire away, partner."

"Back in Baltimore, checking for keister stash was generally something that was, hmm, endured. We did it, but only when we really, really had to."

"And the question is?" Enid readjusted her rearview, took a look, nothing encroaching. "Are you going to tell me how candy-ass bureaucrats in Maryland do a job with Uncle Sam looking over their shoulders, or are you going to put a question?"

"Well, I'm not judging, but you seem to be taking me to a lot of naughty little places."

Naughty little places, huh? Enid said that's where drugs moved, in places folks went to be stimulated. That's where you found out who was dealing to the dealers, which always leads to a bigger operation. She thought Fowler knew that much.

"Course there's action at the ballet." He watched Enid get cut off by one of those new Chrysler products built to look old, a PT Cruiser, the bumper sticker saying, IT AIN'T OVER TIL YOUR BROTHER COUNTS THE VOTES. "But, it's just that you seem to like checking for keister stash. I mean, you really, really seem to like it."

Very seriously, she told Fowler he was playing with the worst of the worst now, Detroiters. Moreover, a DEA agent had greater powers than your garden-variety narc, and that was because DEAs didn't just solve drug cases. No, DEAs solved cases about drugs that were connected to worse things.

"And this is where the terrorism fits in?" Fowler said.

Enid gave the kid a sad smile. Eyes back on the freeway, she said, "That's right, and if we have to snap on the odd pair of rubber gloves to protect ourselves, so be it."

Fowler turned his mouth down, nodding. "I guess you're right."

"You know I am."

"Yeah, you put your hand up enough assholes, sooner or later you're going to pull out Osama bin Laden himself." Fowler snapped his fingers. "Smoke 'em out of their holes, like Bush said."

Enid bit the inside of her cheek, hitting the indicator, pulling onto the shoulder beneath a fenced-in pedestrian overpass. Slamming the Cherokee into park before quite coming to a full stop, lurching, she said, "You, calling me a perv, how dare you."

"Perv?" Fowler looked up at a kid in Pistons gear watching them. "I didn't say that."

"It was implied, Fowler, implied. And look, if a peeler or a girly man is holding, they're most likely holding in the place we least want to check, their ass, okay?"

"Okay."

"Alright then. I don't want to hear anything for the next little while."

"I just—"

"Nothing."

Fowler flashed a glance at her, said, "You got it."

"I told you and I said, stop."

"Fine." He held up his hands, looking away when he couldn't beat back his smile. "I'm not one of those people who can't take a hint."

Enid put the Cherokee into drive, looked in her sideview, hit the indicator. "Goddammit, Fowler, you always have to get the last word in."

Fowler waited, just like the comedian and the drag queen, then he said, "No I don't."

Mitchell thought aloud about how he'd rather be trolling thrift shops for funky cowboy gear, an old-style hat, maybe even a poncho like Clint Eastwood wore in the spaghetti trilogy. But hushpuppies, after managing to get to his remaining three girls in time, he was on the phone, again, making small talk with Phil's wife. Charlene Legace was saying Mitchell would be interested in this. Phil had been given a Diego Rivera original in lieu of payment though one of his biker contacts at the church. What's this, Mitchell wanted to know, when did Phil start accepting art as payment? Was it even advisable?

Well, Charlene said, it was more like the guy owed Phil from a while back, and this was the best he could come up with, a stolen Diego Rivera. Mitchell wondered about what eventually came of the guy who paid Phil with art. And suet, before Mitchell could so much as ask the title of the piece, curious if he'd seen it—must have been a lesser known work if Phil had it—Charlene was complaining about how she hated this time of year.

She'd been giving the field the full treatment, smelly compost, worm droppings. All the while Phil was sitting on his fat ass making like some sort of half-baked Mennonite saint, smoking too much of his own product.

Much as Mitchell was trying to empathize—he was genuinely sorry about that, the injustice—he didn't appreciate Charlene talking openly on the phone. So yeah, he said he had to get around to putting compost down, too. That aside, he did need to talk to Phil. Alright, Charlene got it, Mitchell didn't want to talk to her. No, no, Mitchell said he enjoyed speaking with Charlene, using flowery language to say something about the poetry of her speech. It was just that Mitchell had farmer-to-farmer-type issues. Soon enough, Charlene handed the phone over, and Mitchell was telling Phil he had a hair in the butter. Then, in code, what kind of a deal could Mitchell get on this amount, assuming Mitchell could get it across the border to Phil.

"Hypothetical, Phil. If I was to bet on a team name of the 59ers to win, what would an establishment yonder in Canada pay on a wager like that?"

Phil thought back how it was the 76ers in '94, code. "It is good like last time?"

"Ever introduce Mary to Violet?" Mitchell said.

"I read the article in *High Times*, have heard good things, but does it work?"

Mitchell didn't like the way Phil mentioned *High Times* on the phone, sloppy, but reckoned he better not push Phil around on a pesky etiquette matter just now. "Oh yeah. Makes for a nice, slow creeper. Takes a while to kick in, but when it does . . ."

"Okay, five days it will take me, maybe five weeks, but can do. Same terms as with the 76ers, per 59er, indexed for inflation from '94."

"Favorably?" Mitchell said.

"Favorably, 60 on the 59. Just get your team on the bus."

Mitchell said, "Fair enough, but none of this five-days, five-weeks nonsense. Even indexed favorably, you're getting a deal, means cash on the barrelhead."

Taking a deep breath, a moment, Phil exhaled, said, "Fair enough."

"Yeah, well you just make sure to have that dough handy, you Amish devil."

"We are not Amish, just Mennonite."

"Sorry," Mitchell said. "Also make sure it's 60 American, the bet pays in. No confusion like last time, you saying we didn't say U.S. dollars. And did I also tell you have it handy?"

"Mitchell, you know I have it handy. Why, just the other day, some young man was saying, 'Phil, where do you keep your money?' You know what I told him?"

Mitchell said, "I'll bite, Phil."

"I told him, young man, when I want some money, I just go get some."

"Yeah, well then go get some, in American." Mitchell pinched the bridge between his eyes. "Okay, now we'll see you late tonight, early tomorrow. Be ready."

Late tonight, early tomorrow—that was fast. Phil said it sounded like Mitchell had two hairs in the butter . . . Hello, was Mitchell there? It was supposed to be funny—two hairs. Did Mitchell get it?

Yeah, Mitchell got it. Sorry to be a pill, Phil, but let's just say this wasn't no hootenanny Mitchell was dealing with. And yes, Catori was still safe as an ox on a hobby farm. Then yes again, she was still cuter than a 'lil red truck. See you, bye.

Hanging up, Mitchell watched Catori close the fridge. She was holding a bag of Uncle Herschel's Soya Jerky. Looking at his face then down at his Endangered Species belt buckle—the words "The Giant Panda" engraved above the actual beastie—she asked did the buckle come with a tax receipt?

"I got one rule." Mitchell looked down at his stocking feet. "No contributing to the global slavery of animals. Means no critter-eatin' in this house, none."

"You're telling me you're a vegan farmer?"

"Slaughtering isn't necessary for survival, not anymore." Mitchell pointed at the bag of soya jerky. "All these new products gives one plenty of options over flesh. Besides, didn't your people tell of a time when the land was lived on only by talking critters? I thought First Persons are supposed to treat the land, water, and critters with respect, always. Especially critters—you have got to learn to treat critters as your fellows, to talk to 'em as such. I'm sure it was the First Persons said something about that."

Catori nodded, inwardly saying patience, white man. Telling her what it was to be Native, talking critters—the urban dude rancher had to be high, again. "Look, we don't hunt for sport, no. When we do hunt, we're taught to use the whole animal, not just the meat. See, there's nothing wrong with the eating part. It's the wasting part—like cutting off sharks' fins, then throwing them back to drown—that's wrong. The disrespect."

"Yeah, well I bet the poor little tasties feel slightly dissed on the way down your gullet."

She pointed at his London Calf leathers near the door. "But you wear 'em."

"Previously-enjoyed is okay." Mitchell tugged at his orange-brown leather belt. "Already dead, bought by the pound, means I'm not creating demand, just recycling what's been discarded, political. Won't see any of my greenbacks going to The Gap, Levi's. Now tonight, we're on with Phil."

She crossed the room, sitting in the middle of the loveseat, open palms on each cushion. "Have a plan to get us there?"

"Think so." He picked up the *Free Press* sports, folding the page. "Plymouth Whalers are playing a neutral site game against the Windsor Spitfires at Joe Louis Arena, pre-season action."

"You want to go to a hockey game? Now?"

Mitchell looked at her, back to the paper. "I'm saying we cross over with the hockey crowd heading home to Windsor, blend. Lots of people in Windsor love those Spits, will risk their lives to come see 'em here at the Joe. After the game, they'll be going home together in small mobs." Pointing south. "All we have to do is dress the part like we've been to the game and time it so as we're going back to Canada with them."

All we have to do—she waited for the rest.

Mitchell said, "What do you want, greenbacks?"

She thought quickly, said 25 percent.

Twenty-five—suet, if she helped get his dope to Dresden, she could have 33⅓, wholesale. She did the math. That was like 20-grand, right? Right, Mitchell said. She said that's the first time anyone bargained up. He brought his hands into a praying position, saying, then you've never been to a fire sale, young lady. She just thought he was feeling freakin' guilty.

CHAPTER SEVEN

Second floor, northwest corner of 431 Howard, Fowler was on all fours, spreading buckskin car coats out on the carpet. Now that he'd found the seams, he knew where to find the tiny zippers.

A few feet away, Enid Bruckner spoke into the phone at her desk, saying yes, Mr. Gall, your young son Ivan will receive a plaque. That was indeed valuable information about the cowboy buying up your African Violet Mix. Expect a call for the community service awards. No sir, she wouldn't forget. Thanks again, she said, hanging up, waiting... Waiting until Fowler bit.

"You want to pick me a letter, Vanna?"

Enid's nostrils contracted. Oh, she was going to fix that smug attitude yet. "Listen, if this adds the way I calculate, we've got the middleman, supplier, and grower. And I love that cowboy from the Hoedown for all three, makes him top Sandinista."

"Again," Fowler said, "Sandinistas are from Nicaragua."

"Yeah, so?"

"It's just that . . ." Fowler trailed off. Just for a second he was trying not to be condescending. Really, really trying. "I think he's of Polish descent, Hosowich."

Enid blew that off. "First, I'm pretty sure he's the one wrecked my sign, navy paint. Second, I got a voicemail from Veronica Cake."

"Yet another reliable source. Girl named Cake calls, you put E.F. Hutton on hold."

Enid chopped at the air. "Veronica says the cowboy left with Gina the Ballerina after us."

Fowler sat against the soft blue wall. The shade, he figured, was likely picked by a consultant who surmised that it was balmy, soothing. "So far, you maybe have a cowboy banging a peeler who blows the odd roach." He pointed at the floor, Catori's buckskin. "I found what amounts to an eighth, loose joints, in her coat, simple possession. She'll be long gone when we go back. As for the Polish Nicaraguan, I did run his plates, nothing."

"Thing is." Enid pointed to the phone. "Gall's Hardware has his plates on the list of people buying excessive amounts of African Violet Mix."

"How'd you know where he shops?"

"Checked the phone book, found the closest hardware."

Neat trick, but Fowler still didn't see the point. "He's a farmer, grows things."

She rummaged in her desk, handing him a faxed magazine article, *High Times.*

FLY HIGHER ON AFRICAN VIOLET MIX

Fowler took it from her, reading the lede aloud. "For growers big and small, African Violet Mix is the new elixir." Pointing at a photo of the product near the top of the page. "But then it also says it's for African Violets 'and other flowering plants.' Says so right on the bag."

"So?"

"So, maybe he has lots of African Violets or other flowering plants. That's not cause."

Enid couldn't figure Fowler. This Hosowich buys 25 bags of voodoo steroid dope shit, probably on the counsel of some high-ranking beach boogaloo, and Fowler says it's no big deal. Like maybe he, Fowler, was a pothead, empathetic, advocating on behalf of green fiends everywhere.

She finally said, "Look, Gall's been doing as all hardwares were told—taking plates of those buying too much, suspicious when they ask for it, chatting them up, keeping records." Plucking the article from Fowler's hands, she waved it at him, wake up. "This Hosowich buys five bags in early summer, tests it. Buys 20 a month later when he knows it works. Tyler's son, Ivan, wrote it down, documented it. Cowboy says he's buying it for his portulacas and rare herbs. Ivan tells him that's a lot of portulacas, mister, and what kind of rare herbs was that?"

Fowler scratched his ankle. Maybe the guy did have a lot of flowers and herbs. Fowler still didn't see how that linked this Hosowich to terror, let alone weed. But then what the shit did

Fowler know? "Hey," he said. "Can I do it next time?"

"Do what?"

"You know."

"Can you do what?" Olin Blue walked into the office carrying a dated historical textbook in his right hand, *Detroit: Paris of the Midwest* by Bryce Fields, a green bottle of Perrier in the other. When Fowler didn't answer, Olin had to repeat himself, and that pissed him off, like maybe the young operative was buying time to dream up a lie. "Can you do what, Fowler?"

Originally, Fowler had been asking Enid if he could check the farmer for keister stash, as if he wanted to do that, kidding. But looking at the boss, all serious, Fowler said, "Just asking if I can drive. DEA ran my license, right? You know I have a clean record, no tickets since '91."

Olin looked at Enid. "You don't let him drive?"

"He's not senior agent."

Olin pursed, what a hard case. "Let him take the wheel next time. Might need his skills sharp to drive you to the hospital one day."

Looking at her face, features pretty much gone, Olin thought somebody ought to tell her to stop it with the surgery. While it wasn't going to be Olin, he couldn't help but shake his head at the sight of her. "Business," he said. "What's up with your 50-foot tall dope ring?"

Enid pointed at the buckskin car-coat on the floor, telling Olin about the secret zippers, then the Sandinistas, the labels. She told Olin how the Sandinista part made it political. And it all led back to a grower in the green ghetto, something larger from there.

"Alleged grower," Fowler told Olin. "Should see this guy, right out of Roy Rogers."

Enid shot Fowler a look, shut up. "Important thing is he's buying excessive amounts of African Violet Mix, like an article says in *High Times*. He's maybe also into pimping."

Pimping now? Olin looked at Fowler. What did he think?

Fowler told Olin the same thing he told Enid. "We found a farmer buys farming supplies maybe bangs a peeler blows the odd roach. I still don't see how this has anything to with"—looking to Enid—"what did you call them?"

She contracted her nostrils, said nothing.

Fowler snapped his fingers, said, "Guys that go by Muhammad."

Enid couldn't believe the submarining prick, playing the race card for the black man. "I believe I said Taliban."

"Right. You also said guys that go by Muhammad."

"Where did you say this?" Olin looked at Enid. "In the field?"

When Enid didn't answer, Fowler jumped in. "She asked the cowboy, did he know any guys went by Muhammad?"

"It's 2002." Olin shook his head, no. "You can't say shit like that in representation of a federal office. Happens again, I have to cover my ass, put you in the sensitivity training where the white hippie chick with cat-poop hair, likely a doper herself, tells you, do everything Michael Moore says. Is that what you want? To do everything Michael Moore says?"

No, Enid didn't want to do everything Michael Moore says.

"Whatever," Fowler said. "I don't see as how it has anything to do with terror, funding terror, etcetera. Just some slacker farmer in"—snapping his fingers—"what kind of ghetto?"

"Green," Enid said. Okay, she didn't see malice there.

"Yes." Fowler was into it now, pointing at Enid, looking at Olin. "She said you said something about three kinds of ghettos, green being one." Nodding to Olin's textbook. "That you know the area's history and shit."

Dumbass white boy saying and shit to the assistant deputy director, him. Olin spoke, cautious. "You honestly interested?"

Yes, Fowler was interested, honestly.

Assured the kid wasn't mocking, Olin nodded down the hall, his office. "Happen to have some books you can look at."

"Can we learn this lesson in the morning?" Enid held out her watch, 5:28. "Got to go."

Olin looked at her behind Fowler. "You're off the clock. I'm not approving overtime."

"Not asking."

"I am directing you to attend that farm in the ayem—not

tonight. If your farmer's there now, he'll be there in the morning." Looking at Fowler, Olin said, "C'mon," turning, starting towards his office.

Mitchell had thought about doing a quickie job of shucking everything off the main stems and haphazardly trimming the fruit, leaves and all. But there was no time. He'd best just keep doing what he was doing, working fast. He'd already taken his machete to all 59 plants. After that, he ran over the stubs with the tractor. One good rain would take care of the rest and muddy up any obvious evidence.

He was back in the barn now, jamming entire plants, stem and all, into empty paint airtights he'd put aside for just such an emergency, ever since he had to unload quickly in '94. That load of paint tins Mitchell paid top dollar for yonder at Sears, last minute. This time, he'd planned ahead, bought up a huge lot on eBay for little more than shipping. eBay was proving to be a great source for his cowboy essentials, and who wanted to pay retail?

Before sealing the cans, Mitchell threw in vapor-seal bags of cayenne pepper he'd been using to keep the raccoons away, something that would be equally effective at buggering the senses of any frisky border dogs. Poor things, made to work for the meat-eating man, against Mitchell no less. After the cayenne bags, he'd drop in a couple dryer sheets, something to really mess with the turncoat hounds.

Oh man, Mitchell could hardly afford to do it like this. Eliminating the middleman, having his own group of dealers, freelancing—that was the only way to both stay under the radar and make this work, financially. Mitchell always kept his crop modest, small change in the Detroit dope trade. Maximizing profits, his dealers were getting $3,000 off the sum of each plant in the clubs, Mitchell taking 65 percent for a high five-figure, tax-free income, most years.

But now he was doing it again, counting Phil in, just like when they had the chopper program in '94, and that was about as sour a seed as Mitchell felt the gods of *ganja* ought to make him swallow. Bad enough, because, after packing, Mitchell still had to get his manifest into Canada, then about an hour east to Dresden.

And oh yeah, Mitchell was such a nice guy he promised the First Person of Canada girl, calling him white man now, 33⅓ percent.

Doing the math, down to about a thousand bucks a plant—and that was before paying Catori—he had 40K coming. So, he asked himself, is it worth it?

Not hardly, but then Mitchell wasn't the kind to abandon a crop on account of adversity. Same time, it wasn't like he was connected downtown, and who wanted to deal with the slickers? Yonder, they'd slit your throat for a nickel bag. So imagine if Mitchell drove down, said, hey slickers, here I have 59 tins of delicious Detroit dope I need to move fast. Let me do you a deal.

Do 'em a deal—they'd just take it, so if Mitchell was cutting Phil and the girl in, it was because he didn't see as how he had options.

"Don't even think about it," he said, sealing another airtight, loading it into the van backed up to the barn. "Only six or seven to go. Just keep doing like you're doing. That, and mind getting ahead of yourself. You'll be fine."

Right now, he was just staying focused on the task at hand, forcing wilting plants into airtights like one might stuff a square pizza box into a round garbage can—any way he could. When he was done, he hid his Remington M700 Varmint-Synthetic rifle in a roll of industrial-sized wallpaper, burying it with some other rolls. He cleaned up after that, wrapped any waste in paper bags then fired up the barbecue and burned everything that needed burning.

Olin had nowhere to go, so he suggested the three of them order in. Fowler snapped his fingers, said he'd been wanting to try Zane's ever since he smelled their Peking roasted duck across Woodward last night. Olin was good with that, rounding out dinner with Szechuan noodles, rice, and spicy garlic greens. Enid didn't say anything about the order, *gratis* for the DEA.

Enid was stabbing at the duck when Olin turned in his chair to pull a book from the polished mahogany shelves behind his desk. He pushed it across the coffee table at Fowler—*The New American Ghetto*, photo-essay type-thing by Camilo José Vergara.

Pointing at the book with a chopstick as Fowler opened it, Olin took a pull on his Perrier, said, "Vergara's thesis is that there are three main types of ghettos." Showing a thumb. "First you've got your institutionalized ghettos, projects." Showing an index. "Two, immigrant or racial ghettos like we have in Mexican town, black ghettos downtown, 90 percent black. And Hamtramck was one of the biggest Polish ghettos in North America."

"Cowboy we're pursuing is Polack, Hosowich." Enid pushed her plate aside. "Now let's everyone eat up because we have to go get 'em."

No, Olin told her, tomorrow. Again, that was a directive. Also, don't say Polack, another directive. Then, pointing at the book, speaking to Fowler, Olin said, "Third type of ghetto Vergara ID'd is green. Green ghetto, unlike the others, is marked by a lack of people. Or, as Vergara says, 'by depopulation and by vacant land and ruins overgrown by nature.'"

Enid asked if anyone had a fork. Olin looked in the bag, said no, but there was cutlery in the kitchen. Enid didn't think it was wise to leave Fowler and Olin alone, said she'd make do.

Upside down, Olin flipped pages, showing Fowler a picture of a man harvesting peppers from a plot on Rosa Parks Boulevard. "That's what makes the green ghetto an enigma. Other ghettos, populations vary. Sometimes over-populated, sometimes under, but people live there. Here." Olin pointed at a framed map on his wall, the Briggs neighborhood. "Not so much. Even when people do live there, it's mostly white. Probably has something to do with Briggs, former Tigers owner, said no black would ever wear the Old English D."

"I did not know that." Fowler flipped through pages. "Are you saying I can borrow this?"

No, Olin was not saying Fowler could borrow the book, rare, but he could attend Olin's office to refer to it, if he was careful. Just so Fowler was forewarned, if Olin had a criticism of Vergara's work, it was that the he simply asked questions, such as how do we interpret what's left behind? That frustrated Olin because he paid cash-money thinking Vergara would better serve the reader by answering such queries. Anyone could ask. Vergara was the expert. That aside, Olin thought Vergara's portrayal of the Briggs community—torched houses, vacant lots, failing infrastructure— showed America a ghetto it wasn't used to, something other than black.

"Most folks never even heard of green ghettos, like Briggs and well beyond where you're talking, yet all rustbelt cities have at least one." Olin looked at Enid, then the map. "Show me where's your urban dude rancher."

Enid came around the desk, stabbed the framed map with a chopstick, eight or ten miles northwest of Briggs.

"Just about the ghost suburbs, some Hispanic," Olin said. "It was supposed to be a subdivision proper way back when, Medland Estates, named after war hero, Dick Medland. Leveled a bunch of stuff, including." Reaching to his shelf, Olin pulled another book, mostly text, flipping pages until he came across an image. "This." He pointed to rock formations, something that could have been part of a crude fort. "War landmark back when we were fighting the British, via Canada, circa 1812-13. And did you know they, the Brits, briefly took over Detroit?" Olin waited for Fowler to shake his head, no. "Yeah, bunch of them set up fort here, a fort in a hostile territory. Had it in their heads they were going to take over from Detroit."

"What we do to them?" Fowler said.

Olin coughed into his fist, said, "Eventually beat them back, shot them, with key assistance from Medland, hero marksman. Point is, developers got an order to level what was left of the fort and then they didn't go through with the improvements, the construction. A historical landmark ruined for nothing, disgusting."

"Yeah," Enid said. "Well, that's where we're going."

"Not until morning, as directed." Olin nodded at the window, the sun about to set. "Days are getting shorter, dark soon. Out there, there's not even streetlights. Not a good place to be on a fishing expedition at night. You don't want to drive way northwest of Briggs where you're talking now, the green ghetto proper. Do it tomorrow, first light."

Enid pushed loose strands out of her eyes, said, "You a cop—afraid of the dark?"

Olin didn't hesitate to answer. "Yes, especially when it's dark with wild animals not supposed to be here hiding in the tall grass with their feed bags on. For those animals, coyotes, it's supper." Olin nodded at the map. "Heard they even have a deer now."

"Deer," Enid said. "The fuck did a deer get out there?"

"I imagine somebody put it," Olin said. "They also have foxes, snakes, rattlers."

"Okay, okay. There's no rattlers."

"Goddammit, Enid, stop arguing fact," Olin said. "Deal with it."

"Fine. They have snakes. But maybe if we weren't sitting around here learning all this very valuable historical information, we wouldn't have to worry about it, the dark."

Oh man, Olin didn't like the disrespect. And did she say something about very valuable historical information? As soon as Olin got out of here, he was going to sit down and write a book on the subject, show everybody, if only he could figure out a hook. *The Green Ghetto of Detroit* by Olin Blue? Perhaps, but the certain part was that he was out of here in seven months. Next April, he was retired, and here's this pasty bitch, face tighter than a snare drum, saying he's afraid of the dark.

"Alright," Olin said, nodding to Fowler. "Maybe this has been a time waste, teaching the recruit about communities he's policing. But as much as you question, maybe you'll be the assistant deputy director one day, make the big calls. Until then, it's me saying if you go to the green ghetto now, you could get there but maybe can't find your farmer, and you have animals not supposed to be there, people-hunting. No sense in going to this area when it's dark."

Enid said, "Also no sense in going after he's moved his dope."

"I'm telling you, don't." Olin pointed in stabs, giving it to her.

"I'm ordering you, don't. I'm directing you, don't. Understood? Go in the morning."

Fine, Enid looked at the carpet. But then could they just call it a day already? She'd take Fowler back to his hotel on Cass, the Ansonia, get herself home. Then she'd pick him up in the morning, visit the farmer early.

Olin set his eyes on her, said, "See that you do." Turning to Fowler. "You know about the pheasants? In the green ghetto here, they have so many pheasants the state exports them so as to improve the local gene pool."

CHAPTER EIGHT

Mitchell stumbled on the sinkhole again on his way out the barn. Damn hole had been like that since last summer, so you'd think he would've acted on one of his mental yellow stickies and done a half-ass job of filling the thing in. Just a few shovels would have done the trick. But no, just like the sign in the road, Sadao's phone call, whatever else Mitchell should have paid attention to, he'd let it slide. He was always letting it slide.

Mitchell's ability to make like water off a duck was something he appreciated about himself, never minding inconveniences. Scolding counter girls over tax, how was that going to make things better? But now he was getting cranky over the minutia, some ever-growing prairie pothole affecting him. Cursing as he made his way inside, he passed Catori sleeping on the loveseat. Down the hall, he threw his clothes into the hamper. No sense in calling out to the border critters, hey doggies, smell my threads, come get me.

In the washroom, he placed pages of an edition of last week's *Free Press* on the floor, retrieved his hair kit from a gold gift-box under the sink. Selecting the number-one tool, plugging the clippers in, he cut his straggly blond-gray locks down to nothing, fuzz, in minutes. Then he turned the thing on his 'stache and lamb chops, reducing everything to stubble, neat.

Job done, he collected the newspapers, mindful not to get hair on the floor, dropping the whole mess into a Kentucky Derby garbage can, circa Secretariat, and stepped into his clawfoot tub to shower down. He pulled the curtain around the oval circumference, closing his eyes, letting hot water hit him full on his face, scrubbing with Irish Spring. Next, after massaging his scalp with the Burt's Bees Rosemary Mint Shampoo Bar, he used a small brush and Burt's toothpaste, going to work on his hands, getting the green out from beneath his sticky fingernails.

Cuticles clean but raw, he switched bars again, this time going for his Emu Oil soap bar. It was wrong, Mitchell knew it, and the guilty pleasure stopped him from researching what parts of the poor Emu birds were being ground up for his comfort, the lather. It couldn't have been a nice demise, but Mitchell's hands were always a couple steps from hamburger, this time of year. Emu soap, $1.19 a bar downtown at the Cass Corridor Food Co-op, was the only thing that offered relief.

And suet, why hadn't he worn gloves? The way his hands had been covered in juice, sticky, kind of musky, he had himself a little contact high kicking in. Yes, it was a slow creeper and Mitchell needed to be stoned at this moment about as much as Custer needed a bigger hat when the Cheyenne caught up with him at Little Bighorn.

Whatever, it was what it was, so Mitchell tried singing. He had a Burt's bar for shaving, too, lathering it while he sampled Johnny Cash's "A Boy Named Sue." But it didn't take, didn't feel right the way Johnny was disrespecting the fear, over-confident. That's exactly why Johnny spent three days in the clink after trying to smuggle a few thousand amphetamines into El Paso back in '55, came out for gospel after that.

Next, Mitchell tried "The Beast in Me." Not Johnny's cover he'd heard on Detroit's only country station, but the original by Johnny's former son-in-law, Nick Lowe. Nick's take was more melancholy than Johnny's self-flagellation on the first volume of the *American Recordings* series. But no matter the singer, the songwriter had obviously been beating the hell out of himself, feeling guilty about something, and Mitchell still didn't think he'd done anything mean-spirited. That made "The Beast in Me" unfair to Mitchell, personally.

Kristofferson wasn't going to be of solace and neither was Hank, both of them on too much about the hard stuff, hooch. Eventually, Mitchell settled on "Home on the Range." Not the old campfire version. No, Mitchell was singing the strung-out Neil Young cover he'd played in the van. It was from the soundtrack of that movie about the journalist calls himself Gonzo, played by Bill Murray, who gives a fellow reporter LSD on an airplane when the guy clearly asked for aspirin. Aside from covertly substituting LSD for aspirin being ethically challenged, Mitchell didn't remember much about the flick. But that cut by Neil always felt so good it hurt.

It was the way he was warbling, something between singing and moaning, giving a tired old range tune new meaning in its desperate hopefulness. Especially when he got to the part about how the deer and the antelope play. That always did it to Mitchell, left him on the edge of welling up, wishing he was born 120 years earlier, simpler times. Course, even if Mitchell was born back when, he would have been into some nasty business or another. Probably selling snake oil to solve all your problems, or something, working like hell to get out of work, someone hatin' on him and chasin' on him, no matter.

This time or that, it just comes a day when, like Johnny sang, any person had the man coming around—even the slicker stock-traders—and this was just Mitchell's day.

What, he asked himself, hosing off the last of the lather. Did he think someone was going to do him a solid? Didn't he see, even way back when, that one day the man was going to come around to collect Mitchell for being the only thing he'd ever wanted to be? No, Mitchell thought, stepping out to towel dry. He'd just been hoping, wishfully, that being the lone hand on his own land wouldn't raise anyone's dander.

This was just his turn to pay for all that free living, and he was going through his toilet time deliberately, rubbing Burt's Bees salve into his tender paws, spraying on the same brand pit juice, the oil of sage oil, fresh.

He could now feel how the hot shower had loosened him enough to try that routine he'd been learning from the *Yoga for Rodeo Riders* tapes. The bridge pose, something to relax him and strengthen muscles at the same time.

Spreading out his towel on the floor, he lay down on his back, placing his knees at a 90-degree angle. "Press your navel towards your spine, lifting your hips high off the floor as possible," he said, recalling the tape's instructions. Holding the pose for 15 breaths, he repeated three times, before standing, rubbing some Vitamin E cream into his face, then getting dressed.

He walked into the living room in baggy Lee painters and a

black collared shirt with silver details, calling out to the girl, procrastinating when she didn't answer. He looked out the window and goddammit if she wasn't bareback riding that wild horse of his and whipping around a half-assed lasso in the beautiful pollution of a Detroit sunset.

Kicking into Birkenstocks, he dragged his tired feet outside, mouth open. Almost a shadow in front of the blood-red sun, Catori steered to the pasture's edge, throwing the lasso over his shoulders.

"Where'd you learn that kind of cowgirlin'?" he said, fighting out of it. "Phil said you done hogtied an RCMP lawman..." Trailing off, waving it away. "None of my business. But I mean, man, you do throw a long loop, young lady."

"I'm Ojibway. We work a lot with rope." She smirked, looked down at him, clean cut without his moustache and grizzle. Rode hard, leathery around the eyes, mouth, sure. But he was handsome now, even if he had left her twisting in the wind. His hair was short, bristly, smelled nice, too. Was that Irish Spring? No, Irish Spring plus sage plus something. Almost minty, she told herself, reaching behind his neck, pulling his black collar back for the label. "What Goes Around." Turning her mouth down. "Not bad."

"Also by the pound," he said, pointing at Hasty. "How?"

Catori pressed her lips together.

"Political correct," Mitchell said. "I mean, how did you mount her?"

She scratched Hasty between the ears, said, "Did like you told me. I just talked to her like a fellow creature, talked her through it, and she responded, let me step up."

Bashful, Mitchell covered his smile as he spoke, minding his gold chopper. "Well maybe it'd be different if there was meat for Hasty to smell on your breath. And you're so in touch with the animals—how come you never heard of a cow with three horns?"

"I've heard old-timer, only where I come from it's attributed to birth defects, like I said, downstream from chemical valley. Now let me ask, how come your horse won't let you up?"

Used to be, Mitchell explained, Hasty Kiss was a harness racer. A decent bet until she stopped up short with a condylar fracture—quack talk for busting her head.

Over yonder at Windsor Raceway, they said she needed eight month's stall rest. Mitchell adopted her for the price of a border hassle, bringing her around in half the time with non-dairy calcium shakes he bought on eBay. It's just that, at the track, she was called Bucking Doe, hallmarking her displeasure for two-legged creatures.

"Thinking it was negatory connotations making her mad, I changed her name," Mitchell said. "She's since chilled some, stopped kicking, but I wouldn't step up like you." Petting Hasty's snout. "You're a good pet anyway, a friend." She took a nip, neigh, Mitchell pulling back. "Maybe I ought to rename the pale horse again—Hasty Bitch."

"Talk about negatory," Catori said.

"You don't know the half of it, something wrong with her noggin makes her get snappy. Now listen, I packed the van—everything in airtights, like paint. Bags of cayenne pepper and scented dryer sheets to throw off the turncoat doggies. Plus, I put cans of real paint closest to the door, decoys if Customs snoops." Looking at her sitting up there, he shielded his eyes from the red sun falling into the horizon, serious now.

She was a bit too thin, needed a cabbage roll. Her hair, parted in the middle, kept falling into her eyes, caramel freckles. And man, she had a lot of them, a fortunate buckshot across her face. "Look," Mitchell said, "I am sorry, about before."

She sighed, thinking he must be Catholic, guilt still killing him. "You don't have to be."

"Says who?"

"Mourning Dove." Catori felt a smile creeping, biting her lip. "She said every disease has a herb to cure it, every person a mission to grow it—her theory of existence."

"Yeah," Mitchell said, "and about how long did Mourning Dove exist?"

Catori thought about it, said, "Until she was 48."

Hushpuppies, that meant Mitchell had been too old for this shit for four years now.

CHAPTER NINE

Olin had gone on about the local pheasant population until seven, showing Fowler yet another book, *Wild Nights* by Anne Matthews, a study of depopulated areas, the bible on the subject. Fowler asked if he could borrow that one, too. Again, Olin explained, the books were rare, that they were not to leave his office.

Finally, after Fowler wasted time on his computer—checking email, he said, even though he seemed to be doing more typing than reading—they were out of 431 Howard and in the Jeep.

Enid nodded at an armed guard as they drove past concrete barricades built to surround the place this time last year. She was behind the wheel, despite Olin's edict to let Fowler drive. Heading southwest on Howard toward First Street, on the way, not to Fowler's hotel, no, Enid was taking him exactly where the assistant deputy director had said don't go, this time of night.

Now that it actually was getting dark, Enid wondered when Olin thought drug crimes went down? These people weren't exactly early risers. But then if they weren't early risers, maybe morning was best, like Olin said.

Fuck it, she thought, taking a right onto the John C. Lodge Freeway, glancing at Fowler in the passenger seat. The poor young prick was so far from home, it seemed, saying, "You know the assistant deputy director's going to find out about this." Eyes wide behind his bulky glasses. "Where we're going, when we're going there. He's going to find out we're defying his directive. And defying a directive—that's insubordination, cause."

Enid said, yeah, she'd tell Olin personal as soon as they busted that cowboy, made him divulge his ties. Then, when they made CNN, what was Olin going to say? Nothing. Aside from that, they wouldn't have to go in the dark if Olin had sent them right away. You know someone's holding, you get to it before they move it, make the best bust you can at your first opportunity, now. What does Olin do? He orders Zane's.

Speaking of which, Enid couldn't believe it, the way Fowler kissed so much Olin ass that he might as well wipe his face with Charmin Ultra Soft. Now, after all that, when she finally gets Fowler out of there, he says the assistant director's going to find out. What was Fowler going to do, tell, she thought, merging the Jeep onto I-94 West, passing an obsolete billboard, YOU'VE GOT AN UNCLE IN THE FURNITURE BUSINESS, JOSHUA DOORE.

"So." Fowler looked blankly at the dash, eyes out of focus. "Think we're going to find a bunch of dope-smoking Taliban guys overseeing a massive grow-op while they make letter bombs from African Violet Mix?"

Enid, hitting the indicator, veering off to the right lane, said Fowler could laugh all he wanted, but all signs pointed to that cowboy having something to do with dope, if nothing else. And, in case Fowler hadn't noticed, dope was still a jailable offense. If he was growing, it was as much as a year a plant on this side of the border, no matter what the Canadians were talking about, dumb.

"We're Canada's biggest trading partner, value of goods crossing the Ambassador Bridge is greater than all U.S. exports to Japan, billion dollars a day." Enid took a look in the rearview, a smattering of headlights. "But no, now they're making noises they don't want go to war with us against Iraq."

"Could be they remember we installed Saddam," Fowler said, running fingers over his gelled hair, stiff. "I mean, I just don't see this as their problem to solve, objectively." Adjusting his glasses, looking at the brown grass along the freeway. "Plus, while I was researching for the interview, I read somewhere Detroit once gave him, Saddam, the key to the city."

Enid said that was a fact; 1980, Coleman Young, Commie mayor, rolls out the red carpet after Saddam donates a quarter-million to an Iraqi church out on 7 Mile Road, Chaldean Sacred Heart. But that still wasn't why the Canadians were fixing to not help the States in Iraq.

"Why then?" Fowler said.

"Priorities—Canadians are too busy fixing to make pot legal."

"They're talking about decriminalizing," Fowler said, "a little different."

"Amounts to the same. Why? Don't tell me you think it's a good idea."

Despite being a narc, Fowler came around to a similar way of thinking years ago. He didn't want it legal, either. But he said it was more of a social issue, like booze. That's what he thought. Also, it was a medical thing.

"Medical," Enid pulled a face, sour. "Medical's the thin edge of the wedge."

"What wedge?"

"Wedge that pushes global legalization."

Fowler looked at his four-hole Doc Martens on the floor, utilitarian, said, "You want to write a ticket, fine them, okay. But you shouldn't do time for blowing the odd roach. I'm still in favor of locking up bad guys selling bad drugs to good kids. And that, before you take me out of context, is all I'm saying." Holding his hands like a scale. "We need a more balanced approach."

"Balance—you're DEA and you want to balance it in the criminal's favor. You want to make it more acceptable." Enid hit the indicator again, pulling onto the shoulder below a Marlboro Man billboard, putting the Jeep in park. "A DEA talking like this, it's like a Ford worker joining Greenpeace. Anything that makes it more acceptable is bad for business." Pointing at herself, Fowler. "Our business. Besides, if you can't get anything on someone, you can most always get them for dope."

"Like getting Al Capone on tax evasion?"

Enid thought about it, said, "Like that."

Catori sat at the marble linoleum kitchen table eating leftover cabbage rolls stuffed with tofu, listening to the hockey game on the radio with Mitchell. Thinking the guy did smell really freakin' good, she wondered if maybe Mitchell smelled good for the same reason kittens smelled like vanilla beans: It stopped their poor mothers from killing them.

At least he was gracious. But this guy, it looked like he hadn't eaten in days, the way he was taking another bite before he'd swallowed the last one. And the fear, she could see it in his eyes, tight and jumpy.

Was he stoned, paranoid? Because it sure seemed like it, and that scared her. Nobody had thought this through. Him, her, Phil, probably even those DEAs—they were all just reacting to circumstance. That also frightened her. And who was to say Mitchell and Catori weren't making a bad situation worse? Maybe they should just dump the manifest and save themselves. Looking at Mitchell, still chowing down on the cabbage rolls, she said, "What are you thinking?"

He blinked, dousing some green habanero sauce on his cabbage roll. "Should never ask a person that," he said, taking a bite, chewing as he spoke. "Is impolite."

Impolite? Catori said what's impolite was the way Mitchell was showing her his food as that gold chopper of his worked on it— eat with your mouth closed. She was just asking, you know, trying to have a bonding moment before they pulled this stunt. They were taking 59 plants over the border tonight, making mules of themselves, for what, some money? So, yes, what was Mitchell thinking? She wanted to know.

Swallowing, Mitchell said he was sorry about gabbing and grubbing. As for what he was thinking, she wanted to have a moment, huh? Personal? Okay, it wasn't what he was thinking so much as what he was singing in his head, "Home on the Range." Not the campfire version, no, the Neil Young version was the one Mitchell was playing on the CD-drive in his mind.

"Melancholy," he said, "hopeful." Looking at the ceiling. "The way Neil tells of how seldom is heard a discouraging word, simple, and the skies—the skies are not cloudy all day."

Catori looked at him closely. His eyes weren't just a bit pink, his pupils were dilated, lids heavy. That was it. He really was stoned. "You high?"

Mitchell, holding his thumb and index about an inch apart,

said, "A little."

"When? I didn't see you, didn't smell smoke."

Mitchell giggled, pointing at the cabbage roll on his Little Dick West display plate, said, "Baked in." Taking another bite.

Catori grabbed the last roll on her plate. "You've got to be kidding."

"What?"

"You." She pointed the roll at him, dripping. "Getting us stoned before we do this." Sniffing it. "Did you put some of that date rape shit in here, too?"

Mitchell threw his arms out, innocent. Now hold on, young lady. Maybe he was buzzed, but only because he had a tiny contact high going. In all his haste, he hadn't worn gloves while handling the plants, okay? And date rape drug—Mitchell had never, not in all his days, pulled any *guano* like that. No way he'd ever dust cabbage rolls, blasphemy.

Catori said, "But did you bake anything in?"

"Bought those at Farmer Jack's deli, didn't alter 'em an iota."

"Honest?"

Mitchell pinched up his face. He couldn't reckon it, the girl making him say it. No, he hadn't baked anything in. Honest. He really was joking. Sorry.

Catori called him white man, told him not to joke so much if he wanted to keep his hair.

Still parked beneath the Marlboro Man on I-94, Enid said, if you asked her, the commander-in-chief ought to slap an embargo on the Canadians, socialists, and could someone please tell her the difference between the Canadians and Castro?

Fowler said, "For starters, they let the Canadians leave Canada. They're allowed to travel. You know that, right?"

"But like Castro, they can't choose their doctors."

"Myth. They have more choice than us."

Enid ignored that, saying, also like Castro, Dubya should starve the Canadians out until they just said no, period. Same as their biggest trading partner, the States, had done without fail since pot became contraband in 1937. If Canada couldn't also say no, Dubya should slap an embargo on them, the Canadians.

"Isn't that a little harsh?" Fowler said. "An embargo?"

"Did you hear what their president said? What's his name, Cretin?"

"You mean Chrétien," Fowler felt the Jeep tremble, freeway traffic shaking it. He looked up at the Marlboro Man clenching a cigarette between his teeth, riding, rounding up cattle. "And he's their prime minister, Jean Chrétien."

"Him." Enid looked at her eyes in the rearview. The lines were gone, but she couldn't see how surgery was making her girlish, just a little less human. Perhaps she could get something done to make her look softer, rounder. "Was in today's *Free Press*. On the anniversary of September 11, Canada's frog president says America's arrogant, self-satisfied, over-bearing, and there are no limits to our pursuit of wealth."

"French always hated us." Fowler put his hands on his knees. "Even in the early '90s, when I went backpacking after college, France, they said, if you're American, sew a Canadian flag on your back pack, they hate us so much."

Enid punched the Jeep into drive. Hitting the gas, getting some speed up on the gravel, she watched the sideview mirror for a chance to merge, then jerked back into traffic, saying they might as well make that a Cannabis flag now. Point was, 11 September was an occasion to honor victims, not blame them. And over there, Canada, Enid heard it on the radio, scientific, 85 percent agreed with Cretin that the States brought on the attacks themselves.

"More like 65," Fowler said. "And again, that's not quite the way they put the question. What they asked was, do you feel that the U.S. needs to be a better international citizen? That's a long way from, did bin Laden do good?"

Enid threw her right hand up, whatever, looking down at the speedometer, almost 60.

Fowler went on, saying the Canadian prime minister's name

properly and with emphasis, Chrétien, and could Enid blame him? What about the time U.S. soldiers killed four Canadians in Afghanistan? How long did it take curious George to apologize for that?

Friendly fire happens, Enid said, and that Cretin was using it to weasel out of going to war with Iraq. Plus, Canada hadn't paid its full NATO dues since 1972. Did Fowler know that?

Pounding the steering wheel now, veering right onto Livernois, Enid said they had sleeper cells taking advantage of Canada's so-called multi-cultural society to organize, using it as a channel of communication and transportation to get into the States.

"Well, how'd they get in here," Fowler said, "our security's so good?"

Enid stopped at the light, said, "What do you mean?"

"Canadians let the bad guys into the States, or was it the States who let bad guys into the States? We're responsible for our own border, us. You know that, right?"

"Goddammit Fowler, this isn't something to be smug about." The light turned green. She took it, hanging another right. "On the streets of our country, we're vulnerable, at war. If the Canadians don't want to help, yes, put an embargo on them. See how they like it when the Taliban invades them and we say, 'Sorry, Canada. Not our pig, not our farm.'"

Fowler looked across at Enid, said, "You sound like that nutjob ran for president, Buchanan, called Canada Soviet Canuckistan, but you, you—"

"Pat Buchanan is a patriot. And me what?"

"Maybe it's like that Gina the Ballerina said." Fowler watched Enid take a series of quick lefts. "Maybe you should have done more experimenting back at Quantico."

After Warren, Enid didn't bother hitting the indicator, no one around, turning north on Unassumed Road. Passing the sign, MEDLAND ESTATES, she said, "Listen, I've been patient with your goofs, and that's fine. Keep loose on the job, create some banter. But the moment we step onto that man's land, it's business, serious DEA business, no matter what you think of the commander-in-chief, and I'm the senior partner, in charge, got it?"

Fowler looked down, said, "Yes, ma'am."

"Goddammit, Fowler. Just say yes, you understand."

Fowler made a *pfft* sound, said, yes, he understood . . . Ma'am.

The high-beams picked up the burnt-out house with eyes, STOP
HALLOWEEN ARSON. When the lights hit the Mitchell P. Hosowich
sign, the Jeep went dark, Enid pulling tight to the side of the road,
parking, looking over. "Fowler, you're a little boy on probation in a
new job in a place badder than where you came from, only you don't
know. You want to get into a petty power struggles, remember who
they'll be asking when your time comes, me."

You, Fowler thought, the Chief of Liposuction pulling rank. He'd
heard all about Enid Bruckner. Even Olin had taken him aside,
dropping hints. Fowler knew how much weight her word carried
around 431 Howard, not a whole heck of a lot.

"Your hands, huh?" Fowler rubbed his chin. "And all this time
I thought they were leaving it up to Veronica Cake. Guess I owe
you an apology, pards."

Enid felt her a dull throb in her chest. Calming herself, breathing
deep like she'd seen that Buddhist on channel 62, willing her
heart-rate down, she cut the engine.

Fowler checked his watch, 7:57 P.M. "Now what?"

"We assume positions," Enid said, "and wait."

CHAPTER TEN

Catori sat at the kitchen table apologizing for threatening to take Mitchell's hair. Also, Mitchell pointed out that he hadn't given anybody shit for their gender or skin color. As such, could she kindly stop giving him shit for his? And for the last time, he hadn't baked dope into anything. Alright, Catori said, but the white man still had to be stoned, the way he was shushing her as Windsor radio station CKLW reported rain on the way, returning to Joe Louis Arena. John-Scott Dickson had both goals, Spitfires up two zip.

Mitchell remembered his Spitfires toque, something else he picked up thrifting, and figured it would be a good prop for their story at Customs. Wearing the hat slightly askew, strands of red, white, and blue wool sticking out, he said c'mon. They'd listen to the third period on the way, keep track of the score in case Customs asked who won. Assuming they made it, he'd get Catori some flesh at a drive-thru yonder in Canada.

Catori watched him turn on the TV, mute the volume. She asked why he did that. To create moving shadows, he said, the illusion someone's home. He guided her to the door, locking up, leading her down the poorly-lit path towards his van near the first barn.

She adjusted the knapsack on her shoulder, said, "So I'm your Canadian girlfriend, you're a Detroit contractor, and you're driving me home after the game—that's our story and we're sticking to it. Simple, right?"

"Should work." Mitchell stopped near his van and looked at the gap where her velour vanilla hoody didn't quite meet the matching pants, wondering if anyone was going to believe she was his girl. Then he was thinking he probably shouldn't tell her about the Remington M700 Varmint-Synthetic hidden in the wallpaper roll. One hand, he shouldn't be bringing the shotgun, the way it could up the ante at Customs. Other, he still thought it best to pack a gun on account of the load he was carrying—protection just in case of he didn't know what.

Plus, he didn't see what good worrying Catori was going to do, so he went ahead and did his best to keep her calm, reprising all the work he'd done to get them through. "Airtights are organized nice, marked like paints, sealed with vapor-sealed cayenne and dryer sheets, Bounce, to put off any Customs Cujos. Then there's the decoy cans I told you about, closest to the door, actual paint. Also, we have rollers, brushes, tape, wallpaper—"

Catori stopped him. "But if they open the wrong can?"

Mitchell hesitated, said, "Then to the big pasture we're a goin'."

"At least it'll be a Canadian prison."

"More like Jackson State." That there was a third voice, Mitchell and Catori looking at each other—wasn't them—then to Enid Bruckner stepping out from behind the outhouse, Fowler coming from behind the composter.

"What the . . ."

Talk about discouraging words, Mitchell sagged at the sight. With all he'd done, he didn't want to accept that he had that there Federale on his spread. But there she was, smiling her tight smile, telling Mitchell nice shave, pointing her pistol at Catori and mocking them like a bona-fide cowgirl. "Looks like she done got stirred with a stick, dragged ass backwards, then chewed her split ends off—she worth it?" When Mitchell didn't answer, Enid said, "I want to give the barns a thrice-over, so please, lead me inside."

Mitchell looked over her shoulder, seeing Wolfie chasing Lou over a bale in the moonlight—thanks doggies. Mitchell had not one but two intruders, and those shepherds didn't even look sideways. Laying his eyes on Enid's Les Baer Prowler III, he said, "Just kindly mind your pepper box. My horse's jumpier than Orville Redenbacher in a microwave."

"Sure, Little Dick West. No need to upset the animals." Enid followed Mitchell and Catori to the bigger barn. When Mitchell sidestepped at the door, Enid tightened the grip on her piece, said, "Where you think you're going?"

"Just stepping around the sinkhole." Mitchell nodded at the incline. "Humbly suggest you do the same, careful."

Enid watched him, said, "Aren't we helpful."

Mitchell said nothing, Hasty Kiss kicking up a fuss in her stall, neigh, Enid speaking to Fowler. "Go ahead."

"Go ahead, what?"

"At the office you asked, could you do it next time?"

Fowler crossed his arms, bringing a hand over his face, embarrassed, like maybe the rancher was thinking that he, Fowler, genuinely wanted to check him for keister stash.

"Whoa." Mitchell pointed outside. "Whoa, Nelly. Dope's in the van. I know you done heard me."

Enid looked at Fowler. "Just subdue the suspect."

Oh, that's all, only Fowler said the suspect was telling them where the dope was, doing what he was told, and indicating that he would continue cooperating so long as no harm came to his animals, reasonable. Enid made a noise with her tongue, bringing her gun high above her head, down hard onto Mitchell's collarbone. He crumpled, Enid booting him, keeping him down in the hay where his Spitfires hat fell off.

Covering what was becoming an instant weakness, the spot she kept kicking, it wasn't like Mitchell was fighting back. He was turtling, trying to protect himself, Enid taunting him, beating him down out of principle, rendering him ineffective.

Being cuffed, hands behind his back, Mitchell was saying something about how Enid wasn't fit for a horse-eatin' man to hole up with. Right away, he knew that was a mistake, the way she jerked him up to his knees, turned him around. Facing her, he watched as she brought the heel of her palm back, then bang, she connected sharply with his forehead, knocking him over, telling him, "Just you keep courtin', Little Dick." Grabbing a roll of silver-gray duct tape off the workbench, she knelt in front of him, bit a strip off, taping his mouth shut. "There."

Rising from her knees, checking out that horse bobbing her head in the stall, Enid looked around the barn, wondering whether she'd really found the grail after all, or even a grail.

Dammit, if the cowboy was truthing and everything he had was in that van, this was going to rate for a two-inch blip in the *Free Press*, and now what the hell was she hearing outside? Chickens?

Whatever, waving at herself, she said, "Fowler, lay the gloves on me."

Fowler opened his peacoat. "What gloves?"

"You didn't bring any?"

Fowler shook his head, pointing to a pair of sealed dish gloves on the workbench. Enid could use those. She nodded, starting over, then stopped abruptly. The girl, where was the girl?

Catori slipped into the smaller barn, thinking, chickens, how could she use the chickens? She couldn't, but there had to be something, anything, and now the misfit cow was agitated, snorting, third horn pumping like a piston. Yeah, that was natural, like the cow patty on John Boy's face, huh? What a freak. What a fucking freak.

Spying a generous rope coil hanging in the animal's stall, Catori went in, gingerly stepping around the beast. A bit worried when the cow bolted out the open door, but what the hell? Catori couldn't run. Too much open space. Plus, looking down at her Chuck Taylor high tops matching her vanilla sweat suit, she was entirely in off-white. They'd see her a kilometer away, shoot her for fun. No, her only hope was to wreak havoc and hope to find a way out in the ensuing mayhem, so it was just as well that the three-horned cow was loose. And now that she thought of it, maybe she could use the chickens. Or, was she just stoned? The son of a bitch, he'd better not have baked anything in, but why even say it? Did he have some Spanish fly, too? The creep putting that in her head. Yeah, way to take care of your people, white man.

"You were covering me?" Enid nodded sarcastically, pointing her gun at the girl's knapsack in the hay. "Thanks, Fowler, thank you. Now just you run around the barn, back in. She's still out there. Find her, bring her back. I want that girl."

Fowler clicked the safety on his Glock; 17 rounds, 17 more in his peacoat. What the shit did he requisition this for anyway? Nice, little six-shot was all he needed.

Careful, he decided to clean this situation up then blow the whistle. Sure, it had been fun egging Enid on, but why couldn't they have done this tomorrow? And did she have to pistol-whip the cowboy? No. That's exactly the type of abuse Fowler had been documenting. He was going to put this part in his computer with the rest of it, print it off, give it to Olin tomorrow. Get there first, he told himself, document this crazy bitch right out of there. Then, maybe Fowler could get a decent partner, someone who could teach him something.

Eyes adjusting, he stumbled on the sinkhole outside the barn. He couldn't see anything at first, just vague shapes. But what was with those chickens? Chickens, plus he heard something else—footsteps, rapid footsteps coming from different directions. Couldn't be the girl, so what were they? And how many?

Closer now, it sounded like dogs. Were there really Coyotes here? Because it sure sounded like something panting, bearing down. And did one of them have a cough?

Coming on hard, leaping, Lou knocked Fowler down from behind. Wolfie, the bigger dog, liberated his plastic gun as it fired wildly. One of them yelped. Hit, Fowler thought, picking himself up as the other ran off, spooked by the Glock's report. Then there were more footsteps in the distance, heavier this time.

Fumbling with buttons on his peacoat, Fowler came up with the yellow lighter from an inside pocket. Flicking it once, twice, the Bic caught on the third try. He cupped a hand over the flame, seeing the Australian Shepherd, writhing. Affirmative, it was hit. Then, feeling the ground rumble, hearing a snort, he caught the image of something else coming at him. What the shit was this now? Oh, sweet Jesus, whatever they called it, it had three horns and a full head of steam.

Inside the barn, Enid heard a series of dull thuds, watching the north wall rattle, Fowler screaming something she couldn't understand. As the skirmish continued on the other side, she called to him, calmly, raising her voice. Panicking when she heard increasingly heavier action, the wall giving a bit more, she was shouting his name, throwing items she couldn't use off the workbench, looking for something.

Finding a flashlight, she stepped outside, casting it, stumbling over the sinkhole. After regaining her balance, she saw the orange -and-white dog sidewinding, whimpering, then Fowler being gored up against the barn, shouting, are you happy now? Shoot it, inbred. Screaming something about the assistant deputy director— what Olin had said about the fucking animals out here—by the time she fired.

The cow was still going good, but Fowler had stopped complaining. Enid had hit him, his neck limp. Enid stepped closer for a second shot, putting a hole above the animal's shoulder, staggering it. What a mess, she thought, seeing the cow go down in a heap. All she could do was shake her head, dropping her hands to her sides as Simmi howled.

Enid wondered how to explain all this to Olin, how to blame it on Fowler. Inexperience, she was telling herself, nothing but plain, old-fashioned inexperience—that was the cause of this tragic farm accident. But, of course, Olin was going to ask what they were doing out here, especially when he had told them how many times, wait.

And then there was her bullet in Fowler, how was that going to look?

Goddamn everything and everyone, it was going to look like she plugged him for being smug, fixed his attitude. And who knew what he'd been reporting back? Thinking, no, there wouldn't be any explaining her way out of this, that Olin had her now, Enid felt herself losing balance. Falling, grunting, dropping her gun, gripping the lasso around her neck, tight.

Catori scooped the Les Baer with her left hand, tucked it in her waistband, looping slack rope around her right shoulder and dragging Enid back into the main barn. There, Catori held the rope tight between her knees while she tied the other end to Hasty Kiss. The animal was kicking mad when Catori dropped the coil on the hay, keeping a reign on the DEA woman.

"Do you have any idea what you're doing?" Enid looked up at the girl, careful not to plead. "I'm a federal op, pretty serious offense, you keep going."

"It's already pretty serious," Catori said. "And what? You're going to let me go?" Opening Hasty's gate, Catori reeled in a foot of rope at a time, keeping the DEA lady's leash cinched, inching back to her. "What you did to me, also a pretty serious offense, and you were about to do it again—no way, lady." At that, she drew Enid's gun and fired through the open door, sending Hasty clippety-clop into the beautiful Detroit night—more than half a moon, stars everywhere.

Enid tried to say something but she was frozen, watching the white horse disappear, the coil unraveling.

Recalling a Bedouin legend, Catori said God took southerly wind, blew upon it, and created horse. Then she remembered the new Johnny Cash tune, a bridge to finish her thought. "It was a pale horse, and the name set upon it was death. Then hell followed with it."

"Ooof." Enid felt herself blush, face hot. "You're not Italian, a Gina?"

"Stage name." Catori avoided eye contact, letting go of the rope.

"Then what are you?"

"Canadian."

Enid glanced at the coil, getting to the end. "What kind?"

Catori looked her in the eye this time, said, "The Ojibway kind."

Slack gone, rope taunt, Enid pawed her throat, standing involuntarily. Then she was running, thinking she could keep up with the horse until she hit uneven ground, the sinkhole at the barn door, pinwheeling when her head hit something hidden in the darkness.

Catori winced, tossed the gun aside. Bending over, hands on her knees, she caught her breath, feeling a rush of adrenaline at the thought of what that lady might look like dragged ass-backwards when she remembered Mitchell, turning to him. He was mumbling something fierce, eyes wide, as she walked over and pulled the tape covering his mouth with a rip. Gasping, he chin-nodded, outside. "Two dead Federales, my spread?"

She grabbed her knapsack and his Spitfires hat off the hay, said, "Both of them, gone."

Mitchell shook his head, almost crying. "Then we've got to burn the breeze, now."

"What's that mean?" She placed the hat on her head, leaned over, kissing his forehead. "We in cahoots?"

"Means we got to get gone faster than a hillbilly's teeth, and yeah."

"Yeah to what?"

"Cahoots," he said, watching her.

"Right." She looked away. "Cahoots." Nodding at first, then shaking her head, no. "Only I think that lady cop still has the keys to your cuffs. And like you said, it's time."

Oh man, he could see where this was going already.

Time was, this life of Mitchell's was his juice, being the lone hand on his own land. And for a good long while there, he really was the only thing he ever really wanted to be, his own man. Had quite a run too, a good one. But on his knees now, defenseless, hands behind his back, he found himself accusing her of getting greedy, wanting too much, more than she needed. Like Paul Newman in *Hud*—wanted his daddy's farm so bad every critter was destroyed by the time he got to be big sugar, ruined, no farm at all.

That didn't resonate, so he told her she couldn't pull it off alone. And Phil, he wasn't going to be okay with this. Then Mitchell just said why—why? Maybe this was his fault, but he'd taken Catori in, fed her, was going to give her some greenbacks. Why was she doing this to him? Same time, even as he was saying all that, Mitchell thought it really did make him sound like a mail-order cowboy, nor was it helping his cause any.

Ah, maybe he could have lived another life or at least have

gotten out while the getting was good—put his land to use, legally. Maybe he could have researched the stone formations in the southeast corner and turned the place into a fine, upstanding tourist trap. Set up a U-pick-it for his rare herbs, the legal ones. Maybe, but hearing the far-off hum of industry in the distance, he just looked at Catori and said, "What came first, young lady, grants or farmers?"

She smirked, peeling off 10 inches of fresh tape, biting it off and shaping it against his mouth. Then she peeled off another strip, breaking it with her teeth.

CHAPTER ELEVEN

Catori was still wearing the Spitfires hat when she climbed into Mitchell's van and hit the ignition. Checking the time, 9:14 P.M., she thought she could make the hockey story work at the border, jerking the van into reverse and clipping Mitchell's composter, braking abruptly. She looked at the sideview, seeing nothing but stars, backhanding the tranny into gear, winding down the driveway, and hanging a right on Unassumed Road.

She told herself she needed soothing, hitting play on the cassette deck, Paul Simonon still talking more than he was singing, telling the story of Ivan who gets caught with a gun.

Thinking Mitchell was right about one thing—the song did seem a bit negatory—she hit stop, removing the hat and tossing it on the dash.

Old man like that bellying down in the bush with her—she didn't think so.

The way Mitchell had left her out there twisting, sure, there was a part of her that sort of wanted to rub it in, tell him that he really was just a mail-order cowboy caring for misfit animals on land, stolen, that he never came to understand. In fact, it was probably him being so stupid to be scared that saved him all these years—freakin' green ghetto.

She'd thought about shooting him, putting him out quick, no pain. But when it came down to it, she felt bad enough kicking the farmer, so-called, when he was on his knees like that, hands behind his back. She'd taken the easy way out, nonviolent, almost. Biting off a fresh strip of tape, plastering it over his mouth. Biting off another, pinching off his air supply, his nose . . .

Okay, so he was going to suffer, she thought, checking the rearview, nothing. But she couldn't shoot him. Even when she was a kid, she didn't have it in her to club a caught fish, so did she really just do the DEA lady like that?

As for Mitchell saying Phil wouldn't be okay with this, please. Phil never could stand Mitchell. And why? There really was a sign on his road, yet he'd still left her exposed, quite literally, along with the others.

But did Mitchell have to die?

It wasn't like she wanted to do it. More than anything, she told herself having him around was only going to make things worse, that he was holding her back. And the one with the tight face really did have the keys, so who was Mitchell going to blame when the man came around? Of course, he'd blame her. He'd have to. Whatever, it was done. Now she had to—how had he put it? Oh yeah, she had to burn the breeze.

Even with the headlights, it was still too dark, so she hit the brights, passing Mickey Joseph's Service Station. Further, she drove along the dandelion patch leading to the sign.

IF YOU THINK IT'S DRY NOW
WAIT TIL NOVEMBER.

"Shit, shit, shit . . ." She hit the brakes, sliding on the loose stones. Goddammit, she was heading in the wrong freakin' direction.

Pulling a three-pointer, turning back towards the I-94, only way she knew to Canada, she hit the gas too hard, tires spinning. Quickly, she had the van up to 60, swerving at the sight of an animal zig-zagging in the road. What was this now, a deer? Regaining control, she told herself it couldn't be. Probably a dog or something, but she still thought she better slow down.

While it seemed to be taking longer to make up make up lost time than she'd spent losing it, she brought the van down to 30. As remote as she was—didn't seem to be any speed-limit signs— this wasn't exactly the Autobahn, either, and the last thing she needed was a ticket.

Catching the Mitchell P. Hosowich sign in the headlights, she took her foot off the gas, slowing, almost stopping. Now had the white man baked anything into those cabbage rolls or not? She had to be stoned. How else could she have gone the wrong freakin' way?

Mitchell rolled around in the hay, grunting, sucking hard at the tiny cracks his heavy breathing had puffed out of the tape stuck to his mouth. With panic setting in, he recognized the warning signs from an article he'd read on asphyxiation in *Horse & Rider* —stymied high-pitch screams, gurgling sounds, hands fighting like hell against the cuffs. He was hurting himself, even if he knew, rationally anyway, there was no use.

If he could see himself, he was turning blue. Oh, he was getting some oxygen, but it wasn't going to be enough for long. He felt faint, rubbery. Soon the panic became less urgent, transforming into mild euphoria. Like the article said, he sensed he was coming to the point where he was almost happy to be going to the big boneyard, peaceful.

Was he outside himself? He was sure of it, seeing a light when Lou came whimpering into the barn, her tail stub wagging. She started licking . . . Licking, licking, licking . . . Licking Mitchell's face instinctively, obsessively, compulsively, until the tape began rolling off the left corner of his mouth.

At first Mitchell didn't notice the difference. But as blood returned to his pleasure zones, he came to, shaking out of it, taking enough air to roll over, trying to roll the rest of the tape off on the barn floor. All he got from that was a face full of hay sticking to the tape.

Taking deep breaths through the gap, he walked on his knees to the workbench, trying to peel the rest off by rubbing his face against a rough two-by-four leg. That didn't work, either, the straw stopping the tape from catching on the wood, no traction.

Falling back down, lying sideways, he gasped, drinking in air like a winehead at Grape Fest. When he had enough, he remembered the move he'd been learning on *Yoga for Rodeo Riders*, the bridge pose. Maybe he could at least get his hands in front of his own self, solve two problems at once.

He rolled onto his back, placing his knees at a 90-degree angle, pressing his navel towards his spine, just like the velvet-voiced woman, very crunchy-granola, said on the tapes, and lifted his hips high off the straw as possible. Now all he had to do was step into the hole between his arms. All he had to do—oh man, the common shitkicker didn't suffer pain like this, he told himself, threading that needle, tendons and bones and cartilage creaking. Then he had to bring his arms right through, eyes watering as he did it. Hands in front of him now, still cuffed, he rested before peeling the rest of the tape off his mouth, straw with it. The tape on his nose went next. He could breathe clearly, unobstructed, but now what?

Downtown Detroit, Catori drove through some roadwork, passing a sign.

LET 'EM LIVE, LET 'EM WORK
INJURE OR KILL A WORKER
$7,500 FINE OR 15 YEARS

Why not just stone them, she thought.

Turning off Jefferson Avenue, she saw people in hockey jerseys at the border bus stop and pulled the van over. Rolling down the window, shouting hey, she made a deal to buy a ticket stub off a kid holding a Windsor Spitfires pennant with a red airplane on it.

First the kid didn't understand. Why would someone want to buy a used ticket? Catori said her brother—she didn't actually have one—collected them. The kid said he'd let it go for an American fiver. Catori handed over a ten, never minding the difference. Then she went ahead, paid the toll, heading down into the tunnel.

What with casinos and the hockey people, she'd expected traffic, but found herself breezing through the glowing yellow-white tube at a comfortable pace, 30 MPH. What was that in metric, 50 KM/HR, something like that? Mitchell's van was an American make, speedometer didn't have metric conversion. Passing flags of both countries, back in Canada proper, Windsor, Ontario, she wondered why the two sides couldn't have one uniform system of measurement, something to keep everyone on the same page.

Emerging from the ancient tunnel, winding upwards and right, looking to the console—three pieces of ID, ready—she stopped behind a cream Jetta, the driver being questioned. Catori didn't have a record to worry about, clean, but did Del Ray James back in Kent County have a warrant out on her? If he did and they ran her ID, it would come up. She knew that. She also knew they infrequently ran Canadians through the computer on the Canadian side. She was telling herself the same thing as the Jetta was waved through, pulling up to the kiosk when her light turned from red to green.

"Where're you coming from?" the Customs man said.

"Hockey game. Plymouth Whalers versus the Spitfires, pre-season action."

He looked at the ticket stub and Spitfires toque on the dash, picking her birth certificate out of her hand, motioning that she could hold onto her license and SIN card. "Who won?"

Shit, why hadn't she turned on CKLW coming in like Mitchell had said? "Spits were up two-nothing when we left. John-Scott Dickson scored both." There, nice recovery.

He handed the ID back. Good, she thought, he wasn't going to run it, only now he wanted to know why a Canadian girl was driving a van with American plates. Okay, she'd expected this, no problem. "Boyfriend's van, my turn to be the DD." She tipped an imaginary cup to her mouth. "Also why we had to leave a bit early."

"Damn Americans." He smiled conspiratorially. "Anything inside?"

"Supplies. Boyfriend's a contractor—paints, rollers, tape, brushes, wallpaper."

He pointed at the van's ass. "Let me take a look, send you on your way. Turn it off."

Catori killed the ignition, took a sharp breath, stepped out, around to the back, opened up.

He looked up, down—rollers, brushes, cans, tape, huge rolls of wallpaper—like she said. "So you'll be driving this heap back to Detroit. It's not an American coming here to pick up his work vehicle, take Canadian jobs."

"No, no. Have to have it back tomorrow."

"That's fair. Just let me see your boyfriend's papers, send you on your way."

Papers—shit, she'd heard that they'd been asking drivers for papers, but she hadn't checked. Going for the passenger side, a little herky-jerky, she forced herself to move slowly. Man, she was running hot, racing, heart pounding. The glove box was locked so she tried the ignition key. It worked. Inside, she found a row of country CDs, photocopied liner notes revealing Mitchell had loaned them from the library, burned them, the tight-wad. But thank Christ, beneath some bunched-up Farmer Jack bags, she found ownership and insurance slips tucked inside a City Bank pouch, gold lettering on brown vinyl.

She handed it over, watching the Customs guy scratch a side-burn, taking his time. This was probably just his way to get her out of the van and prancing around in her little velour hoody, matching pants. She figured he was hoping to catch a little midriff, so she ran her hands through her hair, stretching, showing him. "So, will you be sending me on my way?"

Removing his hat, he said, "You say your boyfriend's a contractor?"

"That's right." Goddammit, she was doing it again, biting her freakin' lip. "A painter."

He held the pouch open. "Says this van's registered to Mitchell P. Hosowich Farms."

Catori tilted her head, asking, did he know what came first, grants or farmers?

"Right, farmers are so poor they take side jobs in the winter. I get it." He pointed to the van's ass. "Just let me take a look at those cans, send you on your way."

As he stepped around to the back, reaching inside, Catori relinquished control, realizing she didn't understand this part of the world. She thought about how someone famous said one's level of stupidity depended on which two feet of dirt one stood. That, and maybe Mitchell could have talked their way out of this.

Old man like that bellying down in the bush with her—maybe if she'd taken the time to listen, to actually hear the people who came before, she would have been able to disappear into rural Detroit for months, wait this whole RCMP thing out.

Speaking of which, did she have to hogtie Del Ray back in Chatham? That's what started this whole thing, and now he was going to win, because here she was, not 25 minutes from the Detroit prairie, watching the Customs man jimmy an airtight with his Swiss Army knife. Right then, she knew she was never going to escape the green ghetto and all that had gone on there. She just knew it. It was the way the Customs man opened the tin, peeling back her layers. And look at him, putting his face up to the can. Was he going to taste it?

Taking a sniff, he said, "Paint."

Catori tugged her hair. "What?"

"Paint." He held the can out. "Like you said."

"Of course, it is." Catori broke eye contact, looking at the rows of cans. If she could get out of this, she was going to stop dancing for good, cut the whole thing out. Stop dancing—if she got out of here without doing jumping jacks naked, she was going to join the Peace Corps. "Paint, like I said. Now will you be sending me on my way?"

CHAPTER TWELVE

Lying in the hay, all airholes fully open for the first time in he didn't know how many minutes, Mitchell waited until he felt sufficiently rejuvenated, bringing up his hands to stroke Lou. "Good girl," he said, remembering her little brother. "Wolfie?" Lou whimpered, licked Mitchell.

Hands still cuffed, albeit in front of him, he struggled to stand, minding his balance on the way up. Thinking now he had real problems while he made for the barn door, he stepped into the night and stumbled over the sinkhole again. He looked back, promising to fill that goddamn thing if he ever got himself out of this.

He couldn't see anything at first, just shapes of vegetation, gray-headed coneflowers making the clearest outlines. Nearby, he heard Simmi murmuring, painful, then the clippety-clop of Hasty Kiss moving towards him. As her shadow came into his field of vision, he remembered to talk to the filly nice, like a human, a baby human maybe, but a human nonetheless, calling out gently. "Hasty. Here pretty, pretty, pretty . . . Hasty Kiss, come to Mitchell, baby."

The horse stopped about 15 feet short, pumped its head up and down, snorted.

"Hasty, remember I said a couple days back how I needed you more than ever?" Mitchell blew at a cloud of no-see-ums fluttering about his face. "Well scratch that, because I need you to come here right now, you devil, more than when those government commercials started all this business on 2, 4, and 7, so c'mon."

Closer now, tangled up in rope, the animal stutter stepped, stopping in front of Mitchell.

Looking to her rear, he saw that Hasty had essentially hanged the DEA lady. Enid Bruckner was a lumpy mess of scrapes, contusions, blood, and sundry signs of trail rash, her neck hanging to one side. Broken, Mitchell thought, telling himself to worry about the dead DEA later. He had to get the keys off her belt just to get to the point where he could fret over her and that guy looked like the dude bops his wife's sister in the movies. Or was it the wife's best friend?

Mitchell couldn't remember and that bothered him. But then what was he thinking about that for anyway? He thought maybe he was getting soft like Phil, smoking too much of his own brand, so he did his best to block the nonsense.

First time Mitchell knelt down next to the dead law lady, he wanted to say he didn't think much of her ethics, but when did speaking poorly of a lady pay? Never. So, working his linked hands on her keychain—the mountain-climbing clip attached to her first belt loop above her right pocket—he started to say something about her being a capable adversary when Hasty decided to take a few steps away, neigh, teasing old Mitchell.

Sighing, ready to start over, he walked on his knees towards the animal. Was tempted to start giving her hell, calling her Hasty Bitch, then thought better of it. If he did start getting all negatory, maybe the horse would mosey, then what?

Suet, if he didn't get that keychain off the dead lady, he was going to the big pasture for sure. Either that, or the turkey buzzards would end up fighting over his eyeballs, succulent. And man, it sure got dark out here, so dark that he'd never find Hasty if she wanted to play hide and seek. That's why he re-doubled his efforts to talk sweet, telling Hasty how pretty she was, despite the problems with her head. Even so, she was working at it, trying to get better, and that was all that mattered. Poor thing, now stay.

Hasty huffed but she remained stationary long enough to allow Mitchell to work the mountain clip off Enid's belt-loop, remaining next to him while he awkwardly fitted the skeleton key into the keyhole in the nearby barn light, wrist shackles giving one by one.

Free, Mitchell praised the horse, good Hasty, rubbing his sore wrists then his shoulders, particularly the left on account of that funky yoga move he'd used to get his hands up-front. Falling back ass first, probably sitting on Hasty piddle, the hay rank, he told himself that, if nothing else, the horse had seen enough in his attempted good works—like saving her from the glue factory—to give him a chance.

Just keep moving, deliberately, he told himself. One step at a time like the baseball slicker played right field for the Tigers, name of Gibson, used to say, so as not to compound the first error by scrambling and making additional mistakes. Maybe, just maybe, if he moved forward like that, he'd get this *guano* wiped. Oh man, couldn't be much more than 10, so maybe he had enough darkness to work with.

Pushing himself up, he untied Hasty's rope from the dead law lady, untangling them, then bringing the horse to her stall in the main barn. There, he found Enid's Les Baer Prowler III in the straw. Picking it up, examining it—five bullets left—he slipped it into the waistband of his Dungarees. At the workbench, his flashlight was gone. Remembering Enid had taken it, he went outside, kicking upon it. Soon as he flicked it on, he saw Lou licking Wolfie, just lying there.

Mitchell walked over, felt for Wolfie's pulse, dead. Seeing Fowler's Glock lying a few feet away, he retrieved it. Thinking, as much as he didn't love guns, he might actually need both.

Further back, casting his light against the side of the barn, he saw Fowler clearly dead. Rifling through the DEA's pockets, he grabbed the ID, another clip of 17 shots in the guy's peacoat. Bringing 34 rounds—for someone conflicted, this Fowler seemed to be expecting religious Commies gonna blow up the Ambassador Bridge for sure.

Hearing Simmi breathing, a little labored, he stood upright and walked to her, stroked her gently between the eyes. The cow raised her head weakly, looking at Mitchell, moo. The poor thing, Mitchell could half-see why the DEAers came after him, a dope man, but why'd they have to shoot his animals?

From the border, Catori followed the signs out of Windsor, taking a left on the main drag, Ouellette Avenue. A few miles south, over the Jackson Park overpass, it turned into a winding road, Dougall. Other than two independent pizza shops, Arcata and Capri, it was Southern Ontario's every-city map; Comfort Inn,

Kentucky Fried Chicken, Becker's, Taco Bell, Swiss Chalet, Shell, Walmart, Harvey's, McDonald's, Burger King, The Beer Store . . . After Canadian Tire, she hit Highway 401 east, the main road out of town.

Getting the van up to 70 MPH—roughly 120 KM by her calculations, just enough over the limit so as not to stick out—she approached the most notorious stretch of the 401. So boring it was dangerous, the elders said, stupid white people seduced by their own clear-cut nothingness, falling asleep at the wheel.

Passing Tilbury, population 4,300, she glanced at the sideview. Headlights in the distance, nothing that looked like it was coming for her. But so long as she was driving a dead cowboy's van, carting around his dope, she had to get off the road.

Maybe Phil would know what to do with the van, but she was heading back home where that freakin' Del Ray James—freak being operative—maybe had a warrant on her. Okay, Catori felt justified there, but now she's killing cops, two. The more she thought about it, she'd only killed one, but if this ever caught up with her they were going to blame her for Fowler as well. And again, did she have to do that to Mitchell?

No, and he had to be dead by now. But then maybe he shouldn't have gotten her stoned with those cabbage rolls. Or was she still just thinking she was stoned? Either way, she was pretty freakin' paranoid, which is probably why she promised to join the Peace Corps. The Peace Corps—please, the Peace Corps wouldn't take a girl like her—and that might have been a good thing, except she was a dealer-cum-killer-cum-mule now, having crossed the border with all that dope on a prayer to a god she didn't know.

Alone, being a mule would have been what? Five, ten years? Tack on two dead DEAs, an asphyxiated farmer, and once they heard about what she did to Del Ray James, she was pretty sure Michigan was going to change its capital punishment law just for her.

Alright, breathe.

If worse came to worse, she would just say the cowboy fed her that date rape drug, put it on him. It would be Mitchell's word against her's. Seeing how he couldn't speak, dead, she liked her chances, at least until she started worrying about how she would answer Phil's questions.

She eased off the gas when she passed a sign—60 MPH/100 KM, ZERO TOLERANCE, FINES STARTING AT $100 FOR 120 KM—bringing it down to 60 American. The next marker she drove by was the cutoff to Leamington.

Looking into her eyes in the rearview, she told herself she had simply seen her opportunity and taken it, only after being forced into a situation. That's right, forced, and maybe even drugged.

As for Mitchell, it was a matter of self-defense, almost. She had no choice, right?

When that wouldn't take, she thought maybe some god or another was teasing her, out to get her, maybe not. But coming up with different could've, should've, and would've scenarios wasn't going to help. Shit, shit, shit—she didn't just need to get off the road, she needed to go somewhere, anywhere safe, just to calm down and think clearly so that she might come up with some semblance of a plan that would get her on to the next place.

Mitchell came run-walking from the farm house carrying two kerosene lamps in one hand, an old medical bag in the other. Under his arms, he had bottles of water and vinegar, along with a tattered hardcover, *Medical Procedures of the Civil War*. Again, Simmi lifted her head slowly and let out a low moo.

Putting his things on the ground, Mitchell smiled nice, said, "No, I've never done this before." Lighting a wood match then the lamp, nodding to his text. "But this book here's going guide old Mitchell right through like assembling a barbecue."

The cow let her head drop to the ground, blinking when Mitchell struck another match, lighting the second lamp. He arranged the lights as close as he could to Simmi's wound, minding not to burn the poor thing.

Sweet as Mitchell was talking, he didn't know from surgery. And the directions on page 145, "How To Extract A Bullet," were about as clear as wax paper.

Step one said to anesthetize the patient, but it wasn't like Mitchell kept a bushel of bovine valium on hand. Next best thing, he thought, digging a Ziploc baggie out of his toolbox, was to improvise, use pot, a proven painkiller. At first, he was trying to think of some way to blow smoke into Simmi's pie hole, then thought doing so might rile her. That's why he went ahead and placed a nice wad of Detroit dope into the animal's mouth, squirting some water in to chase it down, holding her jaw bones shut until she swallowed, gulp.

Hoping it would kick in by the time he got to operating, Mitchell went to step two: Clean the wound with a sterile sponge and warm water. This would allow the surgeon, Mitchell in this case, to examine the tissue damage, determine whether the bullet was intact.

Back to the house, Mitchell grabbed a fresh bag of sponges from under the kitchen sink, ran the water hot for three-quarters of a soup cauldron, scrubbed up to the elbows.

Outside, holding the sponges under his right arm, he had his hands up-front like a surgeon, sterile. Then, remembering he done forgot the cauldron, he had to run back, fetching it from the kitchen after washing up, again, on account of touching the door knob contaminated him.

At Simmi's side, he mixed a little vinegar in with the water, having read that article in *Horse & Rider*, "Vinegar: More Than Just a Condiment." Aside from being good on fries, the article said vinegar was the best astringent, natural. War doctors used it to disinfect soldiers shot in the field, so Mitchell reckoned it would work.

Matter settled, he got down to it, gently running the sponge over her wound. At the sting, Simmi lifted her head slowly, looked at Mitchell, dropping her noggin, moo.

Mitchell reckoned it was the pot taking effect that made her eyes droopy, calmer than expected. And that had better be the case because aside from flat-out loving that animal—who else had a three-horned cow, nobody—he just had to get Simmi better.

Not that Mitchell was so impolite as to mention it, but there was no way he could dispose of a critter that size before daylight. Move her by himself? He couldn't. Then how was he going to explain a dead cow, shot? Couldn't do that, either.

Just you worry about the task at hand, Mitchell told himself. And dang if it didn't look like he could see the bullet, a bit shiny, in the lamp-glow.

Back in his medical bag he came up with forceps, running raw vinegar over the big tweezers and his bare hands.

Straddling Simmi—he didn't know if this was a good idea but the book said it was necessary, something about patients thrashing during the procedure—he relocated the bullet, extracted it easily. Holding it in the forceps up to the lamp, yes, it looked to be intact. Likely stopped on account of Simmi's meat wasn't so tender anymore, her age.

"I think you gonna make it, baby."

But Mitchell wasn't finished. Now, according to the book, he had to get control of the bleeding. Same time, there wasn't much new blood, likely on account of the wound was close to the surface. And well, Mitchell figured, one shot with a human gun was probably like getting pinged with a Daisy Red Ryder to an animal of Simmi's stature.

The book said something about an instrument called a tenaculum to hold up the ends of arteries and tie off the vessels. Mitchell didn't seem to have such an item handy, wouldn't know if he did on account of there was no illustration of said utensil. Blood didn't seem to be coming anymore, so he skipped that part, went onto the next step, suture, and if there was one thing this cowboy could do it was sew. It took a few minutes, on account of the toughness of Simmi's skin, but Mitchell got 'er done.

After dousing more vinegar, the book said to apply a bandage to the wound. Simple enough, Mitchell cut large swatches of gauze, white tape, made a Paul Bunyan size bandage and applied it. Just one more thing. Now Mitchell had to get a stoned cow back to her stall for recovery. Book said to stimulate the patient with ammonia salts. Mitchell didn't have any handy. He did, however, have plain old ammonia for cleaning particularly offensive piddle patches, so he ran into the main barn, grabbed a jug from the shelf.

Thinking it would be just as nasty smelling, he returned to the animal, putting some on a rag, the rag under her nose. It was enough to get Simmi's eyes wide open, mooing again, a bit mad this time, on her feet, and back into the second barn.

Mitchell wasn't exactly world-renowned, but it looked like maybe he'd doctored her up well enough, saved her. For a few seconds, he felt proud, until Lou came lumbering back in, whimpering, licking Mitchell's hand. The poor things, Mitchell had brought this whole mess down on his critters, every one of them.

CHAPTER THIRTEEN

Veering off Highway 401, Catori took Bloomfield Road into Chatham, passing the Thames River then a strip of fast-food conveniences on the way to Highway 40. Closer now, Wallaceburg, she followed the familiar landmarks—Sam's Hotel, the Big Chief Drive-In Restaurant—approaching the Walpole Island Bridge. She was back home from another bad trip, wondering whether she was ever going to get out of this place for real.

In a way, the green ghetto wasn't so different. The rez, after all, was by its very nature a ghetto, three main tribes—Ojibway, Pottawatomi, and Ottawa—forced onto another tract of badlands. It had mostly the same animals, too.

But this place, she thought, hanging a right onto River Road, looking out onto the St. Clair River . . . This place could have been so damn pure if it wasn't downstream from chemical valley. And there was the rub, the thing that put the stamp on Walpole as a ghetto—white men devaluing it, belching toxins into the water, letting it flow downstream, killing them slowly, deforming the little ones, ghettoizing them.

Even *The Chatham Daily News*, bastion of conservative thought in these parts, would run editorials saying it was time to build a clean-water pipeline. Since the '80s, politicians of every stripe—former Premier Bob Rae, supposed to be a friend to First Nations, included—promised to pay for it, creatively breaking their vows once elected. No wonder the islanders opted out. They couldn't afford to build it, but then Catori figured they couldn't afford not to.

Whatever was in the water—and reasonable people agreed that there was something—Catori didn't miss rez politics, either, elders asking, where's your mother? And without a mother, how can you prove tribal roots? Even when Reverend Wayne came through with evidence, he still had to guilt them into providing supportive paperwork.

Status or not, she would always have too much cream in her coffee for here. "Walpole Island, the place where the waters divide," according to the sign, population 3,000. Historically known as Bkejwanong, she remembered the elders, their stories about the very name, Walpole, how it was taken from the word for totem poles, warpoles, but nobody said much about that anymore. Looking out across the river at Algonac, Michigan a ferry ride away, she thought how the elders pretty much knew every freakin' thing, which was why she had to file appeal after appeal. Too much cream in her coffee—go to hell.

None of that mattered right now. Only thing that did was that she still had someone here. And man, much as she secretly fancied herself a bad-ass, pot-selling, nude-dancing, half-breed chick, she genuinely needed someplace to hide, a place to think, and someone to provide it.

She took a right onto Dan Shab Road, pulling into the driveway of the Evangelical Fellowship House. Circling around back to the near empty lot, she parked, checked the time, 11:21 P.M., killing the ignition. She threw her knapsack over her shoulder and jumped out when she remembered her clothes in Farmer Jack bags back at Mitchell's. Shit, shit, shit . . . Wondering how was she going to explain her things in a dead man's house, she ran her hands through her hair, thoughts racing as she walked to the door, about to knock when it opened in front of her.

"Catori," Reverend Wayne Rhondeau said. "Catori Jacobs."

"Reverend Rhondeau."

"Call me Wayne." Looking her up and down. "You're a full-grown woman now."

"Well Wayne, I'm 37." She pushed her hair out of her face. "Been full-grown 18 years, and, like, you saw me in the spring."

"Still my child."

She smiled, covering her mouth, bashful, letting her hair fall back in front. "Look, I'm sorry to impose, but I need a place."

"No imposition." Wayne looked past her, crossing his arms when he saw the van, Michigan plates. "And I'm not going to judge. Bible says I'm in no position, my sins." He felt his arms wrapped around himself, protective, so he opened them. "Judge not means judge not, asshole, me being the asshole that is not supposed to judge. It is just I know there was minor trouble in Chatham, have to ask, is this a sanctuary situation?"

She glanced at the church behind him, still no different from a regular house except for the glass cross. "Sanctuary," she said. "One night."

"It's okay. I just need to know who to keep at bay, can do." Reverend Wayne nodded to the vehicle. "May I help you with your things?"

She looked down, said she didn't have any. He said not to worry. She could go through the donation box. Someone had left a clean T-shirt that said Free Newfoundland, nice stuff, radical. Also, there were some jeans that might fit, he said, opening the storm door.

In both arms, Mitchell carried Wolfie onto his field, passing the rock formations. Man, maybe if Mitchell had done like Glen Campbell, made the token compromise, he could've turned the place into a respectable tourist trap, saved his critters all this grief. Maybe, but then he asked the same question he'd been asking since 1974: What came first, grants or farmers?

Thinking of all the stipulations, regulations, and connotations, he gently placed Wolfie on the ground then went about digging his doggie's grave. Carefully, he removed portulacas in shovel-fulls, ensuring he could replant them roughly the same way so the dirt could normalize with the next storm. And man, he was doing a little rain dance in his head. So far as Mitchell's personal savior was concerned—you bet he was coming out for Jesus, just like Johnny Cash after prison—all Mitchell was asking for was a rain storm.

So long as he got that much—and Linda Lau on Detroit's only country station had mentioned that dense air mass moving in—there'd be no problem replanting the sundial-white portulacas he was digging on. Little buggers were prehistoric, heartier than cannabis, indestructible the way they replanted themselves, came back thicker every year.

But the waterworks weren't coming from the sky quite yet. Instead, there were flowing down Mitchell's face as he dug until he had a five-by-three hole, a good four-feet deep.

Done, he lay down next to Wolfie's body as he'd seen his father Morris do back when they had Mitchell's first Australian Shepherd, Angus, put down in '61, head cancer, holding the dead animal, stroking it.

Like old Mo senior saying goodbye to Angus, Mitchell thought he ought to have some words for Wolfie, a friend who'd saved him. Mitchell scratched Lou behind the ears as he spoke, referencing The Cowboy Code. "The primary reward of being a cowboy is the pleasure of living a cowboy's life." His voice cracked, and he was sniffling, blowing out a pinch of snot. "And Wolfie, you done brought this cowboy many pleasures."

Sure, Wolfie was more ornamental than useful, like the rest. Plus, Mitchell would have liked it if Wolfie hadn't chased every stray cat out of the green ghetto. Mitchell wanted some kitties in the mix, but yeah, it was just as well. Cuddly as they were, damn felines would've brought dead mice home, rats. Mitchell had read that cats do that on account of they see human companions as inept hunters, and Mitchell couldn't have taken that—critters killing each other when they really ought to unite against the common enemy, mankind. But then Mitchell remembered how that went in *Animal Farm*.

Important thing was Wolfie had been just like Hasty Kiss, a good friend doing a good job, helping maintain a respectable front.

Now that it was all getting away from him, Mitchell spoke to Lou about her friend, calling Wolfie her life partner, albeit not in an intimate sense on account of Dr. Mallard said the kindest thing was to fix 'em both. And Lou, she seemed to be listening to her space cowboy, floppy ears stirring with each inflection of Mitchell's voice. She made a sad, doggy-crying sound as Mitchell sobbed about how he'd picked Wolfie out of an Australian Shepherd rescue out on 10 Mile, took him in to the vets, got him de-wormed, up and running.

Like Lou, or any of Mitchell's animals, Wolfie wouldn't be trained, four by the time Mitchell got him, set in his ways. Or maybe it was that Mitchell was too soft, paving the way for that phase when Wolfie got into taking a dump on the porch whenever his cookies were late. The bugger was so ugly he was beautiful, and those different color eyes, gray-white and burnt-orange, really did make him look like a canine David Bowie, circa *Diamond Dogs*.

Over the years, Mitchell had chided himself for not being more social with the human persuasion, for not going to the odd mixer and finding a good woman to make an honest man out of him. Yes, Mitchell should've had more to do with people, the socializing alone probably keeping him on the right side of good. But feeling as he did now, placing his doggie in the ground, then picking up the shovel and dropping dirt in, it didn't seem strange that barnyard animals were his best friends. It was the fear Mitchell had in common with them, their vulnerability to so many things out of their control. That's why he'd gone cold-turkey on meat back in '76, same summer Mark "The Bird" Fidrych had his big year with the Tigers.

Critters were Mitchell's friends, and he had every right not to eat them.

Folks waiting at drive-thrus, mouths slobbering, saying eat 'em up, eat 'em up, and the government was after Mitchell? No way that made sense. Same time, Mitchell knew he couldn't spout off like that in front of a judge, if push ever came to shove. Eat 'em up—if Mitchell started talking like some half-assed granola-eater, they'd sit him in the hot seat for sure.

Catori followed Reverend Wayne down into the church basement where he kept a few cots, all empty. On the wall, she noticed a poster of Floyd "Red Crow" Westerman. He'd be appearing at the Fellowship House tomorrow. Wrinkling the freckles on her nose, squinting, she said, "Ten Bears from *Dances with Wolves* sings the songs of Johnny Cash?" Looking at Wayne. "Really?"

Wayne held a hand up, stop. "Floyd's a country singer first, five LPs dating back to 1969. He just loves Johnny. Says he's going to make a tribute album if it's the last thing he does."

"What's he doing here?"

Wayne pointed at the small-print, LâKOTA Topical Pain Reliever. "He has a TV ad campaign dropping. Says he leads an active lifestyle, except pain was getting in the way. Then he found LâKOTA." Looking at Floyd making a fist, virile. "Now he's back to his old self."

Eyes up on Wayne, Catori said, "This pain-reliever thing, does it work?"

"How the fuck do I know?" Wayne wrapped his arms around himself, defensive. "LâKOTA's just a sponsor. Can't hurt, getting him out there before the ads drop."

Catori covered her smirk, the good reverend dropping an F-bomb. "What's your end?"

"My end?" Wayne could barely swallow it—she was judging him. "I get word out Floyd's coming, convince *The Chatham Daily News* to run an advance article, then white people come to hear Johnny Cash songs. After Floyd sings 'Big River,' tells stories, works in some originals—he's a man of spirit, knows the drill—I step in, tell them how expensive it is serving the Lord, then they make community donations and feel better about the stolen land, the white people." Pointing at himself. "That's my end."

Thinking fuck the white people, she told herself they did take the land, and that's why Wayne, Floyd, and even her did what they had to do. Chemical valley was just another term for elimination. They had been comprised, at birth, left to drink the dirty water, bathe in it. How could they be clean? Looking at Wayne, calming herself, she said, "I'm in no position to judge, either. You use it well, your work with youth, at-risk. It's just, there's been a lot of Johnny Cash in my life lately. You hear the new CD? Freakin' Four Horsemen claptrap."

"*Man Comes Around* is not out until November." Wayne looked at her, confused. Was she judging Johnny Cash now? "How did you hear it?"

Catori thought about it, waved it away. "Long story." Blurring her eyes, flashing back. "Remember that guy you had here? Coyne, I think his name was."

"Ronald Coyne? The man who could see through an empty eye socket?"

"Him." Catori pointed at Wayne. "I was here when he was here, summer of 1990. Claimed he lost his right eye in a bailing wire accident. He'd patch up his good eye, take out his glass eye. Then people would bring up greeting cards, pieces of ID, and he'd make like he was reading the info from his bare eye-socket. You know how he did that?"

Wayne nodded, yes, he knew.

Catori waited for an explanation. Getting none, she said, "You going to tell me?"

"No."

"Why not?"

Wayne said, "Because child, it is expensive serving the Lord. It is a trade, and you are asking me to divulge a man's trade secret."

Mitchell walked to Unassumed Road, found the Jeep Cherokee. Wearing work gloves, minding his prints, he located both cellphones, putting them on the passenger seat. He used Enid's keys to start the ignition, steering the DEA vehicle into his driveway, parking near the main barn. Next, he pulled Fowler into the back of the Jeep, then Enid. It wasn't until now that Mitchell realized he'd have to transport the bodies without a trunk. At first, he was more worried than a soldier's wife, but then decided he didn't have a choice, something that seemed to dull his worrying.

Just keep moving forward, he told himself, going behind the main barn and grabbing a green tarp off a mess of fire wood. He threw it over the bodies, doing it in such a way that he didn't look directly at them, before heading back towards the house.

Standing in the nutmeg thyme, he placed the DEA lady's keys on the porch along with the weapons, cuffs, and IDs, stripping out of his blood-stained clothes, throwing his threads under his porch, making a mental yellow sticky to dispose of them later. How? Probably burn 'em in the barby, but later.

Inside, he ran the shower hot, hosing down the blood and the sweat and fear. Singing a little song for Wolfie, "Home on the Range," Mitchell felt a good cry coming on, so he went ahead and had it. It was the way Neil Young sang to the simplicity of animals being allowed to play, to be left alone. And oh man, Mitchell was hoping that there really was a hound heaven, that his innocent friend Wolfie was in a better place.

Turning off the taps, stepping out dripping wet on the ceramic tiles, he toweled dry with thoughts about rolling a fatty and getting higher than downtown's unemployment rate, then remembered the paranoia that would surely follow, time like this.

From his medicine cabinet, he grabbed a tube of LâKOTA and applied it to his sore points. He wrapped the towel around his waist and shuffled to the kitchen where he cracked open a bottle of Atwater Block Lager, local brand, taking a pull, then another when the phone rang.

Mitchell looked at the answering machine, a tiny red light flaring with each jingle. Call-display showed a 519 area code. Mitchell didn't know the number. Whoever it was, they were phoning yonder from Canada, and while Mitchell still didn't like the feel of it by ring five, he figured he might as well know. Plucking the phone off its cradle, he pressed it against his ear, speaking tentatively. "Hello."

"This is Bell Canada," an automated voice said. "You have a collect call from (Sadao's recorded voice now) Sadao Saffron." Mitchell heaved as the automated voice went on. "To accept the charges, please press one." He stabbed the one button, pointing like Sadao could see him. "If I could reach through this here phone, I'd ring your yellow neck."

"That some sort of Asian crack?"

"Goddamn you, Sadao, I'm talking metaphorical for chickenshit. I'm disappointed. You turned on me."

"Look, I didn't give them you, I wouldn't. But I had to give them something, gave them the girls, not you."

"That's nice." Mitchell rubbed his eyes with a thumb and middle finger. "But I'm still madder than Paul Newman in *Hud* when his daddy called in the government man instead of just offing the mad cow, burying it. You know how many hairs I got in the butter?"

"I know," Sadao said. "I know, and I'm sorry."

"You know—do you know what you've caused?"

"Only that it's bad. Look, they put something in my ass made me talk, the DEA woman. I admit it, okay, I told her about the dancers when she was in my ass, wiggling it."

"And Envy?" Mitchell said.

"No, no. I didn't say her name. Why, they get her, too?"

"I think she got out of Dodge, but yeah, she said something about her whoopsie-daisy."

"Well, I'm sorry," Sadao said. "Envy works for charity, actually does good, deserves better. Me, I just gave them enough to get the lady out of my ass and it's a miracle I didn't lose my shit. Get it? I didn't lose my shit. Like, I think she had her whole hand up there, yet I didn't actually shit myself. She was looking, she said, for keister stash." Pausing, clicking his tongue into the mouthpiece. "So, what's goin' on?"

Much as he couldn't reckon how the guy just asked what's going on, casual, Mitchell thought about how he might put this whole mess over the phone. Realizing he couldn't, what with the killings, he said, "I'll pull your coat when I get there."

"Get where?"

"Wherever you're staying," Mitchell said, "Canada."

"Oh no, you're not bringing it to me, dragging me further in. You hear me? Whatever the frick is going on, I'm in seclusion."

"Seclusion—goddammit Sadao, you done brought it on all of us. This is your fault."

"Japanese people, we don't put the onus on others by assigning blame. Just make the problem go away, solve it as a team. Putting the onus, that's white, Judeo-Christian."

Mitchell wasn't having it. "And that's about as convenient as a 7-Eleven at the top of Monteagle Mountain. Now listen, because, of what you did, you're going to help me. Also, I know you're in Canada without a lot of money, and I've got your number, can track you down through reverse look-up."

"Fine, I'm broke in Windsor, okay?"

"Windsor, where?"

Sadao pulled back the curtains to reveal a yellow and red sign. "Travellers Choice Motel, 3665 Sandwich."

"How do I get there?"

"Riverside Drive turns into Sandwich west of the Ambassador Bridge. After that, you pass Wally's Baits, a Home Hardware, then a thrift shop, see it on your left. Only hotel around."

"Okay," Mitchell said. "See you, early."

"Fine, what time?"

"When I'm done what I've got to get done, I'll be there."

"What do you got to get done?"

That was it. Mitchell shouted the guy's name. "Sadao!"

"Fine, keep an asshole in suspense, but Mitchell?"

"Yeah?"

"What size are you—pants, shirts?"

Mitchell closed his eyes. "The hell's that got to do with anything?"

"I need a fresh change of clothes."

Mitchell, trying to blink Sadao away, said, "XL in the shirt, 36 waist, pants."

"Got any 34s?"

"No, Sadao. Why would I have any 34s when that's not my goddamn size?"

"It's okay, alright, 36 is fine. Just bring me a belt. I'll cinch them."

Chapter Fourteen

It was almost 1:30 in the morning, and Phil Legace was waiting on Mitchell. For the moment, Phil couldn't decide whether to use his corncob or fancy papers. Pipe would have been easier, faster, except Phil was the kind of man who liked to change the ritual, so he opted to twist one. Sitting as his desk, tasting Juicy Jay's Super Fine papers, very cherry, he rolled and glued, sparking a match, drying his saliva, solidifying the glue, lighting up and inhaling, holding the smoke as his wife morphed from plain to beautiful.

With one foot on the couch, Charlene pulled a shapeless black dress from her ankles inside-out over her head, dropping it. Barefoot, tan marks from her sandals, she faced Phil in a black bikini, Monarch wings over her 36-Bs. Reaching down to her right thigh, she pulled a rectangular gadget the size of a TV remote from her black bride-style garter. Placing it on her husband's desk, she said, "Why do we need these anyway?"

"Because it is a gun that does not look like a gun." Phil hefted Charlene's piece. "Cop finds this, he sees a garage opener." Aiming it at Charlene, she said get it the fuck off her. Phil complied, placing the prototype AFT Credit Card Shotgun on the desk, recounting its merits.

Phil said the muzzle-loader was key. See, despite having shot-gun in its name, the AFT did not use shotgun shells. This was inconvenient because the user had to measure gunpowder and pour it into each barrel, along with seven .177 caliber bullets. But then that is what made it small, and it had decent power, so long as your adversary was within 10 feet. No, it did not have the kick of Charlene's Browning Hi-Power BDA, and the Browning was more aesthetically pleasing. Phil said Charlene should keep it for use around the house, but she should carry the Credit Card Shotgun into town for self-defense, because, again, it was nearly impossible to ID as a firearm.

One button was marked safety, another shoot. Phil was the first to admit he was looking for an excuse to test it, said maybe he would get up early, look for an opossum.

That's what Charlene always wanted in a man, a guy who shoots opossums. She was standing over Phil now. "So how are you going to screw over Mitchell?" Pointing one hand out at her Credit Card Shotgun on Phil's desk. "You gonna zap him?"

"It will not come to that. I am giving him payment in Canadian, that is all."

She did the rough math, round numbers, said, "Exchange figured, that's almost 20-grand short. I heard you working it out, 59 plus one, 60 in Uncle Sams. He gets Canadian, he's going to see the pretty colors, then what do you say?"

"That he misheard." Phil sucked on the spliff. Dammit, with the distraction of his woman's buzzkill, he had not nursed the jay. Out, Phil struck another match, putting it to the wrap, inhaling. "What am I, Phil's Bank?" Exhaling. "I keep U.S. currency lying around? British pounds? Or is it Yen I hoard?" Waving a hand over his imaginary shingle. "Phil's Bank." Lost in the nothingness of the stucco ceiling. "No, it should be The Phil Legace Bank of Commerce. We make your green grow."

"Focus," Charlene said. "Do you think he's just going to take Canadian, walk?"

Phil took another tug, smoke spewing. "Mitchell Hosowich is nonviolent. Cannot eat animals, his weakness."

"I'd say it's admirable, Phil."

"Perhaps, but it also telecasts the man's underbelly." Phil hit the joint again. "It tells what he is going to do, how he is going to do it." Flattening his hands, raising them above his head, standing, and turning himself into a giant Y, an antenna. "He telecasts it."

Charlene waited, said, "Mitchell puts it on TV?"

Phil brought his hands down, the joint still burning in his right. "You can see his next moving coming, is what I am saying."

"You mean telegraph, that he telegraphs his next move."

"That is what I said."

"No, Phil. You said he telecasts it, made yourself into an antenna and everything."

Phil took another toke, sitting. "He is vegan, hardcore, and what is a vegan to do? Strike up a committee, stage a boycott?" Shaking his head, no. "At worst, maybe he threatens to take it, smuggle it back to Detroit." Looking at Charlene, his eyes half-shut. "He is crazy enough, no doubt." Pointing the joint at her. "But the one thing you know about Mitchell is that he will not hurt, maim, or otherwise injure you. It is not his way."

Phil remembered when he met Mitchell at the *High Times* conference in Detroit, 1989. Phil smoked some of his, Mitchell smoked some of Phil's, then Mitchell rambled on about being vegan. Said he had eaten meat, enjoyed it, tasty, but that critters would never again cross his lips.

Yeah, well Charlene just hoped Mitchell hadn't fallen off the Chuck Wagon and let his heart run cold.

"Do not worry, he is still vegan." Phil noticed the joint, out again. He might as well have used the pipe the way this was going. He struck another match, inhaling, letting it out. "Last time he consumed meat, he ended up at White Castle, that did it, the processing of creatures in a factory setting. He said it was doubly a sin, disrespectful in that it was so bad. Tells me, 'Phil, there's no critter eating on this ranch,' after he invites me for dinner. That is two messages right there, both strident, yet nonviolent."

Yeah, Charlene thought, this was going to be okay because the guy swore off sliders. "Why do we need his dope anyway?" She looked around—a Mac computer, a Bose stereo, stacks of CDs, DVDs *Happy as the Grass was Green*, *Breaking the Ice*, *Catch-22*, and other Mennonite movies Phil tried to learn from. On the blue-gray wall, along with some other originals, hung the Diego Rivera she told Mitchell about. It was titled "Peasants," slightly Orwellian like the old paperback editions of *1984*, the only good book she recalled from school.

Anyway, this guy in the Diego Rivera painting was wearing a sombrero, digging in a field under the watchful eye of a farmer. And Phil, Charlene knew he couldn't see himself in there. Not that it mattered. Phil didn't know Diego from Dago delivering for Family Pizza.

"This thing with Mitchell," Charlene said, "it can't be about money. We are fine, don't need more things."

"Need." Phil looked at her black dress on the floor. "Where do you get off, questioning my decisions?"

She looked at him, eyes wide. "Yours?"

"Mine. In a traditional Mennonite family, the man makes decisions, woman accepts."

"Phil, please." She ran a hand over the contour of her torso. "Under my garb, as you can see, I've been wearing a black triangle halter-style bikini top with matching tie-side bottoms from the Road Angel collection by American Rebel."

Phil gave her a look, thinking she had a nice round ass. Small tits though, even if they were firm, what letter writers in *Gent* often called perky. And yes, Phil could see that it was getting cold out here in Kent County night, perkier still.

"Phil?"

He looked up at her face, the part he liked best. Any wife of Phil's had to look good without make-up, and the achingly beautiful thing about Charlene was her face, the way painting it would have been a sin in any church. Full lips, eyes so brown they were black in the dim light, slightly alien. And Phil liked that she was naturally a bit out of this world in such a way as no one at the Dresden Mennonite Church could question it.

"Phil," she said, clapping. "Phil, Phil . . ."

"What?" He came out of it, blinking. "What are you telling me?"

She reached down on his desk, snatching the book of very cherry papers. "That this is not a traditional Mennonite family."

He stood, pawing at his night-shirt depicting a cartoon chicken opening its wings. The caption said no one coats chicken like Shake 'n Bake. "What kind of family are we then?"

"We're a drug family, Phil. We grow and trade in dope."

Phil, stroking his beard, said, "What do you call this?"

She reached out, pulled his facial hair, hard. "It's our front." Letting go. "And I hate it. You wonder why I don't kiss you? That thing burns, Phil. It burns."

Phil masturbated the part of the beard she'd yanked, sore,

watching her undo that—what had she called it? Oh yes, her Road Angel bikini by American Rebel. "Why are you wearing swimwear?" Pointing out the window to his fields. "Out there."

She dropped her top on the floor, said, "Because it gets warm around noon, and I need color, can't wear make-up." Wiggling out of her bottoms, kicking them to him. "Like we're from British Columbia, didn't want real jobs, so we went into dope. Is any of this coming back?"

Phil held her panties to his nose, sniffed.

"Pig." She turned her mouth down, sour. "You are a pig man."

"Does Aurelio see you out there, sunning?" Phil held the briefs out to her. "In this?"

"Yeah, so?"

"So, Aurelio is real, and it does not look good at Dresden Mennonite, by which I am doing Pastor Baker a personal favor by keeping Aurelio in our employ. And you, turning this into *Temptation Island*, tan lines."

"Personal favor—they get you cheap labor. You make a donation to the church, pay Aurelio three bucks an hour, then you insult the kid, tell him he's picking cotton batten."

"I keep Aurelio in the country." Phil looked at Charlene's stomach, navel pierced with a surgical steel ring. "Besides." Tossing the bottoms back at her. "Why would you want to corrupt him, tempt him?"

Charlene caught the bottoms, shook them, said, "If you don't start using contractions I'm going to shove these down your throat."

"It is for consistency. I keep it simple, always talk like this. You slipped in front of Pastor Baker, saying 'it's' and 'that's.' You should talk this way at all times for consistency's sake."

Charlene watched Phil folding his hands like some preacher who bought his credentials from a *Rolling Stone* ad. When did he start taking the whole thing this far? He was rambling, the windbag, about how it had better not be Aurelio corrupting her. In other words, if she was parading around in front of Aurelio like that, maybe Aurelio had done something to tempt her.

Charlene simulated male masturbation. "You mean did he *viva* his Guadalajara?"

Phil looked away, said, "Do not get in the habit of joking in that fashion." Pointing at his desk now. "We cannot risk any transgressions here. Not now, when we are getting so big."

"That's another thing, Phil. Why are we getting so big? We're into coke now?"

"New world order. Same things are happening in corporate culture as drug culture. You cannot just participate in your market any longer." Phil crushed an imaginary globe with his hands. "You have to control your market, and in order to control pot, we must control coke."

She bowed, holding out an open hand. "And that's why you donate to candidates who oppose decriminalization?"

"We can only control it if it remains criminal. That is also why we need Mitchell's product." Phil held his hands far apart now. "To get bigger with an eye to controlling our market." Hearing tires on the gravel, he stood, moving away from his desk, looking out the window, down his private road, headlights.

Charlene said, "That Mitchell?"

"Probably Dago from Family Pizza." Phil said. "I had the munchies, ordered in." Turning to look into her eyes, entirely black the way the light hit her at this angle. Down, her pussy hair was trimmed into a perfect triangle, the hoo hoo, just like he had her do it after seeing that girl who looked like Charlene in *Gent*. He pointed to their room, said, "Go to bed."

"Fuck you, Phil."

Looking out the window, the dinged-up yellow Ford Mustang getting closer. Yeah, it was Dago. "Then go put something on. I can now see Dago which means Dago can see you."

"Yeah." Charlene started down the hall. "Wouldn't want any more transgressions."

Phil watched her walk, ass wiggling, yelling after her. "What do you mean any *more*?"

"What?"

Phil, heard the car door slam, hesitated. He was about to repeat his question when the doorbell chimed. Relax, Charlene said, she'd get it. And oh man, working his skeleton key into the keyhole of the brass bust next to his desk, getting his money, Phil could hear her at the door now, answering it. Was she covered? No way she was standing there talking to Dago without throwing something on, but then Phil could not see how she had time.

Chapter Fifteen

Mitchell drove the Jeep Cherokee from I-94 east to I-96 east. Merging onto I-75 south towards the border, he shook out of his right glove, found his Camels in his buckskin, a few left, put one in his mouth, his glove back on, pushed the lighter in, and powered down the window. Hearing the click, ready, he brought the glow to his cigarette, inhaling when he heard the tarp taking the wind. And suet—looking into the rearview he saw the cover blown askew. Fowler's head was exposed, gelled hair everywhere, his forehead glaring in the night lights.

Eyes back in front, Mitchell watched an optic-green Dodge Neon pass. A little kid was looking out the back at him, laughing, carefully mouthing words. Mitchell was no lip-reader, but the message couldn't have been that the kid had seen dead people because he was waving. Mitchell figured he probably shouldn't wave back while he's driving this stolen Jeep with dead DEAs. No way. Safest thing was to refrain from responding, rude as it felt.

As for Fowler's exposed head, it wasn't like Mitchell could pull over and fix the tarp without drawing attention, so he just smoked his cigarette, taking the Porter Street exit near the border. Pulling over in Mexican Village—they were calling it Mexican Town now—he parked behind Los Galanes on Bagley.

With the lot near empty, five or six vehicles, Mitchell stepped out, keyed the back, fixed the tarp. No sooner than he had it over Fowler, two city coppers walked around the corner. Frozen, Mitchell talked himself into motion, fluid as he closed the hatch and started around the building. By then, the coppers were moseying, Mitchell making for the patio at Los Galanes. Lady there, nice, said she was sorry, the kitchen was closed, past last call. Mitchell waved a twenty. Might he get a quick drink? Yes, the nice lady said, a quick one. And did he want to come in? It was getting chilly.

Mitchell said thanks, the fresh air would suit him, ordered a tequila double. As per the rule at this establishment, Mitchell's double was served within two minutes. He thanked the nice lady, paid, tipped her the twenty, and waited for her to stop smiling and mosey herself. She took the hint, said *gracias*.

Looking through the yellow liquid, holding it to the moon, Mitchell started singing "Luck Be a Lady" under his breath. Wasn't cowboy music per se, but Mitchell thought it could be a cowboy tune in a situation like this, especially when one considered that Sinatra acted in Mitchell didn't know how many westerns, most infamously, *Dirty Dingus Magee.*

Out back, Mitchell had himself two dead DEAs, so you bet he was taking the time to lick the salt, down the drink, and bite the lemon. He was still singing that Sinatra tune softly, sending it out to his high-school flame, Vi, when he walked onto Bagley. Stopping, looking about, alone, he cupped the lemon slice in his right hand, tossing it into a bin.

At La Carreta Market, he stepped inside to buy three packs of Camels when he noticed a red candle emblazoned with a hot hippie chick standing in flames. Picking it up, reading the other side: "Listen Mortal to the lament of an imprisoned soul . . ."

"Can I ring that up for you, sir?" the lady running the cash said. "Only $1.29."

"Thank you, but no." Mitchell put the item on the counter. "Message is a bit negatory."

The lady, likely Catholic, shot Mitchell a look, evildoer.

Outside, he scanned for those city coppers. Clear, he re-gloved, walked to the Jeep, climbed in, and hit the ignition.

Driving through Mexican Village, Mitchell headed west on Fort Street to a mostly abandoned industrial park near the Detroit River. As he passed Fort Wayne, built as a line of defense in response to how the Canuckleheads briefly took over Detroit, he noticed the place covered in weeds and thistle, overgrown trees doing a number on the walls, unkempt. Mitchell found it all fenced off. Suet, he was finding most every route to the river fenced off, like maybe they planned it this way on account of other people had the same idea.

About the only possible point of access was the abandoned Boblo ferry dock. That was fenced off, too, locked, so he backed up a good 200 yards, stomped on the gas and smashed the gate. Bouncing on the way through, he regained control of the vehicle, pumping the brake, slowing, coming to a stop near the water. He wanted to rest, to think this through. Same time, he felt locked into a course of action. If he had any chance, he just had to do it, keep moving.

He reached in for the cellphones on the passenger seat, breaking them with gloved hands, stepping out, tossing them into the water. Without thinking, cold, he pulled his tarp off the bodies and let it go in the river for a DNA bath. He grabbed his military bag off the passenger seat, flinging it over his shoulder as he rounded to the driver's side. Stepping in with his right foot, left foot on the pavement, he put the vehicle in drive, stepping out, pushing the Jeep when it hit the low curb, giving it something extra, another 25-feet or so, then over the edge and into the river.

Mitchell watched the Jeep float, the undertow, one of the strongest in the world, it was said, taking the vehicle west. He looked all around, figuring somebody must be watching. And what if the Jeep washed back to shore? Goddammit, why had he shut the windows tight? The vehicle, to Mitchell's horror, was floating, spinning. Finally, it filled with water, submerging front bumper first, bringing it further away from shore, bubbling under.

Done, Mitchell hoofed it north on Clark, passing the old Community Justice Building. Taking the train tracks, he walked a half-mile to Grand West Boulevard, *The Detroit News* paper warehouse, then left at a dilapidated house without a roof. He grabbed a cab at Fort and Grand in front of the Crest Motel. Dude up front, wearing a backwards Tigers home cap, navy with a white Old English D, looked through the Plexiglas and said, "This's not a good place, this time, especially for you."

"Especially for me, why?" Mitchell said.

The guy stifled a laugh. "You don't want to be caught in a cowboy get-up, these parts."

Oh, Mitchell smiled tightly, saying that's some very valuable slicker guidance, thanks. Hand on the military bag next to him, biting the inside of his cheek, he told the guy to take him to the

MGM Grand Casino.

A short ride later, Mitchell dropped a twenty into the cash box, keep the change. Out on the street he lingered long enough to smoke a Camel, people watching the line-up, then hired a Dependable Cab to take him to Canada, negotiating a flat $40-fee up front. The ride through the tunnel was swift, no traffic, this time of night. At Customs, Mitchell caught the officer on his cellphone, like he was being interrupted. Right away, Mitchell knew he lucked out, that the guy wanted to get this over with, get back on the talker with his girl.

When asked, Mitchell said he was going to Casino Windsor, open 24 hours. After what he'd been through, he didn't even worry, not much anyway, about the guns and badges in his bag. He would have been a goner if this guy had looked, found the artillery. But Mitchell, he was too tired to be nervous. Resigned to whatever was about to happen next, he calmly answered the Customs man, said he wanted to try the Canadian casino, change of scenery, maybe a change of luck, plus the exchange rate was favorable, and was sent on his way, too easy.

Taking Ouellette Avenue north, back towards the river, the car right-turned onto Riverside Drive East, dropping Mitchell off at the gaming facility, Canada's number one tourist destination until Detroit brought in casinos of its own. Mitchell deposited two twenties in the cash box, thanks. Outside, he smoked a cigarette, marveling at another line-up of folks aiming to gamble their groceries away.

Just you keep moving, he told himself, not too much thinking.

Smoking the butt to the filter, he hired a Vets Cab, Canuckle-head driver never minding with a bullet-proof divider. Mitchell said kindly take him to the Travellers Choice on Sandwich.

Backtracking west along Riverside Drive, Mitchell looked across the water to Detroit. Less than a mile of *agua* separated the two countries, but Mitchell was starting to breathe a little easier. He wasn't out of the honey pot, but he'd put some serious space, a border, between him and those dead DEAs, given himself a chance.

Driving below the Ambassador Bridge—big, ugly mess of iron

in the sky, sturdy—the cab passed Wally's Baits, a Home Hardware, like Sadao said, then a thrift shop, Second Time Around. Arriving at 3665 Sandwich Street, Mitchell doubled the fare, another American twenty.

In all, he'd dropped $80 in less than an hour on cabs, which is something he, as a budget-conscious man, would never do. Main thing was he'd changed taxis so often that he couldn't have left a scent, right? Right—who knew? Suffice it to say that's what he'd done.

Mitchell figured he'd probably left some morsels of popcorn along the way, but what the hell? He was doing the best that he could, circumstances considered.

Finding room 304, he knocked three times, hearing some rustling inside, seeing the curtains break. Sadao opened the door trying to smile. "You made it."

"Yeah, I made it. Now where's the bed, funny boy?"

Sadao pulled his head back, looked at Mitchell. "There's just one, mine."

"Yours." Mitchell walked in. "Thanks for keeping it warm." Dropping his military sack on the floor. "Listen Sadao, I got some jobs for you."

"Jobs? You mean gigs, right? A stag?"

Mitchell looked at the clock radio, thinking yeah, he came all the way here at 3:54 a.m. to talk about the Ohio wing of the Sadao Saffron tour. "No, I mean jobs, as in jobs for me. You listening, Sadao?"

Yeah, he was listening.

"Good, because job one is to rent a car, two is to get us some chow, vegan for me." Mitchell took a roll of cash out of his pocket, counted out $400 in twenties, handing the stack to Sadao. "Put the car on your VISA, keep the cash."

"Alright." Sadao thought he could might make money here. "But what's your job?"

"Goddammit Sadao, I've already done my jobs, plural. Now my job is to get a couple hours shut eye, so go, man, get the car, some vegan grub."

"What kind of car?"

Mitchell thought about it, said, "Something economical, good on gas. And Sadao?"

"Yeah?"

"See if you can get the Detroit paper. Pretty sure they sell *The Free Press* here."

"Fine, what about the clothes? Did you remember my clothes?"

Mitchell ran his tongue across his front teeth, digging into his pack, tossing Sadao some rolled-up items. Sadao caught the pants, looked—black Buffalo brand jeans with blue patches—picking up a faded coral paisley shirt off the floor, American Eagle Outfitters. "The hell's this?"

"Range clothes," Mitchell said.

"For who? The lavender cowboy?"

"Name of a song," Mitchell said. "Point of fact: Vernon Dalhart recorded 'The Lavender Cowboy' in 1938, ended Vernon's career, blacklisted on account of cowboy culture was not ready to come to terms with its homoerotic roots."

Sadao threw the clothes at Mitchell. Asked if that's why Mitchell came over, to dress Sadao up, no thanks. Mitchell reminded Sadao that he'd asked after a clean set of clothes, and he didn't have to wear them. Sadao said okay, took the clothes back. At least they were clean.

Eventually, Mitchell reluctantly agreed that it was too early for Sadao to rent a car. That rental places would be closed until seven, three hours from now.

Mitchell didn't like the reality of that. He just wanted the space to himself, privacy, but he couldn't argue Sadao's spurt of logic. He told Sadao to quietly slip out as soon as places started opening, and again, that was vegan chow for Mitchell. Until then, Mitchell was taking the bed. He said Sadao was just little, to push some chairs together, and was that alright?

Sadao wasn't in a position to say boo. So yeah, he'd push some chairs together as long as he could have one of the covers, a pillow.

Mitchell gave the so-called comedian that much, got himself

tucked in. But Mitchell couldn't get any shut-eye. Tossing, turning, and sweating . . .

Hearing thunder, rain pelting the roof, he relaxed a little, believing a good storm would wash away the footprints, tire impressions, the blood and sundry incriminating DNA splotching his landscape. The rain would quickly re-establish the portulacas he'd replanted over Wolfie, the poor thing, and smooth over the area that used to be his pot patch. Yep, just like the old cowboy proverb said, timing had a lot to do with the outcome of a successful rain dance.

Still, lying there in that musty room, the vacancy sign outside changing the curtains red, Mitchell couldn't help but think how, just yesterday, he'd told himself he was happier than a puppy with two tails. But then he'd also told himself he didn't have the right. Maybe that was the part he should have minded, for he may as well killed two law officers, appearances considered. Now here he was bellying down in the bush with Sadao, of all people, chasing a First Person of Canada girl he'd known less than two months, left him for dead and stole his dope.

All of that was bad enough. And okay, if he somehow got out of this, maybe he'd buck up and get eligible for some kind of grant or another, get old peacefully. If that didn't work, maybe he'd raise critters. Not minks on account you had to skin them. Mitchell could, however, raise alpacas, supposed to be the new sheep. See, you didn't need to kill alpacas, just shave them, and Mitchell thought he could live with just shaving them.

Maybe, but Mitchell had also heard alpacas were notorious biters, and until he made a commitment, he genuinely needed the cash coming to him on this deal with Phil.

Of the 80- or 90-K or so Mitchell cleared most years, a real nice chunk went to keep the animals healthy and general upkeep on the farm. Replacing planks of wood, maintaining the rare herb collection, tools, insurance, vet bills—that took money. And suet, he was still paying taxes even though the city didn't service Unassumed Road anymore.

Thank Christ he didn't have a mortgage. Still, other than the pleasure of his critters, he lived a spartan life. And who was to say weed-growing was the toil of evildoers? Mitchell didn't blow his money on luxury booze, slicker women, cars, or powerful vice. People all coked up, eating critters, no way that was Mitchell. He was a marijuana man, and as far as he was concerned, the whole world would've been better off if everyone took a toke once in a while, the commander-in-chief included.

As for cultivating, Mitchell may as well be growing basil, it was so simple. And now the DEA had him and every person in the industry lumped in with bin Laden?

Reality was, as much as he enjoyed shopping for his cowboy outfits by the pound, Mitchell knew to be frugal for when a day like this came.

Back at the farmhouse, he still had five-grand in walking around money stashed in his stereo speakers, a little nest-egg in his ethical fund, which bought stock in "green and clean" corporations developing recycling and healthcare initiatives, shit like that. Uh-huh, he'd done some modest life planning. But if he had to be on the run, he couldn't exactly show up at the bank, saying, hey, let me cash those bonds of the company's gonna stitch up that hole in the ozone—I got to go.

Oh man, maybe he should have just cut his losses, taken what cash money he had and headed the other way on the I-75, FLA, started over under an assumed identity.

And that was truly it for this dope-growing business. No way he was going to try his luck next year. Goddamn African Violet Mix—Mitchell knew that Gall kid, name of Ivan, just like the Clash song, wasn't right. Pimply as he was, baby fat, probably horny as a three-balled prairie dog, no sexual outlet other than Miss Michigan, his right hand. Yeah, Mitchell remembered that age, so he knew the kid was looking to bugger someone's tar pit.

Speaking of Gall's Hardware, wasn't that nice? Mitchell, spending he didn't know how much over the years, supporting a struggling independent in the bad part of town. Then Gall himself lets young

Ivan sick the Federales on Mitchell. Yes sir, if Mitchell got out of this one, he was going to set that hardware on fire, torch the place.

"Sure," Mitchell whispered to himself. "Sure you are."

"Sure you are, what?" Sadao said from the pushed-together chairs.

"Nothing. Go to sleep."

Main thing, Mitchell thought, was that he was out for good as soon as he tracked down that First Person of Canada girl and got either his dope back or 66 and two-thirds percent of the price. That's all he needed, enough money and time to figure out what to do next. Even if he couldn't be a regular farmer, turning the place into a fine, upstanding tourist trap—a U-pick-it, mayhaps—had to be easier than this. And now that he thought of it, how hard could it be to get folks to pay for something they could just as easily grow themselves? Shit, Mitchell had been doing that for 28 years.

CHAPTER SIXTEEN

Hunkered down on a cot in the basement of the Evangelical Fellowship House, Catori didn't sleep much, either. Thinking she better get rid of the van and its contents as soon as possible, she pulled back the sheets minutes before seven, according to the wall clock.

Dressing in her vanilla velour pants, the matching top, she looked at herself in the mirror, caramel freckles the only sign left of innocence, purity. Purity—there was no way she was ever going to be pure again. Okay, so if the purity bus left as soon as she killed that DEA, what was left, survival? Yes, and that was enough to get her whispering, asking her reflection, can you do this? Well, she'd better freakin' do this, and then—how had Hosowich put it? Oh yeah, she'd better burn the breeze, and never come back. But where would she go? She still didn't know, didn't have a plan for that.

First, she was going to call Phil from the church kitchen, then figured she didn't need him to know where she was staying, no reason to drag Reverend Wayne into it. Who knew what Phil was going to do anyway, especially once she told him her version of why she was here without Mitchell. Phil didn't exactly like Mitchell, no question, but did he want him dead?

Creeping up the stairs, walking out to the van, she wondered how she was going to spin it, justify it. Told herself to figure that part out later. For now, she had to make contact, feel Phil out. But what if she couldn't get to Phil, then what was she supposed to do? Hang around the church with that dead cowboy's dope-filled van? She didn't want to put that on Wayne, either.

Keying the ignition, she backed out, put the van in drive, west along Dan Shab Road. She left-turned on River Road, the St. Clair River next to her, hooking another left on Dufferin. At the fork to the bridge, she passed the sports complex, The Penalty Box Restaurant. Thinking it wouldn't be open, she crossed the bridge to Wallaceburg, the Big Chief Drive-In on Dufferin Avenue.

Parking, she jogged in, seeing somebody she knew already—shit, shit, shit . . .

"Catori?"

She brushed the bangs back from her eyes, forced a smile, thinking, was he still working here? "Greasy."

He looked at her, running fingertips over today's fresh bib, crisp white with that stupid name patch above his left breast, Greasy Spoon, concern creasing his eyes. "What are you doing back? You know Del Ray's still asking after you, right?"

"I heard he has a warrant," she said, "official." Reading a homemade poster advertising the Farmer's Cholesterol Explosion Burger Deluxe Combo (fries plus shake, $5.99), she waited for Greasy to confirm or deny the existence of a warrant. When he did neither, she pointed at the payphone, said, "I have to make a quick call, get some breakfast, then out of your hair."

Greasy nodded, go ahead.

Catori turned, picked up the phone, plugged in a quarter, but it took so long to find the little blue book in her bag that her silver was spit back, an automated voice telling her put in a quarter, insert a card, or hang up. Reloading, keeping a finger on Phil's number, she punched his digits. He answered on the third ring. "Mitchell?"

Catori said, "It's me."

Phil hesitated, said, "Where is Mitchell? Mitchell is supposed to be here." Irritation rising. "Something happen? Something must have happened."

"That's what I need to talk to you about, Phil."

"Where are you?"

"Never mind. Just I need to see you, now."

"Do you have a way of getting here?"

"Yes."

"Then get here. How soon can you do it?"

Catori looked at the Coco-Cola mirror clock, 7:20, buying herself a few seconds to think. "What time is it?"

"It is 7:21," Phil said. "Can I ask, are you in Canada?"

"Yes, Canada."

"How far are you away then?"

About 20 minutes, Catori thought, remembering that she still hadn't filled the holes in her story, that she needed time to think. She said, "It'll take 40 minutes to get to you."

"See you then," Phil said. "I will be waiting." Then he hung up.

Putting the phone back on its cradle, she saw Greasy Spoon walk out from behind the counter holding a plate of scrambled eggs, bacon, hash browns. "Was just making something up for myself before you showed." He nodded to a booth. "Sit, you have it."

She smiled, said thanks. Hiding behind her bangs, shy now, she realized that she looked so fucked up that Greasy Spoon, pure Ojibway, had gone ahead and whipped something up to make sure the dirty half-breed girl on the run had a nutritious breakfast, wholesome.

She grabbed a slice of bacon, put the whole thing in her mouth, trying to eat slower but tightening as Greasy sat across the table peppering her with questions.

When did she get back?

How long was she staying?

Did she have a lawyer lined up in case Del Ray caught up with her? He really was looking, Greasy said, asking around like there wasn't another crime in Kent Country. It was personal with Del Ray, she knew that, right? Story was county-wide that she—what's the word they were using?—emasculated him.

Yeah, Catori knew, which was why she ate as fast as she could. Finishing what was left of the eggs, she washed it down with OJ, rising up from the table. "What do I owe you?"

"On the house." Greasy Spoon shook his head, no, when she pushed a Yankee fiver at him. "You'd do the same for me."

"Thanks, Greasy, thanks."

Then he said, "I'm doing this thing on the side." Standing, pulling a dime bag from beneath his bib, moisture inside, too fresh, maybe mold.

"Thanks." Catori held her smile as she rose from the table. "I'm good for now."

The bell jingled as she went out the door, Greasy following several steps behind. Waving as she put the van in reverse, he noted the Michigan plates, The Great Lakes State, wrote the sequence of numbers and letters on the back of his wrist. Then he mined his jeans for silver, digging out a quarter.

Del Ray James cruised towards Wallaceburg on Highway 40 in his unmarked Chevy Cavalier. Checking himself in the rearview, pushing his International Harvester cap high on his head, he figured his soul patch, little upside-down triangle below his lip, was coming in nicely.

Almost to the point where I'm going to have to shape it, professionally, he thought, reaching into the glove box. He found the bottle of generic codeine aspirin, 222s, Life brand, working the childproof cap and taping out three onto his lap. Clicking the bottle shut, tossing it in the glove box, he reached for the loose pills and plopped them into his mouth, grinding them with his teeth, bitter. What was he tasting, orange zest and chalk? Would it kill them to make the 222s taste good like those grape vitamin Cs? No, Del Ray didn't think it would kill them.

Swallowing the powder, dry, he heard the cellphone ring from the compartment between the seats—reaching, flipping it open, checking call display. Big Chief Dr was all that fit. Hitting the talk button, he said, "Greasy Spoon, what's shaking, my man?"

"She's b-a-a-a-a-ck."

"Back?" Del Ray swung into the oncoming lane. "She, who?"

"Catori," Greasy Spoon said. "Catori Jacobs."

"She there?" Del Ray passed a tractor easily, easing off on the gas as he fell back into his lane. "The Big Chief?"

"Just left."

"Well, why didn't you phone me then, when she was there?"

"She was using the payphone," Greasy said. "Then she ate quick, left. I couldn't call you when she was here. Giving her to you wouldn't stand well in the community."

Braking now, pulling onto the gravel shoulder near Country View Golf & Country Club, Del Ray said, "Why're you telling me anyway?"

"You know. I help you, you let me do my thing. Everyone's happy."

Del Ray watched a lady, late fifties, dressed in a gray pull-over with "Titleist" across her tatas, whiff on the tenth tee. Nice ass in those tight red Bermudas. "Except don't you pilgrims stick together?"

"It's not politic to call us that, pilgrims," Greasy said. "Historically false, has implications of cultural genocide. But yeah, that's the other thing, she's not entirely one of us."

"What do you mean?" Del Ray squinted as the tractor lumbered by. "Not entirely?"

"Too much cream in her coffee, is what they used to say. Looks more Italian than Ojibway. Frowned upon because of having the advantage of being Indian, plus the privilege of blending in the Italian community. Makes colonialism work for her. Probably wouldn't even have status if it wasn't for Reverend Wayne."

Del Ray said, "Sounds like she doesn't fit anywhere, like one of them bisexuals."

"Kind of," Greasy said. "Anyway, she wouldn't say how long she's staying, but she's here for now, easy to find."

"And how's she going to be easy to find? Could be anywhere on the island."

"Point is, she's staying on the island. There's only one way on and one way off, easy to find, if you care to put in the time. Me, I just provide information. Please use it with discretion, which reminds me, I believe she's holding, your end."

"You believe?" Del Ray said. "What makes you say that? You believe."

"Because, when I asked if she wanted to score, she said she was good for now, like that's the one thing going for her. She has enough dope for now, thanks. Means she's not worried about her next baggy. Means she's dealing, holding more than a small amount, gives you cause."

Del Ray watched another lady step onto the tee. Looked like that Nancy Lopez played the lady's tour, a little cream in her coffee, too. This one was about Nancy's age now, forties. The way she was pushing her tee into the turf, ass high, Del Ray couldn't figure out why these gals hadn't learned to bend at the knees. And man, if the last lady's ass was nice, this Nancy Lopez mama was bodacious, had something to grab onto before you pressed the start button—go.

"You there?" Greasy said.

Del Ray said, "Yeah, listen. Did you see any drugs?"

"No."

"Well then, what makes you so sure she has drugs?"

"Like I told you, she said she was good for now. Means she's holding."

"That it?" Del Ray was watching the next golfer tee up, and damn, it had to be lady's day. "She looked stoned?"

"No, but let's just call it dealer's intuition."

"Okay, never hurts to be able to say that you've actually seen the dope. Visual contact."

Greasy said, "Bet that's what you told yourself last time, too."

Twitching at the smirk in his voice, Del Ray said, "Where's she been? You get that?"

"In the States. Where, I can't say."

"The fuck you mean, you can't?"

"She tried paying in American, means she only had American. Also means she's coming from the States, driving an American van. Just one thing. I don't want her here competing, but I want her to think she's my friend. Means you didn't get this from me, as per our arrangement."

"Alright."

"I mean it," Greasy said. "This is on the QT."

"Alright, on the QT, and when I say QT I mean QT. I'm a Mountie, you pilgrim."

Greasy said he didn't hear that, letting Del Ray know what the girl was driving, reading her plates off his wrist.

CHAPTER SEVENTEEN

Sadao parked a green-on-white Austin Mini Cooper in front of his room at the Travellers Choice Motel. Checking the dash, 7:44 a.m., he stepped out carrying two McDonald's bags, keying room 304. Inside, Mitchell was half-dressed, watching the News 4 morning show report that a lot of nothing had happened, despite the red terror alert. Face flushed from his shower, Mitchell said gimme the paper, but Sadao done forgot that part.

Scowling, impatient, Mitchell took his coffee, peeling the lid, sipping, scorching his tongue, ouch. He dug into the bag, partially unwrapping his breakfast sandwich thingy, taking a bite. He'd seen the processed cheese, some egg, neither of which he preferred to eat. But he still thought, okay, it's just animal by-products, not animals, close enough. Chewing, he turned sideways when it occurred to him, spitting onto the carpet. "Goddammit, Sadao."

"Goddammit, what?"

"What—it's meat." Mitchell held the sandwich up, sniffing it. "Pork, if memory serves."

Sadao held up a finger, swallowed. "Memory serves. So?"

"So." Mitchell didn't get it, the guy making like he couldn't recall. "You know I told you, get me vegan."

Sadao, tired of being afraid, said, "Well I take it you saw the egg and that's pre-meat. I did my best, this time, this town. You don't want it?" Reaching for the sandwich. "I'll eat it."

Mitchell pulled back. "I've got to." Taking a bite, closing his eyes, chewing, swallowing. "Only I do it under protest on account of I'm out of fuel. From now on get me vegan grub." Looking at what was left of his sandwich. "I still don't know what God was thinking."

"What?"

"God." Mitchell took another bite, savoring. "Making the critters so dee-licious." Swallowing. "Poor things're downright succulent." Washing it down his gullet with another gulp of coffee, still hot. "It's wrong, man. Anyway, we got to burn the breeze."

"Your shit ready?"

Mitchell patted his military bag on the bed next to him. Wolfing down the last of the sandwich, he snap-buttoned his navy-and-tan Wrangler shirt, slipped into his leathers, put on his hat and stood, slinging his bag over his shoulder. "Now let's get gone."

Sadao scanned the room for yesterday's clothes. Mitchell picked up on that. Said Sadao's dirty things were packed in a plastic bag inside his military bag so as not to come into contact with Mitchell's clean things.

Sadao said, "You going to tell me what this is all about?"

"Later." Mitchell walked to the door, working his tongue against a piece of pork stuck in his teeth. "On the way." Turning the knob, and what the? "Goddamn you three times, Sadao."

"Goddamn me what now?"

Mitchell stepped outside, looking the car over. "I'm six-two and you got a Mini, you stupid sumbitch."

Feeling rightly pissed, Sadao had one hand on his hip, the other in Mitchell's face. "You said economical, and it's got like inner bigness. Wait 'til you get in."

"Inner bigness?" Mitchell said. From now on, if there was a job to be done, he was going to do it himself, much as possible. "Gimme the room key, I'll check out. You drive."

Sadao dug the key from his pocket, handed it over. Mitchell took it to the lobby, rang the bell. The manager emerged scratching his bed head, wearing a T-shirt with the letters BFA. Bad Fucking Attitude, old ska band in these parts, Mitchell thought, pushing the key across the counter. "Just checking out."

The manager looked at it, turning to a row of mail slots on the wall, pulling out a piece of paper. "Rounded off, you owe $16 on the phone."

Mitchell slapped an American twenty on the counter. "Keep the change."

The manager took the bill, held it to the light, looking at it, back at Mitchell. "Hey, wasn't it a China guy checked into 304?"

"My partner, Japanese."

The manager smiled, waved to himself. "No wonder you're generous, couple dudes shacking up at the single rate." Placing a calculator on the counter, punching numbers. "I want another $31.87. Knob jockeys check in single, out double—I don't think so."

Now, Mitchell was in no position to judge the man-lovin'-man people. Being what he was, a dope farmer, he tried to live and let live, did so for the most part. Asides from that way of thinking being nothing but good for his karma, out on the lone prairie, men did outnumber women something like ten to one, point of fact. So cowboys were, as per The Lost Dakotas song, frequently, secretly fond of each other. Just part of the cowboy way, historical, and now this manager was talking down on the cowboy way.

"You and your friend." The manager pointed, seeing Sadao parked outside the office. "There he is. Should've known, walking in late like he just got off his Clydesdale." Turning back to Mitchell. "You and your friend pay or I call the cops."

Mitchell cupped an ear, leaned forward. "Pardon?"

The manager pulled a bored face, casual. "Look, I don't care what you did in there." Pointing to a row of rooms. "But I have to pay someone to clean up. For two, the price is more. So yeah, you don't give me another $31.87, I'm calling 9-1-1."

"9-1-1, huh?" Even if Mitchell paid, the manager seemed pretty bent on bringing down the hammer, just like that Gall kid, Ivan, so Mitchell figured he'd best nip this boy plant in the bud, scare the bejesus out of him. He nodded, yeah, uh huh, going into his pants, pulling Fowler's ID. Careful to cover the headshot with his thumb, he dug deep for the sheer audacity to push the shield into the manager's face. "You know what kind of badge that is?"

The guy looked at it. Yeah, sorry officer, he knew.

"You know what that means?"

Shaking his head yes, then no, the guy didn't know what to say.

"Means U.S. Drug Enforcement Administration, or Do you want an Enema, Asshole?"

"I didn't mean to say you was a gay guy." The manager held his hands high. "It's just—"

Mitchell pointed outside at the Mini. "That I referred to my partner?"

"No, it's just that you sort of look like that dude from the Village People. You're undercover, right? That's not your own clothes, right?"

Slowly winding past the Sydenham River, a few clicks from Dresden, according to the sign on Bass Line Road, Catori had her story as straight as she was going to get it. Kind of flying by the seat of her velour vanilla pants, a bit dirty now, she was going to tell Phil the truth, as close to it as she could anyway. Mostly, she was going to talk about Mitchell ignoring that sign. Then the prick who sicced the cops on her, that comedian, Sadao Something. Phil would understand. Mitchell had exposed her, or at least left her exposed.

Clearly, she would tell Phil, Mitchell fucked up, got old, smoked too much of his own shit, got himself killed. Otherwise, she could tell the story pretty much as it happened. And that part about the cow with the third horn—how was she going to make that up? She couldn't. Phil would know that. But what was she going to say happened to that other cop? The one with the tight face. It would be in the news soon, so she'd have to tell Phil something, but she couldn't admit to it, not even to him. Coming to his farm with a truckload of dope after she offed a fed—he'd say thanks, Catori. Thank you. So, there was no way she was copping to that.

As for Mitchell, Phil really didn't like the way he came around with his zippers, spurs, and flashy shirts, generally insulting the Mennonite way of life. Mitchell, bringing his transgressions onto Phil's farm, attracting attention, flaunting his pursuit of the American dream. Yeah, maybe Phil actually would be happy about this, like someone had done him a personal favor, as Phil himself would say. Plus, Phil genuinely had a soft spot for Catori. He took care of her, making sure she got away to Detroit after that incident with Del Ray James.

Speaking of Del Ray, Catori couldn't believe he was still getting paid to look for her, the creep. That was just another reason she had to get the cash, get out of here. But again, where would she go? Where could she go? And what could she do?

Taking a left on Hughes Road, passing a sign promising premium prices for milk-fed chickens, she couldn't go back to the States, so it had to be somewhere in Canada. Winnipeg? No thanks. What was the next town—15 hours? Too isolated. Toronto was out. She'd worked the Zanzibar on Yonge Street for a few weeks until someone's husband was shot in the VIP room, and she wasn't liking Toronto before that, too many people in too small a place. But then if she didn't like Ottawa or Hamilton or Vancouver or Edmonton, where could a girl like her blend?

With Sadao driving the Mini east on Highway 401, Mitchell flipped through the Thursday, September 12th *Detroit Free Press* he'd picked up at a box on the way. There was a story about false alarms, a speech the president gave about terror, drugs, and getting Saddam, evildoer, but nothing about Fowler Stevens and Enid Bruckner. Even if they had found the dead DEAs, Mitchell thought, it would have been too late to get the story in the paper.

Inside the local section, Mitchell said suet when he read the headline, "Coleman Young Community Center to rise in place of Detroit's last burlesque."

"What?" Sadao glanced over at the paper in Mitchell's lap.

Mitchell closed the broadsheet, folded it. "After all that kerfuffle, going to the highest level of alert, red, it looks like nothing happened. No terror yesterday."

"Looks like it."

At Belle River, 20 minutes east of Windsor, Mitchell switched on the radio, finding 99.5 WYCD on the tuner. Hearing Tim McGraw fade out, Shania Twain in, Mitchell flicked it off.

"Hey," Sadao said. "I was hoping to listen."

"Shania's just a girl needs a cabbage roll in a too-short dress, ain't even close to real music." Mitchell went for the Top papers and baggie in his jacket, preparing to twist one. "Aside from Johnny, Loretta, Tammy, and a little Kristofferson, it's just a bunch of tight-jeans-wearing slickers been processed and branded on Detroit's only country radio station these days. Imagine Shania playing the Opry. It's no wonder those people didn't get along with J.C."

"Jesus Christ?"

"Close," Mitchell said, "Johnny Cash."

"Shania's better than nothing." Sadao pointed at the radio. "Can't we have some tunes?"

They could, Mitchell said, if they were in his van. Bad enough that First Person of Canada girl took his dope, his ride, but she done busted his loops, too.

"Busted your loops?"

"Took my tunes, my CDs." Mitchell broke up a bud, sprinkling it onto one of his papers, chin-nodding up the highway. "Let's us stop at a pump-and-dump yonder, get some real vittles, some music, something classic." Rolling, licking the glue. "This thing got a cassette, CD?"

Sadao looked at the console, said CD, back to the road. Mitchell said they'd have some real country at the pump-and-dumps. Then he sparked up, closing his eyes, taking the smoke.

"So," Sadao said, guiding the Mini past the Town of Tilbury sign. "How much longer you going to keep an asshole in suspense?"

Mitchell opened an eye, blowing smoke as he passed the dutchie. "You the asshole?"

"I told you last night." Sadao took the twisted cigarette in his fingers, hitting it. "Yeah." Holding the smoke as he spoke. "I'm the asshole, alright?" Exhaling. "Can we move on? I'm trying to redeem myself, your eyes. Tell me what I have to do to fix it, make it right."

Leaning back with the seat reclined, Mitchell held up an open hand, saying, "Sadao, I got like five hairs in the butter, and the day just started."

"Specific." Sadao took another hit, giving the car more gas, bringing it up to 70 MPH, setting it to cruise. "Bring me up to speed. So you have DEA chasing you, us —"

"Not no more."

"What do you mean?" Sadao handed the joint back to Mitchell. Reading a sign, Metric conversion 100 KM = 60 MPH, Sadao tapped on the brake, disabling cruise, taking the car down to 64, cheating a bit like everyone else, hitting reset. "Not no more?"

Mitchell reached his free hand into his military sack in the backseat, digging around, coming up with a handgun, checking the safety then placing it on Sadao's lap. Sadao picked it up, cocked it, checking the brand name. "Les Baer Prowler III. Neat."

"Neat." Mitchell managed a sad laugh. "I don't think so, especially if you're talking tidy." Then he took a hit.

Sadao placed the gun in his lap, picking at a tiny piece of paper stuck to his tongue, then spitting it away—*pft, pft, pft.* "I mean neat, as in cool, Daddy-O."

Mitchell blew out a sticky cloud, rolled down the window, took another hit, then let the roach fly. "Yeah, well get ready, because this entire predicament—set in motion by what you done—is about as cool as a broken fridge. Now brace yourself, son. You braced?"

Sadao nodded. He was braced.

Mitchell pointed at Sadao's lap, said, "Good, because that Les Baer Prowler III belonged to the law lady looked in your butt." Rummaging around for something else, coming up with a badge. "Name of Enid Bruckner."

Thirty-three-and-a-third, Catori thought. Hell, with Mitchell out of the picture, she could get a hundred percent, about 60-grand, more or less, American.

Coming up on Phil's farm, everything guarded by rows of evergreens growing into each other, she turned up the drive, passing a sign, Dresden Mennonite Harvest. Around back, she parked, stepped out. Phil's wife Charlene said hi, leading Catori past the good-looking Mexican dude—what was his name again? Oh yeah, Aurelio—in plain black pants and a white shirt, sweeping the cobble-stone patio.

Phil was out there in the same two-tone outfit, taking tea, hands on his belly when he saw Catori. Up from the table, he took her arm, said, "Mitchell?"

Catori looked down, shook her head, no.

"I do wish there was a Mennonite curse for situations like this." Phil looked out on his field, somber. "But even when persecuted, Christ's disciples curse not." Lifting his shoulders, letting them fall. "Not even when in pain. And when you go through mental anguish like this, you know it is God's will to make a punch-line out of physical pain. Anyway." He yanked on Catori's arm. "I assume they got the dope."

Catori shook that off, pulling away. "I have it."

"You have it?" Raising his brow, interested, Phil looked around, leading her towards the house. He split from her near the door, called Aurelio over, whispering. Then Phil walked up the steps, painted gray, opening the door. He led Catori through the kitchen, into his study, a computer, some farm art, all signed originals, and a big Mennonite bust next to his chair. "Okay, brass tacks," he said, sitting behind his desk. "Mitchell, what happened?"

Catori sat across from him, closing her eyes. "Dead."

"I just talked to him." Phil pointed at the phone on his desk. "You mean dead, as in he is in trouble? He is caught, dead in the water?"

"Just dead." She crisscrossed her hands like a referee waving off a touchdown. "D-E-D, dead. And it gets worse."

"Worse?" Phil scowled. He still didn't see how Mitchell could be dead, or what could be worse than that. "Worse, how?"

Chapter Eighteen

Sadao looked at the gun in his lap, glancing at Mitchell, back to the highway. "The DEA lady, you killed her?"

"No, no. Catori's the one did that."

"But a dead cop, your land, and you get me high before you tell me?" Sadao delicately placed the gun on Mitchell's lap. "Like, this is where I decline, opt out."

"No son, this is where you opt in." Mitchell was a little giddy for the first time since yesterday morning. He put the piece back on Sadao's lap. "And there's no sense in fretting over biting off more than you can chew on account of your mouth is bigger than you thought." Eyes glassy, watching Sadao. Funny boy wasn't laughing now. "Time for you to step up, yep."

"Oh Christ, this means you killed two of them."

No, Mitchell didn't kill anyone, ever, nor did he wish to start, clear? Clear, Sadao said, and that was good. He wasn't riding with a murderer, but what happened? Mitchell said it was complicated. First, his cow Simmi done gored the guy looks like the guy got caught videotaping sex he has with Andie MacDowell.

Sadao said, "You're talking the guy who looks like James Spader?"

"Yes, then so far as I can tell the woman DEA shot him, accidentally or not. He seemed conflicted about the whole thing, so I can't tell her intentions. But she shot him."

Sadao took his right hand off the wheel, holding it out. "Then you're okay."

"Not really." Mitchell shook his head. "Could still look like I did it if someone traces them back to my spread."

Sadao was afraid to ask, but he had to. "Why's that?"

Mitchell came out with it all as-a-matter-of-fact. "On account of how Catori killed the lady. Tied a rope to my horse, Hasty Kiss, the other end to the lady's neck, shot off her gun, spooked the horse. Hanged the DEA lady, essentially." Getting a case of giggles, trying in vain to fight them off on account of subject matter. "Would have died from the trail rash alone."

Sadao couldn't believe what he was hearing. Couldn't believe Mitchell found it funny.

Man, in just a few hours Sadao was going to be pussy for perverts, he knew it. A gun, Jesus H. Christ, Sadao had a dead cop's gun in his lap, and why did he need a gun anyway? "Okay, okay, so what am I doing with you, with this?"

Mitchell hit the button on his chair, popped up. "You owe me for starting all this, getting the wheels in motion by sending them to Catori, the other girls."

"That's not the question," Sadao said. From the corner of his eye he could see Mitchell, watching. "What do I have to do?"

"Help me get my dope back." Mitchell read the sign in the road. Wheels Inn, Chatham—mini-golf, indoor/outdoor pools, waterslides, shuffleboard, pool tables, Wild Zone, and sundry honky tonk. "The dope or the money. You help me get either back, and I'll see you get a square deal—a full one-third share."

A third—man, Sadao was afraid to ask what he had to do for that third. But yeah, he could use the cash. And who, exactly, were they going after?

"Catori first." Mitchell, opened the glove box, pulled out the road map. "She's the one stole it. Also the one left me for dead."

"She tried to kill you, too?"

"Tried," Mitchell said, reading the map. "Thinks I'm dead, so we have that going for us."

"She thinks you're dead and that's in the plus column? What else?"

"Well, I think I know where she's going. Best guess is she's gone home, Walpole Island, near Phil's. That's where people tend to go when they're in trouble."

Sadao showed his upper row of perfectly white teeth. "People go to Canadian Indian reservations when they're in trouble?"

"No." Mitchell couldn't believe how long it was taking to explain. This was the last time he smoked Sadao up. "Home. People tend to go home when they're in trouble. Plus, Phil's the only one she knows can handle this load. If I'm right so far, we find her, we find it."

"What makes you so sure?"

"She's driving my van."

"You got a Lojack?" Sadao said. "Some sort of tracking device?"

"No, no. We're going do it detective-style, dog her footsteps." Mitchell held the road map up, pointing at Walpole Island. "Seems there's only one bridge in and out—unless she takes a ferry back to the States, which I highly doubt, scrutiny—and she doesn't know what we're driving." Looking out across the hood. "Is that the engine or the trunk?"

"Engine's in front," Sadao said. "Not much of a trunk in the back. That's how they made room for the inner bigness I was telling you about, new model." He looked in his lap, the dead cop's gun still there, jerking the wheel when he heard Mitchell screaming.

"Sadao—the road, goddamn you. Watch the road."

Sadao swerved on the gravel shoulder—left, right, left, right—catching the right tires on the pavement, finding his lane again. Checking the rearview, he said, "Sorry, man."

"Sorry," Mitchell said, disgusted. He hit the recline button, lying back. "Just you keep it in the fairway, Sadao." Pulling his hat over his eyes. "Also, if you see a pump-and-dump, stop. Got a case of cotton mouth something fierce, and on top of that, the munchies."

Sadao couldn't figure how Mitchell had the munchies already.

Phil had to hand it to Catori, the way she laid it out. There was an actual sign in the road—If You Think It's Dry Now, Wait Til November—and Mitchell still did not deal with it. That was so him. The part about the three-horned cow carried, too, because Phil knew all about Simmi, another freak for Mitchell to play with.

"Just one query." Phil twirled an index. "What happened to the female DEA?"

Dammit, Catori hadn't quite figured how to spin that part, so she said what made sense, mindful of the consequences of Phil

Legace catching her in a lie. "I did it." Pointing at herself with a thumb. "Had to."

"You had to?"

She shifted in her chair, said, "No choice."

Phil said, "Alright. You should have never been put in that situation, sorry. No sense in worrying about it now, done, so what is the deal?"

"Same as you had with Mitchell, only you pay me."

"And what did Mitchell think he was getting?"

Given that Mitchell was going to give her 20K, 33⅓ percent of 60K, Catori figured she should up the price in case Phil wanted to negotiate down. Street value had to be $2,500 a plant, more, so she gave him a figure of 70K for the 59.

Thinking that was her first mistake, price-gouging, Phil stroked his beard, said that would be high under normal circumstances. Only with Mitchell and the DEAs dead, there was nasty business to be concerned with, risk, meaning the dope was tainted. Catori had increased Phil's exposure tenfold by bringing it here. Also, Phil knew she had nowhere to go, so he would be give her a nice finder's fee, do her a personal favor. How did nine-grand sound?

Nine? In other words, Catori's dime, which started out at 20-thou, before ballooning to 60 or 70 in her mind, had now been whittled down to nine. "Sounds like shit, Phil."

"Okay." Phil was entertained, hearing her out. "Reasonably, what could you want?"

"Same as you were giving Mitchell, 60. No more, no less."

"Sixty now, already coming down 10." Phil looked right into her golden-brown eyes. "Besides, you think I just leave that kind of money lying around?"

"Actually, I do, and not just because you said you'd have it." Catori bobbed her head side to side. "Also, because when Phil Legace needs money, he just goes and gets some."

Phil chuckled self-consciously. He had to admit, she had him there. How about 10-grand? Again, Catori would take 60, same as Mitchell. Phil said she would take 10, and he would not even bother to inspect the merchandise—that was that.

Standing, Catori told him to keep the money. She'd sell it to someone else. That's when Phil pulled what appeared to be a TV remote from his back pocket, telling her about the Credit Card Shotgun prototype. See, it was the muzzle-loader that allowed them to make it so small. An inconvenience to load, sure, but at this range, it would put a nice a hole in someone, stop them. Besides, Phil said, looking out the window, Aurelio and Charlene were already unloading the van in the distance. The deal was done and Catori would take 10. One day, she would see that Phil was doing her a personal favor.

"So you keep telling me," she said.

Phil made a face, leaning over the large bust of some guy's head—looked like ZZ Top at a funeral, staid—working a key into the back.

"Who the fuck's that?" Catori said.

"Martyr, Dirk Willems. Convicted for being Anabaptist when Netherlands was Spanish-ruled." Phil flipped the top of this Dirk's head open. "Before they executed Dirk, he made a prison break across some ice. Might have made it, too, except a guard chasing him broke through. Dirk, being an honorable Mennonite, stopped, saved the guy." Reaching inside. "The guard thanks Dirk by apprehending him, burning him at the stake."

Catori, thinking Mennonites weren't supposed to have icons, said, "Look Phil, I need that money to get away."

"And that is why I am giving it to you, despite your disrespect. And despite, as well, that this dope is tainted, devalued." Phil lifted a bound wad, holding it in front of her. "Ten-thousand, I am telling you what it is worth."

"It's not enough."

"There is something I think you glossed over." Phil dropped the money on his desk, leaning back. "Now tell me again, if the cow killed one DEA, you killed the other DEA, who killed Mitchell?" When she hesitated, Phil stroked his beard, said, "Thought so."

Near the border of Chatham-Kent, Mitchell jogged out of the 18-Wheeler Truck Stop carrying a CD. Jumping back in the Mini on the passenger side, he fiddled with the shrink wrap.

Sadao said, "Where's the food?"

"Grub line's too long, hungry truckers. We'll try somewhere near the reservation."

Putting the Mini into drive, Sadao headed down the ramp, merging with east-bound traffic on the 401. "This year's batch, it's a slow creeper."

Mitchell said yeah.

Sadao nodded at the CD as Mitchell read the liner notes. "What'd you get?"

"John R. Cash." Mitchell looked for somewhere to dispose the plastic wrap, dropping it over his shoulder, the back. He held up the jewel case, Johnny wearing a black trench coat, pit bulls, dark and light, sitting on each side. "*American Recordings*, volume one."

Sadao looked in the mirror, eyes red. "Is there even a place we can both eat?"

"We'll find a burger joint," Mitchell said, sliding the platter into the player.

"You going over to the dark side? Becoming carnivore?"

"Just for now, convenience." Mitchell hit the advance button, bumping it to track five. "They have nothing else good, and I use the word loosely, except meat. I get home, it's back to Uncle Herschel's Soya Jerky and other soya products. Funny, they seem to grow a lot of soya around here, but no soya products at the 18-Wheeler."

Mitchell eased into his seat by the time Johnny started strumming like he was a sitting around a campfire. Stripped-down—unplugged, the MTV girl had called it—plucking the odd raw note, he was singing "Why Me Lord?" It was a song about being spared, the tortured chorus wondering what Johnny had done to deserve even one of the blessings he'd known.

"It's church music," Sadao said. "Not even country. It's like gospel."

"Gospel, blues, and country all tie their metaphorical horses to the same post, rural music. Better than what you wanted, Shania. Steve Earle says she's the most expensive lap dancer in Nashville, and while I won't go that far, disrespectful, you know she's not making real music."

Whatever, taking the Bloomfield Road turn-off into Chatham, Sadao still couldn't figure why Mitchell was thankful. Left for dead, his dope gone, why was Mitchell so quick to put his soul in Jesus' hand? Mitchell said Sadao missed the point, which was that he, Mitchell, was alive enough to go after his dope. That's right. Given the killings, Mitchell thought himself a fortunate man, and Sadao might do himself a solid by coming out for a little Jesus and improving their overall karma-quotient. Sadao thought Mitchell was mixing religions, but didn't mention it.

Through Chatham, Sadao hit the indicator, approaching McDonald's. Mitchell slapped it off. So long as they were eating critters, they might as well hold out for something nutritious.

As Sadao took King's Highway 40 towards Wallaceburg, Mitchell looked out at field after field of soya. He'd heard about grants for Canucklehead tobacco farmers to convert. Ah, getting them to stop growing an evil weed in favor of something wholesome. But it wasn't in the cards for Mitchell. Compromising aside, he'd never heard of a program to convert to soya from dope, not one.

Nearing Wallaceburg, he navigated Sadao to Dufferin through town. Johnny was singing how he got the number 13 when he was young, born in the soul of misery.

Sadao glanced at the stereo. "There's another nice little upbeat number for the road."

Mitchell thought about schooling Sadao on how Johnny was exploring his dark side in song instead of acting it out. But then, approaching Walpole Island, seeing the Big Chief Drive-In, Mitchell said, "There."

"The Big Chief?" Sadao said. "Really?"

Mitchell said they stood a better chance of getting something nourishing at an independent. Sadao said alright, hit the indicator, left, pulling in. When he turned off the ignition Mitchell told Sadao to stay there and keep a lookout for his van, to hit the horn if he saw it.

Stepping out onto the gravel, Mitchell went inside. Behind the counter he saw a kid with a Greasy Spoon name patch. "What can I get you for?"

Mitchell looked up at the sign, said, "Tell me about the Farmer's Cholesterol Explosion Burger Deluxe Combo."

Greasy Spoon looked at the Coke clock. "Not even 9:30. You want a burger?"

Mitchell nodded, said he had a taste for it.

Alright then, Greasy described the Farmer's Cholesterol Explosion Burger as a nine-ounce patty smothered in cheddar, mushrooms, and bacon served on a Kaiser, *avec* fries and shake. Mitchell made a peace sign, two orders, make the fries spicy, the shakes vanilla.

Greasy was good to go with that, dunking the fries in oil. He was tossing the patties on the grill when Mitchell noticed a familiar series of numbers and letters on the kid's wrist. "Wouldn't suppose you could help me with some information."

"I can try." Greasy lifted the spuds out of the oil, checking, letting them fry.

"You know a girl, name of Catori Jacobs?"

"Can't say as I do."

"Point a fact?"

Half looking back, Greasy said, "Point of fact."

Chapter Nineteen

Driving away on Phil's private road, Catori looked in the side-view—Phil in his two-tone get-up, waving like he really had done her a personal favor, growing smaller. At Hughes Road, she pounded the wheel. "Shit, shit, shit . . ." Ten-grand, Canadian, how far was that going to get her? Not freakin' very, she thought, right-turning the van.

Okay, so it hadn't worked out and that was that. Much as she wanted to pout, there was no sense. By now, she knew she'd made a mistake with Mitchell, no doubt, but first things first. She had to go back to Walpole, which is where she was headed, passing the sign to Uncle Tom's Cabin. Okay, she'd pick up some fresh clothes from the church—some jeans, maybe that Free Newfoundland T-shirt Wayne mentioned—and get her head screwed on, get rid of the van.

She couldn't just dump it near the bus station. She did that, they'd run the plates sometime over the next 24 hours, have no trouble tracking it to her. Driving the Ram much longer wasn't an option, either. Soon as they found out Mitchell was dead, they'd figure out his van was missing, and once they figured out his van was missing, they'd be chasing it down, chasing her. She had to get rid of it, but where? She hadn't thought that part through, either.

Mitchell, watching Greasy Spoon flip the burgers, took a step back and looked both ways on Dufferin. Clear, he reached for Fowler's badge in his pocket, thumbing the head shot. "Now I'm asking questions about a girl goes by Catori and you're lying to me, son, disrespectful."

"Yeah?" Greasy, casual, looked at the shield. "What makes you think I'm lying?"

Mitchell nodded at the kid's wrist, said, "Because the plate number of a vehicle I'm actively pursuing matches the sequence written on your arm. That's why."

Greasy opened his mouth, let it hang. Okay, he put up his hands, busted, he knew her. Mitchell said good, to get his hands back to food-making while he answered some questions, such as when did he last see her?

Cutting a Kaiser in half, leaving it on the grill to toast, Greasy said earlier this morning.

"Say where she was going?"

"No."

"Don't lie to me, son."

"Not lying, she didn't say. Only thing I know is I saw her driving away from Walpole."

"Okay," Mitchell said, "Only why are my plates written on you?"

Greasy froze, dropping his spatula. "Your plates?"

"Mine, as in the plates of a vehicle I'm pursing, makes 'em mine."

"Oh, I get it."

"Good, then get on to answering the question."

"What was it?"

"Goddammit, that plate number—why is it on your wrist?"

Greasy closed his eyes, said, "Because I already told the RCMP about her."

Knowing enough of what that might be about, Mitchell dropped his eyes, said thank you. But Greasy wasn't to speak of this DEA visit on of account of it was a highly sensitive mission.

Greasy said, "I told you what you wanted to know. Can you tell me what it's about?"

"Classified," said Mitchell. "Sensitive, like I said."

When the burgers were ready, Greasy wrapped everything, bagged it. Mitchell said he assumed it would be on the house on account of the kid had lied—and don't forget, zip it. Fine, the kid said, but this being a small town, he wanted to be sure the DEA guy wouldn't use his name, that he'd keep it on the QT. Mitchell said sure thing. He'd keep Greasy's name out of it, then he left, walking to the Mini holding two brown paper bags.

Sadao said, "What'd we get?"

"Farmer's Cholesterol Explosion Burger Deluxe Combo. Spicy fries, vanilla shakes."

Sadao eyeballed the dash, said, "It's morning, 9:36."

"So it is," Mitchell said, reading a street sign. "Drive up and pull over there in the rough, behind those maples on St. Clair. We can get a view of the traffic coming into the island."

"Why coming in? She could just as easily be going out."

"No way she's heading out." Mitchell chin-nodded to the Big Chief Drive-In. "Kid inside narced her, and not just to us. Also narced on her to the RCMP, which means a guy goes by Del Ray is looking for her. Main point is, she was last seen leaving the island. If we're going to see her, she'll be coming back, returning, or not at all."

Mitchell handed out the food and drinks, then Sadao watched Mitchell put the bite on his Cholesterol Explosion Burger, washing it down with a pull on the shake. "Goddamn, that's good." Mitchell smacked his lips. "Good, but ethically reprehensible. You know how many cows McDonald's sent to the big boneyard last year?"

"No." Sadao chewed on his burger, swallowed, took a pull on the shake. "How many?"

"Let's just say a lot. You know in India, cow's sacred?" Mitchell watched Sadao nod. "In India, McDonald's can't serve burgers."

Sadao sucked on his straw, swallowed. "Like, I'm not having a conversation about cows while I'm eating them. Just tell me how you knew she'd be coming here."

"Done already told you."

"Tell me again."

Mitchell took another bite, chewing as he spoke. "Because when you get in trouble, you go home, here for Catori. I reckon she already beat us to Phil's, not far, and that Phil cheated her on account of she's not a certified grower, won't have to buy from her again." Sucking on his shake, swallowing. "Means by my calculations we're going to catch her heading back here to regroup. Kid in the Big Chief said he saw her leaving, not coming. In other words, she was last seen heading attaway." Mitchell pointed his shake at the road away from the island, back at himself. "If she's coming back home, she has to be headed this way."

Sadao pulled his head back, focusing on nothing. "What do they like her for? The dead cops? Cause if it's the dead cops, then they know about you, and if they know about you, they maybe know about me. And if they know about me—"

Mitchell told Sadao to shut it, said the RCMP was onto Catori for a different matter: Back when she was dancing at JRs in Chatham and selling on the side for Phil, she'd hogtied a young RCMP. Shit, Sadao said, what'd she do that for? Mitchell said he didn't know, that Phil didn't out and say it and neither did Catori, so it must've been bad, whatever the Mountie did.

"All I know is what was vaguely implied," Mitchell said. "And that's why, even if she comes back, she won't be here long."

Greasy Spoon fished a quarter from the till, walking to the payphone, plugging it in, punching digits. Del Ray answered on the other end, what? Greasy said, "I told you, keep me out of it."

Parked, Del Ray looked at the phone, little confidential informant getting uppity. Bringing the talker back to his face, Del Ray shouted over the static. "Out of what?"

"Just please promise you will not share the source, me, of that information with anyone."

Del Ray said, "You stoned?"

"No."

No, well Del Ray had positioned himself on the Island side of the bridge right after Greasy's phone call. Hadn't had human contact since, why, what happened?

Greasy said, "Oh well then, must just be a great big misunderstanding, but some pretty important people are suddenly looking for Catori, and they're coming right for me."

Del Ray caught it, Greasy's dig, even over the static, the way he said suddenly, passive aggressive. And yeah, there sure as hell was a great big misunderstanding, because Greasy now seemed to fear these pretty important people more than him, Del Ray. Or maybe the kid was coming off like that because of the static. What were they? Not even a click apart and the phone was breaking up. "The fuck are you talking to me like that? I'm a Mountie." Del Ray waited for a response. Getting none, he said, "Are you there?"

"Yeah. What I said is . . ." Greasy's voice was breaking up again, but Del Ray was sure he said the PTA had come to the Big Chief looking for the girl.

Holding the phone to his ear, tight, Del Ray could barely hear now, every other consonant fractured. He was telling Greasy that he must be stoned, because the PTA didn't have a say here. That girl was in her thirties, done with school, so clearly, the PTA was out of its jurisdiction.

"Good choice by the way." Sadao held his burger up as he chewed, swallowing. "So how are we going to find her?"

Mitchell took a sip of his shake, shot Sadao a look. "You still stoned?"

Sadao thought about it. "Somewhat."

"Somewhat—she's driving my goddamn van, and I done told you like three times now." Mitchell took another sip of his shake, pointed it at Sadao. "You have got to look alert, son. Find my ride." Looking back at the Big Chief, Mitchell saw Greasy on the phone. "You were keeping a lookout when I was in there, right? We didn't miss her, right?"

"No." Sadao pointed at the Big Chief. "I remembered when you were in there. Then, when you came back, that's when I forgot. Speaking of which, something else I missed."

"Here we go," Mitchell said, waiting for it.

Sadao said, "Why do we need guns?"

"Catori has my varmint rifle. Might not know it yet, but she's armed."

"How does she have your gun, doesn't know?"

"I hid it in a wallpaper cylinder. Didn't want her riled."

Sadao frowned. "You stoned when you did this?"

"A little." Mitchell held his thumb and middle finger a pinch apart. "Had a contact high from handling the plants, packing them. And like we both said, it's a slow creeper."

Looking at the baggy jeans gathered around his thighs, Sadao said, "It's like, you get only a little high when you smoke it, then even higher later, a second wind."

"Smells nice too."

"Almost citrusy." Sadao shook a finger at the stereo when Johnny Cash started singing "Bird on a Wire," track eight. "This isn't country music. It's urban folk."

Mitchell took another sip, said, "Cowboy music comes from all places, is influenced by all things, rural and urban. It's also an influence to all things."

Sadao wanted a for instance. Mitchell said, okay, take the punk rockers. To most, Johnny Cash was the first punk. Some said it was Eddie Cochran on account of the holler he raised with "Somethin' Else." But, for the most part, the punk community was settled on the man in black. It was the way Johnny busted up the Opry, got himself banned, just like Hank.

See, it was what Johnny, especially early Johnny, had in common with the punks—too many cigarettes, gravel roads, and the blood and the guts and the beer.

That old photo of Johnny flippin' the bird over his guitar helped. But it was the Folsom Prison concert—most important LP of the '60s —that cemented Johnny's bond with punks. That explained the Sex Pistols playing Chelmsford Top Security Prison, 1976. Where did the Pistols get the idea? Johnny's Folsom Prison show, 1968.

Also, Mitchell said, you had bands like the Pogues and Social Distortion covering "Ring of Fire." Johnny paid the punks back, too, covering "The Mercy Seat," a death-row ditty by Nick Cave and the Bad Seeds on *American Recordings* volume III. On the new album, Johnny does his rendition of "Hurt" by Nine Inch Nails.

"Except," Sadao said, "Nine Inch Nails aren't punk."

"Goth," Mitchell said, irritated Sadao would split the hair so fine. "Close enough."

"Point is, Johnny Cash just does that shit to appeal to the MTV generation, sell records."

Mitchell said Johnny was never one to mind sales, barely what you would call a popular artist in 2002 terms. That mindset informed Johnny's take on "Hurt," which Mitchell said was regretful enough to make your garden-variety slicker take a dry dive.

CHAPTER TWENTY

Staked out in his Cavalier on Walpole Island proper, Del Ray surfed local radio. He couldn't find anything he liked, so he flicked it off, dropped a couple 222s, thinking that girl was crazy to come home. How did she think she was going pull that off with a warrant over her head? Or was Greasy Spoon so deep into the dope he didn't know what he was seeing? Since the guy called babbling about the PTA, Parent Teacher Association, Del Ray was having doubts. Was this some kind of set-up? No way. Greasy didn't have it in him.

The hell was Del Ray supposed to do anyway? Wait here all day like he didn't have leads on a dozen more important busts? More important, shit, they were still making jokes about what that girl had done to him back at JR's, so the only thing that mattered was doing something to make that whole scene go away, saving face.

Busting her ass, bringing her into custody—Del Ray didn't know if that would make him whole again, but it would sure as shit send a message. It'd be like, yeah, maybe someone could sneak up on Del Ray, get him from behind. But eventually, Del Ray was going to gumshoe your ass, take your pride, and that kind of thinking wasn't going to do anything except win back cred in the Kent County drug community. Yeah, Del Ray wished the world wasn't that way, but he had to hit back, show everyone who ran things out here. Del Ray, that's who.

The point, Mitchell told Sadao, was that cowboy music occurred in all genres. For Butch and Sundance, "Raindrops Keep Fallin' On My Head" became a cowboy song. Flash to the '90s, the Lighting Seeds doing "The Life of Riley." A techno ditty, yes, but cowboy music just the same.

Sadao said, "How so?"

"Just the way it felt." Mitchell let his eyes out of focus. "Lost in the milky way, open land, cowboy pace. Even Dick Dale, king of surf guitar, was influenced, covering 'Riders in the Sky.' Pere Ubu did a techno version, dreadful, but Dick's interpretation is my personal favorite."

"Yeah," Sadao said. "Elyce sometimes uses Dick Dale for her opening number, 'Pipeline' with Stevie Ray Vaughan."

"Elyce, she your for-always girl now?"

"We've been living together." Sadao raised his shoulders, dropped them. "She moved in a few months back."

Mitchell patted Sadao on the shoulder. "There you go."

"There I go, what? I'm a third-rate comedian working a fourth-rate club about to go under shacked up with a glorified peeler past her best-before date."

"Sadao." Mitchell pulled back, a little shocked and appalled. "You have got to reshape your attitude towards women folk."

"Women folk? Seriously?"

"All I'm saying is there's nothing wrong with what you do, or your girl. Why, Wyatt Earp met his third wife, Sadie Marcus, at a burlesque, The Birdcage in Tombstone, Arizona."

Sadao looked over. "And how the hell do you know that?"

Mitchell raised his brow, said, "On account of I'm a cowboy with a library card."

"Yeah, well, I wasn't mining for advice. Just saying she opens sometimes with Dick Dale, usually 'Pipeline' but sometimes with 'Miserlou,'"

"'Pipeline,' you know where that's from?" Mitchell said. Sadao shook his head, no. Mitchell said, "*Back to the Beach*. Bad picture, great soundtrack. Stevie Ray obviously came from cowboy roots. Country and blues influenced each other, and, to this day, some great urban music is influenced by shit-kickers."

Okay, okay. Sadao's leg had been pulled long enough. He'd lived in Detroit since he was born, 1965, had been exposed to a lot of quote-unquote urban music, namely the guitar of Grant Green, and he didn't see how rednecks influenced urban culture.

Mitchell said, "Even Grant Green, father of acid jazz, was a cowboy fan, as evidenced by his *Goin' West* LP. Also, point of fact:

Detroit's own Donald Goines honed his skills writing westerns in prison before posthumously becoming the premier author of what academics now call black-experience fiction, laying the foundation for hip-hop, gangsta rap."

"You saying Donald Goines was a cowboy?"

Mitchell said, "In his own right. Shaft, too. Take the theme by Isaac Hayes." Holding up a thumb. "One, he's a complicated man." Showing an index. "Two, he's a sex machine." Middle finger. "Three, risks his neck for his brother." Ring finger. "Four, won't cop out when it's danger. Now who does that sound like?"

Sadao said it sounded like Shaft.

Mitchell looked past him again, nothing coming, said it also sounded just like Clint in *Fistful of Dollars*. Also, except for the absence of woman folk on account of it was a prison flick, all-male cast, Shaft could have been the Paul Newman character in *Cool Hand Luke*. That was another thing. Shaft was both sheriff and outlaw, making his movies, basically, urban westerns, and did Sadao know dusters were the first PIs?

"No," Sadao said, looking at a soya patch, eyes tired. "I did not know that."

"Well there you have it then." Mitchell squinted, looking through the gap in the trees. And yes, yes, he was seeing his van blow right past them. "Here she come and there she goes."

"Huh?"

Mitchell said, "Hit it."

Sadao looked at the console, confused. "What?"

"The ignition, Sadao, hit it."

The van was getting smaller, Mitchell holding what was left of his vanilla shake in one hand, punching Sadao in the shoulder with the other, telling him to start the goddamn car.

She had a 400-yard lead by the time Sadao got the Mini fired up, on the road, then the bridge. On the island, Mitchell pointed at a shit-brown Chevy peeling out in front of them. "Goddamn you two times, Sadao."

"Why twice?"

"It's another car you done let shoot our gap."

Del Ray looked in his rearview, one of those newfangled Minis gaining. What were they doing chasing him, a Mountie, in pursuit of a criminal? For a second, Del Ray thought maybe these were the PTA people Greasy was on about. Why was the PTA investigating Catori? Overdue books? And did the PTA even have investigators? Del Ray didn't think so. It couldn't be the PTA, just another impatient speeder who didn't know who's ass they were on, Del Ray's.

Steering high, Del Ray followed the navy van with Michigan plates hightailing it across the bridge, back to the island. Oh man, Del Ray didn't know how long that little squaw had been lamming or where she'd been doing it. Must have been seven weeks, but no matter. He had her now, trapped, and look where she was heading. She was taking a right on Dan Shab Road—the Evangelical Fellowship House, that's where she'd been staying. The coward, staying at the church where the law couldn't touch her, nice.

And hey, hadn't Del Ray heard that a Hollywood Indian was going to be there tonight singing Johnny Cash? Probably, that church, if you could call it that. Technically, the law did, legally a sanctuary. That being the case, so long as Del Ray got to her before she went in, it was fine. Hell, even if she managed to get inside, there was no way she was going to get away, and just think of the fun he could have waiting on her. Worse comes to worse, Del Ray told himself, you do like little George Bush said, smoke her out. He laughed as the Mini loomed larger in the mirror. Obviously, they didn't have the slightest.

Catori cursed herself, circling into the parking lot. Okay, maybe it wasn't so bad. She had 10-grand, Canadian, nine times more than she had yesterday. She could still get out, for a little while anyway. But what was she going to do when the money ran dry? Go back to dancing?

Killing the ignition, resting her head on the wheel, she couldn't do that. The way the clubs were regulated now, girls had to be licensed. She had another few months left on her last permit, but sooner or later someone would run a check. If Del Ray had a warrant, they'd find it. Once they did, they might even find out about the green ghetto, then what?

Just get some clothes, she thought, a good lunch, throw a dart at a map, and be gone before nightfall. If she could bring herself to dump the van, get on a bus or a train and go, she was going to be alright for a few months. She was telling herself she might even be able to build on that as she stepped out onto the gravel, hearing a car door shut behind her.

Slowing down near the church, Sadao said, "I saw her pull in here." Reading the sign. "Evangelical Fellowship House. The car that was behind her, too. They're going to pray?"

Pray—that didn't merit a response. Mitchell reached into his military bag, pulling out the Glock.

"Now where'd you get that?"

"Other dead cop." Mitchell checked the safety. "Seventeen shots less one in the clip." Patting his military bag. "Another 17."

Sadao threw his head back. "The hell you need 33 shots for?"

"Never can tell, situation like this. Just pull over, get this settled." Mitchell pointed the gun out the window, testing his aim on a speck of blue paint on the cream gold bricks.

Sadao parked at the side of Dan Shab Road. "You going to shoot the church?"

"Trying not to." Mitchell held the gun loosely now, opened his door, looking across at Sadao. "That's my goal, get out of this with a square deal without doing any shooting, nonviolent. Now, you got that DEA's ID?"

"The hell for? Like, we're impersonating cops now? Even here,

Amsterdam North, it has to be highly illegal to impersonate dead cops. The Canadians are a reasonable people, until—"

"Sadao, don't tell me I have to worry about you," Mitchell said. "Just follow my lead."

When Sadao opened his door, the console started beeping. Mitchell said kindly take the keys out of the ignition, then sighed. Sadao did as he was told, looking out to the river, following Mitchell around the house with a glass cross. On the other side, they saw a young guy, closely cropped white-blond hair under his mesh trucker hat, pushing Catori against the van, randy the way he was patting her down, asking where's the dope?

Mitchell approached, clearing his throat. "Ahem."

Catori, looking over her shoulder as soon as she heard, couldn't feel Del Ray's hands on her, just the horror of what she was seeing, Mitchell, alive. How the freak did that happen?

Pulling his brim low to his eyes, Mitchell said, "I said, ahem."

"Mountie business," Del Ray said, his back still to Mitchell. "Keep moving."

"Oh, I'll keep moving soon as you stop feeling up my prisoner, my witness."

Del Ray turned, seeing this wannabe John Wayne with a skinny Asian in a pink paisley shirt, standing there like some half-assed pilgrim posse. These couldn't be the dudes Greasy Spoon was on about, could they? Tentatively Del Ray said, "Are you with the PTA?"

Mitchell narrowed his right eye, said, "Pardon?"

Del Ray was pissed, the cowboy stalling. "I said, are you with the PTA?"

Mitchell dug the badge out of his pocket, thumbing the headshot. "DEA, Agent Stevens." Nodding at Sadao doing the same. "My partner, Agent Bruckner."

"Oh, it's DEA." Del Ray nodded, of course. "Shit, I thought you was PTA."

Mitchell looked concerned. "PTA?"

Del Ray laughed, everything becoming clear. "Got a call about you from my CI. You been to the Big Chief?"

Mitchell nodded, said they had the Farmer's Cholesterol Explosion Burger Deluxe Combo, then Del Ray explained the call from Greasy Spoon, that the phone was breaking up. And Del Ray, he couldn't see what the PTA could possibly have to do with it.

Everyone except Catori seemed to get a kick out of that, Del Ray checking out the little Asian guy. The pilgrim's jeans were too loose in the waist, hiked up with a belt. Inseam was also too long, cuffs turned up, cigarette style. It didn't seem that those were his pants, and what was with the yellow golf hat? Didn't look right, either. Del Ray thought maybe this was the DEA's idea of UC, sending in pilgrims so visible that no one would make them. He looked back at the guy seemed to be head pilgrim, Stevens. "PTA or DEA, you're out of your jurisdiction. This is Canada, eh, and in Canada, it's RCMP turf, drugs. So?"

Oh man, what was Mitchell going to say to that?

Right here in front of him, he had the rattler by the tail. It was just a Canadian narc, sure, supposed to be peace-lovin', but a narc nonetheless. And here's Mitchell coming off like PTA, watching the Mountie saying "so?" As in, so, what did Agent Stevens have to say about that?

"So." Mitchell took a stance, pointed at the guy. "You're out of your jurisdiction. That's the only thing so around here."

"You're in my country," Del Ray said, pointing his piece at himself. "How can I be out of my jurisdiction in my country?"

Mitchell tilted his head, said, "Did you speak to the Walpole Island Police Service about your investigation?"

"No, I did not. Why?"

"Well, we did, and you'll need to do likewise, get permission. First Persons police have jurisdiction on First Person lands, sacred."

Del Ray thought about it. Dammit, the pilgrim was right. Still, Del Ray figured RCMP had more jurisdiction than DEA. Mitchell said that would normally be true, except this case connected drugs to terror, and the DEA had jurisdiction in all such cases.

Mitchell wasn't sure if that was so, but it seemed to stop Del Ray. Mitchell pointed to Catori, said, "This here woman is wanted for questioning in a major drug investigation, possibly involving Taliban gonna blow up the Joe Louis Arena."

Del Ray squinted. "Taliban wants to blow up where the Red Wings play?"

"Taliban finds ice-hockey decadent, according to our people in the field, lots of chatter." Man, now Mitchell was really stringing the guy a whizzer. "Even as a fellow law officer, what I told you is more than I ought. I do so in the name of cooperation with the betterment of both countries at heart. So, please keep it under your hat."

Fine, Del Ray would keep it under his hat. He looked at Catori. Girl had herself in all sorts of trouble, but Del Ray was going to deal with her first, get his. "We have a warrant. You can maybe have her after processing. Do the paperwork. Liaise with our Chatham office."

"Don't think so, son." Mitchell put a hand on his chest. "I've done all the liaising I need." Pointing at Del Ray. "You must liaise with Walpole, comply with local treaties. We've done so."

Del Ray looked the cowboy up and down, said, "You do what I tell you, my country, and I'm telling you pilgrims liaise with Chatham. You don't want to liaise, fine. But if you think I'm just handing her over you can start picking the peanuts out of my shit right about now."

Whoa, Mitchell said, getting up in Del Ray's face. Whoa fucking Nelly. Did Del Ray know who he was dealing with? No, well he was dealing with a two-time winner of The Kiki Camarena Award.

"Kiki," Del Ray said. "What's a 'Kiki?'"

Mitchell, recalling the synopsis of a 1990 movie of the week, *Drug Wars: The Camarena Story*, said Kiki Camarena was played by Steven Bauer. When that failed to ring Del Ray's bell, Mitchell explained how said award was named after the real-life Enrique "Kiki" Camarena, DEA man killed in Guadalajara, now given to the agent best exemplifying perseverance and distinguished leadership to solve a really big dope case in a foreign land.

"That's my specialty," Mitchell said, "drug cases revolving around international security." Moving along before the Mountie could quiz him, Mitchell said he'd also been featured on *America's*

Most Wanted, *Cops*, and *Bad Boys*. Moreover, he had a quarter century's experience, and he was over here working directly with the same agency Del Ray purported to represent, albeit at a much higher level, and that was on top of liaising with Walpole.

Del Ray was a bit pale, thinking maybe this pilgrim had done all the right liaising. Del Ray was also thinking about the last time he took on some high-ranking dink, made that CSIS guy take a breathalyzer. And well, while it wasn't a career-ending move, it hadn't fast-tracked Del Ray, either, the way he had to hightail it to Toronto to explain himself to RCMP brass. Fuck it. Thinking there was no way he was going to pull rank on another senior officer, Del Ray found himself conceding, apologizing, groveling, stepping aside, and telling this DEA pilgrim, please, take the prisoner. But could he, Del Ray, get credit for the collar, a good word?

"Can do," Mitchell said, taking the cuffs from his belt, tossing them to Del Ray. "I'll even let you have the honors." Nodding to the van. "We're taking it back with us, evidence. Put her in the back, lock her to the side bar. Would you like to do that for us?"

Yes, Del Ray would like to do that.

CHAPTER TWENTY-ONE

Olin Blue flashed his shield, nodding at one of the armed guards, pulling past the concrete barriers. Seconds later, he arrived at 431 Howard proper, a modern blond building with green piping and mirrored windows, driving into a tunnel to the underground lot, parking his BMW wagon four spaces from the exit. After an elevator ride to the second floor, he was late, pushing 10:30 by the time he made himself a latte in the kitchen, brought it to his desk. Of course, he'd also stayed late last night, something he figured justified being late now.

He spent the first part of his morning sipping from an oversized mug, Michigan Historical Society, Detroit Chapter printed on the side in Old English, going through the daily newspaper articles circulated by the national office.

Across the country there were stories place-lined from Seattle, San Francisco, Tampa, Miami, and Buffalo vaguely linking every illicit substance Olin ever heard of to something bigger than those substances. Notably, *The New York Times* was reporting that sleeper cells responsible for recent train bombings in Russia had financed their plot by dealing hash and E.

"Ominously," *The Washington Times* said the Islamic Movement of Uzbekistan and rogue states like North Korea were learning that trafficking provided "large amounts of cash for nefarious purposes."

No doubt, Olin thought, highlighting key phrases in fluorescent yellow. Except how did all that heroin find its way into every black community in America? With cooperation from members of the U.S. Government, that's how.

Now, in his 21st year with the DEA, after 14 with the municipal force, Olin couldn't help but feel head office was turning every person who ever inhaled against them, and who hadn't? Even Bill Clinton had copped. Course, he'd also copped to more side-banging than all of the Kennedys, so what did a toke matter? It didn't. Still, ever since this time last year, the National Drug Control Policy Group had been running those TV ads linking the sale of a dime-bag back from user, to dealer, to smuggler, to some vague bin Laden character who uses the money to do barbarous things to your garden-variety infidel country.

A gripping message, no doubt, and there were kernels of truth to it. But every other day, there were also clippings saying the lion's share of American weed was coming from Canada, and what nefarious activities were the Canadians financing, jay-walking?

The Taliban was indeed processing poppies out of Afghanistan, Kurdistan, countries like that, so maybe Olin was going soft. He knew drugs financed some pretty bad stuff—pimping, for instance—even plain old pot, which is why he was sympathetic to a Nebraska lawyer saying it was time to stop mob and terror organizations from controlling the market. If that meant a little decriminalization, Olin thought giddy up, tax the shit out of it, earmark the windfall for treatment and social programs so the DEA could focus on real drugs. The latest thing was hillbilly heroin, Oxycontin. That was the shit the DEA should be on.

As for the pot spots, Olin didn't like the way the propaganda was pumping agents like Enid full of piss and vinegar. And what she was thinking strip-searching a young woman in a washroom at the Joe Louis Arena during the KISS reunion tour? Enid getting off because the woman was too frightened to testify.

Talk about terror, just a few months back, there were allegations of similar conduct at a fetish party hosted by Noir Leather in Royal Oak. Enid had spied a bottle of amyl nitrate worn by a *femme dom* on a necklace, proceeding to check her for keister stash. Trouble was the amyl nitrate had been sold in a store as boot cleaner, said so on the label, leaving Olin to smooth things over with a defiled woman with a power predilection.

Worst part was, nothing had changed. In fact, Enid was probably out there right now, looking up the butt of that poor farmer who bought too much African Violet Mix.

That's exactly why Olin had been quietly lobbying Chief State Director Jerome Dumont to find a way of chaining her to a desk —she was out of control. Jerome, he was worried about being seen as disloyal, that bringing Enid to heel would handcuff good agents.

To hell with it. In a matter of seven months Olin would be able to turn this off, all of it, sit down and write a book about local history. He'd better have an of angle by then, an outline. No, he'd read that you were supposed to be able to say it in one sentence before you even started.   Until such a time, it was Thursday, September 12, 2002. And as dire as the warnings had been, terror meter at red, it didn't seem that anything of consequence had managed to happen.

Back in the saddle, Mitchell drove his van south along River Road, looked in the sideview to check on Sadao following in the Mini. So far, the Mountie wasn't tailing them. Mitchell scanned ahead then refocused on the rearview, Catori cuffed to the sidebar. "Remember what I was telling you just before you left me for dead?"

The van hit a bump, Catori struggling to keep balanced on her knees. "About the Paul Newman character in *Hud*?"

Mitchell nodded, left-turning at Dufferin, toward the bridge off the island. "Specifically, Hud's greed being the moral lesson."

"You gonna teach me good this time, white man?" Catori looked at her hands, cuffed. How was she freakin' going to get out of this? "That why you kidnapped me? So you can do the job yourself?"

Again, Mitchell looked in the sideview. Sadao was following a little too close in the Mini as they crossed the bridge. A little too close—he was riding Mitchell's ass. So, just as they came on the Big Chief Drive-In, Mitchell gave the brake a little tappy-tappy, watching funny boy react too slowly, swerving. Once Sadao regained control, he was hitting that cute little Limey horn—beep, beep—shaking his fist. Good on 'em, Mitchell thought, speaking over his shoulder. "Sadao and I seem to be the only ones haven't killed anybody. Not looking to start."

"That him?" Catori twisted, looked through the back, the guy in a stupid hat shouting into his windshield. "The prick started all this?"

"Yeah, he's still mad I called him yellow for chickenshit, like it's a slur. Same time, you have to remember the DEA lady put a hand in his tar-pit, made him talk."

"What do you think they did to me?"

Mitchell glanced at her in the mirror, back to the road. "You just tougher than a mountain boot, tougher than the comedian anyway. Probably why you done tried killing me. We'll make nice after you tell me what happened at Phil's. I'm assuming he strung you a whizzer."

Catori said, "You talk to him?"

"Negative, we came for you, figure out the lay of the land before I go see him. What'd he give you? Anything?"

Putting the news clippings aside in a folder, Olin switched to the local *Free Press*, reading a few paragraphs on The Gentlemen's Choice Burlesque Revue and Show Bar. Apparently, a deal had finally been reached to turn it into the Coleman Young Community Center. Wonderful, another landmark destroyed, gentrified. Olin thought the *Free Press* was missing the point—celebrating because the community center was for the kids.

Other than the city issuing the destruction permit, there wasn't anything of consequence in the local paper that Olin hadn't read somewhere else. Nothing to get worked up about, because it wasn't going to affect him, his job, or his ensuing exodus from this place, just another fort in a hostile territory with guards all around making sure no one exploded it, nice.

Self-briefed, as per routine, he checked messages on his private line, nothing important. His butt was covered on intel, but now that he thought of it, where were Fowler and Enid? If they'd gone to that farm at first light, shouldn't he have heard something? Probably, but then it was just as probable that they'd stumbled onto nothing, that Enid was figuring out how to explain the wasted time. Or, maybe they were already chasing someone else.

Olin was about to yell out a directive to his secretary, Diane, whom he called Di, tell her to call them. Then she barged in anyway, saying, "I just wanted to remind you, Olin, you have that

2:30 with the chief director and his crew, boardroom five. You read the clips, right?"

Olin picked up his folder, dropped it back on his desk. "Do I ever not read the clips?"

She smirked, said Ruby's sister called, turning away. Olin said, "Hang on," watching her stop to look back. Man, she was one fine piece of white woman for 63. Going old gracefully with all those gray flecks in her brunette bob, bangs. Nice teeth, too, and that made her a unicorn, their age. "May I ask, have you seen or heard from Enid and Fowler?"

Di shook her head, no.

Olin said, "Please see if you can get them on the cell, tell them I want to be briefed."

"Will do. What are they working on?"

Olin said he didn't hardly know himself, it was so complicated, but it had something to do with a Nicaraguan farmer out in the green ghetto. Or was the farmer Polish-Nicaraguan? Whatever, they were supposed to go to his farm this morning. So, Di was to advise them that Olin was directing them to report back to him, Olin.

"Ten-grand?" Mitchell slapped the dash. "I was going to give you 33⅓ percent, 20-grand, double. Greed, see what it gets you?" Glancing at her in the mirror. "Just like Hud, every critter dead by the time he got his hands on the deed. His relationship with his daddy? Also ruined. Bad blood, just like us."

"What're you saying? You my daddy?"

Mitchell controlled his voice, tight, saying he didn't care for the connotations, young lady.

Catori looked at herself. Yesterday the vanilla outfit was athletic, fresh. Now she was dirty, grass stains on her matching high tops. What did white boys call girls like her? Oh yeah, blueberry blondes, and who taught them that?

"Two-part question," Mitchell said, taking Highway 40 towards

Chatham, a green haze of soya. "Where's the money you got so far? And, was it worth it?"

"It's in my knapsack right here, and no, okay?" She felt herself flush, voice quaking as she looked at the back of Mitchell's hat. "Look, I'm sorry."

"Sorry?" Mitchell glanced at her in the mirror. "It was accident, you left me for dead?" Back to the road. "'Like, I didn't mean to cut off your air, Mitchell.'"

"I panicked, alright, bad decision." She paused. "What are you going to do with me?"

"Nothing like you did. You've just got to switch sides, again, help me."

"I still get my 33⅓ percent?"

Mitchell laughed. Here he's going to spare her after what she done, and she was still angling. "You'll get yours, only now it's a three-person split. I get paid first, then Sadao, you."

"Sadao gets paid before me, why?"

"Why?" Mitchell looked in his sideview, checking for Sadao in the Mini, still there. "Because he didn't try to kill me, and that goes a long way at this very point in time."

"And why do you get paid first?"

"On account of I'm the grower and I need 20K to get my critters through winter."

Catori looked past Mitchell through the windshield, just passing Country View Golf and Country Club, a man in a Gilligan hat dragging his pullcart. "Where are you taking me?"

"It's a treat" Mitchell smiled. "Somewhere I always wanted to stay. I'll admit it, it was the commercials on channel 9 during Hockey Night in Canada—miniature golf, water slides. Saw a billboard up the way, reminded me."

"Oh fuck."

They didn't talk for a while, Mitchell humming "Home on the Range" as he approached the city limits. Hanging a right on Grand Avenue, he guided the van into Chatham, along the Thames River, turning left on Keil. At the outskirts of the other side of town, Richmond Street, he pulled into the lot at Wheels Inn, parking.

There, he crawled into the back, taking Enid Bruckner's keychain from his belt, uncuffing Catori.

"Thanks, white man," she told him, rubbing her wrists. "Thanks a lot."

Mitchell looked away, crawling out as he said, "Just you keep sassing, young lady."

"Or what?" Catori said, following him. "You gonna hit me?"

"Hit you?" Mitchell didn't get it, all this attitude after everything he was letting slide. Talk about turning the other a cheek. Dammit, he'd just about turned all the way around, like that Linda Blair in *The Exorcist*, he was turning the other cheek so much, and she was still disrespecting him. "Simmer down or you're fired."

"Fired?"

Mitchell said, "Look, if you need me less than I think you need me, walk." Pointing down Bloomfield Road, out of town. "Just walk."

She looked down the road, said nothing.

By then Sadao was parking next to them, getting out of the Mini, kicking about how Mitchell slammed the brakes back in Wallaceburg. What did Sadao do now? Mitchell told Sadao he was bumper-lovin', illegal in Canada, pointing at him, then Catori, back and forth. "Sadao, meet Catori. Catori, Sadao."

Sadao extended his hand, said, "How you doin'?"

Catori left Sadao hanging, looking away.

Mitchell grabbed his military bag, told them they better work it the fuck out.

CHAPTER TWENTY-TWO

Phil Legace sat at his desk ogling his Diego Rivera original. All Phil saw was a lazy spic in a sombrero watching another spic in a sombrero work a hoe. It was fine, sure, and Charlene liked it. But Phil could not see how it was worth a couple hundred K. Funnily enough, now that the piece was stolen, it wasn't, its outlaw status driving the price down to a tenth of its value. Even at 20K, Phil could not see it, just a migrant dumb enough to work hard. He had been misled. And why did Charlene butt in and say take it lieu of cash? What were they going to do with it? Nothing, Phil thought, deciding to see how Charlene and Aurelio were doing with the plants.

Locating an Altoids tin in his pocket, opening it, pinching off a bud, Phil packed it tight into his corncob, grabbed a box of matches and headed down the hall. Outside, he sparked up, taking the smoke deep, holding it as he walked.

Exhaling, head rush, he found the barn door open. Inside, Charlene and Aurelio were hanging Mitchell's plants upside down from the ceiling. After the plants dried for a few days, they would cut off the fruit, depositing it into brown paper bags to sweat before curing it.

"How is it coming?"

"Fine, Phil," Charlene said. "What'd you expect?"

Phil opened his arms. "Just asking."

"In what world could we manage to fuck it up?" Charlene drove her knife into the table. "We're hanging plants upside down. It's just boring, mind-numbing work."

Phil, looking at Aurelio then Charlene, zipped an imaginary zipper on his mouth.

"Oh, I'll zip it." Charlene pulled her knife from the wood, pointing. "Soon as you help."

"Gender roles are a social construct." Phil turned sideways. "This has always been your assigned role. Now that we are getting bigger, you have a helper." Nodding to Aurelio. "Additional responsibilities."

Charlene said, "What's your role, Phil?"

Striking a match, re-lighting the corncob, inhaling, Phil said, "To oversee, to delegate." Exhaling. "To run our business."

Charlene placed the knife on the table, said, oh good.

Phil told her she could say what she wanted, because there was no way she was doing that feminist buzzkill thing to him today, not after the deal he had done.

Ten-grand for 59 plants—this was right up there with the time the Indians sold Manhattan for some pretty beads. Too bad about Mitchell, whatever happened, but then Phil noticed something else wrong. How many times was he going to tell Charlene and Aurelio? Why were they not wearing gloves?

"What's the point?" Charlene said, hoisting a plant to the rafters.

"You will get high that way. A contact high."

Charlene bunched her lips to one side of her face, telling Phil that drying, trimming, sweating, and then curing the fruit of 59 plants was just another shitty job. So long as Phil was making his life partner, her, do a shitty job, she was going to get good and stoned.

"But Aurelio."

"Goddammit Phil, he knows you're not growing cotton batten."

Phil had another thing or two to say, but stopped himself. Of course, the kid knew, being Mexican. They were the first stoners, right? Or was it the Mesopotamians? Phil couldn't be sure. "Fine. He knows, so how is it?"

"Sticky, smells citrusy." Charlene held up a bud. "Like Velvet Vida's Smooth Silver we bought up a couple year's back."

"Velvet Vida." Phil strummed his right thumb against index and middle fingers, money, talking about how Mitchell had used that African Violet Mix. Phil read the same article in *High Times*, and now he wanted to sample Mitchell's batch to determine whether the mix made a difference.

Oh, it made a difference alright. Charlene hadn't seen buds this size since the heat wave of '99. Phil said big buds were an excellent sign, quantitatively speaking, but he wanted to know if it was any good, qualitatively.

"Seeing as how you are not wearing gloves," he said, "can you feel anything?"

Charlene said, "Just kicking in now. I think it's like a slow creeper."

"That is what Mitchell had said."

"Yeah, what happened? Why wasn't he here?"

"Dead."

"Dead?" Charlene couldn't believe Phil hadn't told her this part. "How?"

"Not sure, but from what I can gather, Catori killed him. Something about Mitchell missing a sign." Phil waved at himself. "C'mon, let me have a pinch, professional purposes."

"Professional?"

Yes, professional. Phil needed to know what flavor they had here, how to best market it.

Near the front desk at Wheels Inn, Mitchell slid Sadao more cash, told him to register, put the whole thing on his card, seeing as how the comedian was the only one probably not wanted at this point. Also, Sadao was to get a place on the ground floor—two beds and a cot.

Doing like so, Sadao made friendly with the nice blonde with big teeth behind the counter. Even made her laugh when he asked, where's the beach? She told him no one swam in the Thames River, basically a ditch, that Chatham was otherwise landlocked. Small talk aside, check-in wasn't until 3 P.M., but she said they had a double room, *avec* cot, available now on the ground floor, and would that be okay? Perfect, Sadao said. She ran his card, signed him in. Sadao said thanks, followed her directions, leading Mitchell and Catori through the putt-putt course.

Mitchell said, "Get the arrangement I asked for?"

Sadao nodded. "Two beds, a cot, ground floor."

Catori watched Sadao key the lock to 133, saying, "So who sleeps on the cot, me?"

"Young lady." Mitchell followed Sadao as he opened the door, inside. "I still don't think you get it." Slinging his military bag onto the cot. "Cot's my crib, because I'm trying to be a gentleman." Pointing out the door. "You can still walk."

She looked at the door, back to Mitchell. "You have a plan?"

Mitchell sat down next to his gear, working off his left boot. "Part of one. We'll flush it over dinner. I want to sleep on it, calm now that I'm off that island of yours."

"White man doesn't feel comfortable on the rez?"

"White's got nothing to do with it," Mitchell said, kicking out of his right leather. "I'm talking about getting away from that Mountie hatin' on you. And you're welcome, by the way, Sadao and I busting you out of custody, breaking I don't know how many laws." Nodding to Sadao standing there in his yellow pork pie, pink paisley shirt, and ill-fitting pants. "Plus, there was no way me and funny boy here was going to pass for DEA another five minutes."

She looked at Sadao, then down at the carpet. "Alright."

"Alright." Mitchell mimicked her, shaking his head. "Well that's why I don't want to be there, sticking out." Waving at himself. "Now, kindly pay me my 10-grand."

"Thought you said I'm getting a third."

"When we collect, I said." Mitchell waved at himself again. "Until then, I get paid first, I also said, so pay me my money."

Back at his desk, Phil worked Mitchell's bud into his corncob, putting a couple matches to it, flash drying it until it burned, then inhaling. Holding it, Phil noted the fragrance. Nice, but not citrusy like Charlene said. It was more pine meets skunk meets maple, funky and sweet. Still, as pleased as his olfactory glands were, Phil was not getting the immediate satisfaction preferred in such a product.

It was not personal—personally, Phil could afford to sit around waiting for the kick. No, it was about the market, because the market consisted of low-brows who wanted to get off as soon as the THC hit their blood, like they were mainlining. Back in the barn, Phil could see that this specimen was hardy. That was good, fine. The only problem being that African Violet Mix was maybe a concoction that grew you a great deal of pot, quantitatively speaking, while resulting in an inferior smokable, qualitatively.

At best, it was probably the type of thing one would use to grow weed for making rope, not dope. Giggling at his little rhyme—Phil figured that was more from his brand, the pipeful he had smoked just before this pipeful—he decided, yes, it was time for a Snickers break. Rooting around in his desk, empty, he went for his key and opened up his Dirk Willems safe, lifting the martyr's head back, pulling out a candy bar.

Cash, candy, grass—Dirk always held the goodies. And that was true about Dirk rescuing his executioner, Dirk's fatal flaw, too much faith in human nature. Phil figured the guard faked his inability to swim so he would not have to chase Dirk, that the guard knew Dirk was a pussy.

Catori reached in her knapsack, handed Mitchell the stack. He looked at it, said, "It's Canadian. Only worth like six thou in American, less fees." Counting vaguely. "Yeah, it looks like 10K in pretty money." He peeled off a twenty, holding it out to Catori. "Here, get yourself an outfit. Look like shit, dirty white pants."

She took the bill, looked at it. "What am I supposed to buy with this, a sexy gitch?"

Mitchell told Catori to take Sadao to the local clothing-by-the-pound, meaning Catori could get three outfits, if she spent wisely. As for Sadao, Mitchell said he needed a new hat, peeling off another twenty. Mitchell gave them both another twenty after that, told Sadao to find pants that fit. Then he put his head back on the cot, pulling his hat over his face and allowing himself a smile. Yeah, he still liked talking about saving. Speaking of which, they didn't need that Mini anymore, so could Sadao please return it.

"But I rented it in Windsor."

"From what company?"

"Budget."

"Well, I'm sure they have a Budget here in Chatham," Mitchell said, lifting his hat. "Be a little service charge, but you can absorb it with the money I done already gave you." Facing Catori. "You follow him, take my van. And young lady?"

"Yeah?"

"Don't go acting alone anymore."

"Meaning what?"

"Meaning I tracked you once, so just you bring my van back."

She nodded, said, "Mind if I catch a cat nap first? Didn't get much sleep."

"Fine, but don't sleep the day away." Mitchell pointed back and forth at them. "You both got jobs." Thumbing his chest. "And I want 'em done, no matter, before six."

"Anything you say, white man."

Mitchell looked her up and down. "Aren't you half white?"

She sighed, said yeah.

"Then kindly get off me."

"You saying I should stand down?" Catori looked at the Polack, a little shocked that he'd challenged her, a First Person of Canada or however the fuck he said it. "On account of what?"

"On account of what a wise lesbian shitkicker, name of Adrienne, once told me."

"Yeah, and what did this dyke tell you, she's so smart?"

"That good people and bad people come from everywhere."

CHAPTER TWENTY-THREE

Charlene blinked, turning to Aurelio. "Can you feel it, the contact high Phil was talking about?"

"Oh, *si*." Aurelio put his knife on the picnic table, looked at his hands, snorted out a laugh. "And it is a slow creeper."

They looked at each other, eyes relaxed, dilated. Charlene nuzzled her head between Aurelio's neck and shoulder. He let his head tilt against her, warm, said, "Do you think Mr. Phil knows about we, suspects?"

"If he does, I mostly don't see it." She kissed his neck. "Too arrogant."

"Is why is so hard to take." Aurelio pushed her away. "Which is why, sometimes, I feel him suspecting. Is like he tries to get a height out of me."

"You mean a rise?"

"That, too. Is like he wants to see if I am reacting. Is the way he treats you in front of me. Disrespect to you, disrespect to me."

Charlene flipped her right leg over the bench of the picnic table, saying Phil treated her that way all the time. He treated everyone that way. Sitting side-saddle, running her hands over Aurelio's white shirt, moist, her fingers climbing into his hair. "You tense?"

Aurelio closed his eyes, said, "*Si*."

Yeah, running her other hand over his lap, she said she could feel the tension, and maybe she could help work that out.

"Now, while Mr. Phil is present on the property?" Aurelio opened his eyes, blood vessels crowding the whites. "You would like to *viva* my Guadalajara?"

Charlene nodded, said, *si*.

Mitchell lay sideways on the makeshift bed. Goddamn bar sticking into his hip, a wafer-thin pillow—he said cot, not the bottom half of a Folsom Prison bunk. Then, thinking of how they slept on the lone prairie, the cold ground, he felt guilty for griping, even internally.

With Catori and Sadao somehow sleeping soundly in opposite doubles, Mitchell crept to the washroom. Running the taps cold, he threw some water on his face. He was drying off with a hotel towel, making a mental yellow sticky to steal it, luxurious, when he caught his reflection.

Oh Mitchell, he thought, what are you going to do now?

Deep down inside, there was a part of Mitchell that saw Johnny Cash as a bit of a mama's boy, the way he was always singing mama songs. And when Johnny wasn't singing songs about mama, he was singing songs he'd learned from mama's hymn book. But it wasn't until now that Mitchell understood what that could've been about.

Looking at himself, standing in his house shorts, Mitchell saw the fear in his eyes, skittish. Poor Petra Hosowich would be rolling over if she could see what her little boy had done. Bad enough he'd been growing the evil weed, but it was Mitchell's feral eyes that would've hurt his mama so. Yep, just when most men Mitchell's age were attending graduations, kicking back, Mitchell was more afraid than ever. No longer on the move, it was starting to settle in, the death he'd caused, even if he hadn't pulled a trigger. His throat was scratchy, eyes hot. Goddammit, he was getting old, and dope was a young man's game. But the thing that hurt him was this vision of Petra looking down, seeing him like this.

Suet, Mitchell was going back to bed, deal with this mama business another day. He had to be on, man, and the only way he was going to be on was if he caught some winks.

Phil chewed on the last bit of his candy bar, folding his wrapper into squares, wishing Dirk Willems had a bigger head. Phil wished for a beer, too, someone to get it for him. Now that it occurred to Phil, this pot of Mitchell's really was a slow creeper. Phil had stopped smoking some time ago, and he was still getting higher.

Maybe that wasn't such a bad way to market this particular product. He could tell his dealers this was an artisanal batch, sell it at 20 bucks a quarter more. Tell the market this one sets in mellow and then, wait for it, because just around the corner is the Jimi Hendrix Experience, everything warm and fuzzy. That was the truth, too—Phil feeling every tiny pore, flushed, skin moving just a little. No, his skin was pulsating.

The nice thing would have been to stay in that space, but then Phil started fretting over what Mitchell might have done to make it so good, building the high into a crescendo, manipulating it like big tobacco. Could this be a time-released thing? Because, if it was a time-released thing, it was not natural. Top growers kept their cannabis off drugs, so to speak, using only the finest fertilizers, worm poop. Phil was a big believer in worm poop.

But okay, so Mitchell had done something different, used African Violet Mix, flavor of the month. Phil was willing to admit it had in fact made some significant differences, but it had to be African Violet Mix in conjunction with something, so what was Mitchell's secret sauce?

On a recent episode of *Six Feet Under*, Phil remembered that skinhead skate kid with the fancy shave stealing embalming fluid from the funeral home run by his red-haired girlfriend's family. The skinhead was soaking his dope in embalming fluid for an extra-special high. Phil had since read in *High Times* that dipping dope in embalming fluid was bad news. Would Mitchell have stooped to that? If Mitchell would not eat meat, he could not use embalming fluid. Phil was certain of it, but he was just as certain that Mitchell had done something, and now how the hell was Phil going to find out?

He was trying to figure out a way of getting it analyzed, broken down, wondering whether such a place existed for a man like him. He was thinking that he could probably find a disgraced scientist to do it on the Internet when he remembered Charlene and Aurelio. They were still in the barn, working without gloves. If Phil was starting to freak on a pipeful, just imagine Charlene and Aurelio, letting it soak into their pores like that, into their hands.

Worse, if they were getting hopped-up on some necromaniac chemical Mitchell dusted the plants with, then maybe it was something that should not come into contact with live skin. Looking at his own hands, and oh Christ—shit, Phil was not supposed to curse—his hands were red. No, they were purplish.

Down the hall, into the washroom, he scrubbed with Dove, water as hot as he could take it. Rinsing, he held his hands up. They were not purplish anymore. No, they were goddamn eggplants. He cursed again, fuck me, when he remembered that hot water opened pores, that he might be making everything worse. Instinctively, he ran the tap cold, only to fear he had closed his pours, sealed the poison in. Standing there, looking at himself, double-taking, he turned and headed down the hall. Throwing the door open, he broke into a sprint at the porch, shouting something about the arrival of the Trojan horse when his right foot clipped one of the planters.

Mitchell rolled one way, the other, then repeated the ritual. No way he was getting shut eye in this crib. Spying the clock radio, he sharply said, "Sadao!"

Jolted, the comedian sat up. "What?"

"Told you. You have jobs."

"You also said do them by six." Sadao looked at the bedside digital, 2:48 P.M. "Lots of time."

Mitchell sat up, said yeah. And if he stayed on Sadao, then maybe, just maybe, everything would get done before end of business.

Sadao looked at Catori in the other bed, sleeping. "Fine, but why aren't you on her to get going like you are me?"

"Because, Sadao, she's not the one started this."

"True. But I didn't try to kill you. Also, I think you're trying to play us off each other."

Mitchell said maybe he wouldn't have to play them off each other if they could just do their goddamn jobs. Could Sadao just do his jobs and like it for a change? Yeah, Sadao could do his jobs and like it, but he was taking a shower first, and was that okay?

Charlene had her black dress cinched above her hips with one hand, using the other for leverage against the picnic table. She sucked air through her teeth when she felt Aurelio's hand on her ass. Oh yeah, she was ready, pushing up against him, counter-clockwising her hips, losing herself. Only goddammit, was Phil calling her name now? Aurelio closed his eyes, *si*, Mr. Phil was screaming, something wrong.

Straightening her dress, telling Aurelio to pull his pants up, she briskly walked outside, around the barn. She found her husband stretched out closer to the porch. He'd fallen on his way to her, thank Christ. Soon as he saw her, he was saying something about how she should wash her hands in cold water, not hot.

"My hands," he said, palms open. "Will you look at what it has done to my hands."

Charlene, leaned in next to him, kissed his forehead. "What is it?"

Turning, watching Aurelio jog out of the barn, Phil looked up at his wife then Aurelio again, getting closer. Pointing back and forth at them, their faces perspiring, he had trouble finding the words, his mouth hanging open. "You are both sweating," he finally said. Aurelio and Charlene looked at each other. "I told you how many times, wear gloves."

Charlene closed her eyes, said, "So?"

"So, Mitchell dusted the plants with something. That's what I ran out here trying to tell you. You don't want to sweat and handle it. It gets into your pores."

Charlene softened. "It's okay." Petting Phil's hair. "It's just a slow creeper, honey."

Aurelio turned, walking back to the barn. That crazy old gringo still didn't know.

CHAPTER TWENTY-FOUR

As State Chief Director Jerome Dumont's bum boy went on about the results netted by the national campaign linking drugs to terror, Olin took a sip of Perrier, feeling his eyes glaze over at the eight-by-ten of George W. Bush. It wasn't that Olin thought Junior was more or less malevolent than anyone else who held the job, with the possible exception of Reagan. Just that Junior had been a problem child himself. Even if some of the rumors were false, now the guy was driving hard policy when he really ought to back off and let law-enforcement do its job.

Trouble was, 9/11 had politicized everything and everyone, especially folks like Olin who felt more effective back when his job description was that of a bureaucrat, not an activist. Now it wasn't enough to find dope. No, they had to find dope with ties to something bigger than dope itself, evildoers, then trot the shit out for news conferences, pumping street values as high as plausibility allowed.

Back in June, Olin himself stood in front of a garage in Inkster, telling News 4 he didn't know how many thousands of dollars worth of plants the DEA had found in there—and what was that money going to be used for? Nefarious purposes, Olin told News 4.

Nefarious, indeed. No wonder Enid was going off on that farmer. Poor guy had himself caught up in something, but had Enid found anything connecting him to terror? Olin didn't think so. Neither did Fowler, not a bad recruit, if Olin said so himself. And hey, where were they?

Checking the wall Wesclox, past three, Olin looked at Jerome's bum boy, thinking, you're talking, but all I'm hearing is Charlie Brown's teacher—wah, wah, wah—when he, Olin, quietly rose from the table, heading for the door, down the hall to his part of the building.

At the front desk, he saw Di, asking, had she been able to track down Enid and Fowler? Di shook her head, no. She left messages on their cells. Tried Enid at home then Fowler at his hotel, the

Ansonia, where he was staying until he moved into his condo—nothing.

"Huh," Olin said. "Enid must have some egg on her face, hiding this long." Clapping his hands together. "Our vehicles have that doohickey now, Global Situational Something."

Di nodded, said, Global Positioning System. All she had to do was put a call in to the garage and they would send out a specially coded satellite signal, which would feed back to the receiver, the garage in this case, determining position to within a few yards. Olin said he didn't need to know how it worked—his age, how many more shopping days until retirement?—he just wanted Di to go ahead, put the request in. And how long would that take?

Not long at all, Di said. She just had to get in touch with the guy who ran the garage. He'd do it special for her. Hopefully, Olin pushed, before end of the day? End of day—if Di caught the guy, she might be able to get him to run it while they were on the phone.

Olin asked her to make that happen. Di nodded, said Ruby's sister called again. Olin said he was about to call her, then went in his office, sitting and checking his messages to see if Enid or Fowler called his private line. They hadn't, but Doug Henderson, top man at the Detroit chapter of the historical society, had some for-Olin's-ears-only-type information. Potentially good news about old Tiger Stadium, call ASAP. Given that it sounded like something Olin wished to discuss, he closed his door, called Henderson back.

It was too bad about Gentlemen's Choice Burlesque, Henderson said. He would never forget seeing Lottie the Body there in 1961, the way she moved. But on the good news side, apparently, a group of investors was trying to ante up the cash to save Tiger Stadium.

From turning it into condos to renting it out to slow-pitch leagues, Olin had heard it all, so he didn't allow himself to get overly excited while Henderson went on about the new angle.

This group, Henderson was saying, wanted to buy a minor-league team, single-A, and hire former Tigers pitcher Mark "The Bird" Fidrych as manager.

Henderson said they could rent the place out for slow-pitch, too, but Fidrych's involvement would make it viable, financially.

Did Olin remember how they flocked to see The Bird back in 1976? Fifty-two thousand watching him three-hit the Yankees—and Detroiters, they still remembered him. Sure, he only had one good season, but it was a hell of a season.

Del Ray had dropped by the Big Chief to get settled with Greasy Spoon, find out what had gone on with those DEAs. But the dink had called in his relief, reported himself sick, so something must've spooked him. After that, Del Ray crunched down a couple 222s and tooled around Wallaceburg in a dreamy pout.

Sure, there was a grow-op Del Ray could bust in Blenheim, and he was positive about that E-lab Greasy told him about near Tilbury. But, cruising Main Street Wallaceburg, a Walpole Island Police SUV parked outside Tim Hortons, Del Ray's heart wasn't in any of it. And why should it be? The way those DEAs could come here and tell Del Ray what to do in his own country. Maybe he should have at least called it in to ensure everything they were saying was so. This was Del Ray's jurisdiction. But that last time he challenged anyone's authority, back when he made that CSIS dude take the breathalyzer, he had to take it from that uppity Toronto RCMP, the guy reminding Del Ray of the fanatical pecking order within federal law-enforcement organizations. And did Del Ray know his role? Yeah, Del Ray knew his fucking role.

The other message, even if they didn't out and say it, was that CSIS dudes weren't supposed to be put in a position where they might blow over. That's exactly why Del Ray shouldn't have called in the local detachment. What, did he have a hard-on for authority? If that was his thing, he could just turn his campaign hat in and save everyone the heartache.

So, if Del Ray was wrong for calling in the local detachment back then, he couldn't see as how it would be right now. That wasn't Del Ray's fault. Even for a guy with his record, if you wanted cops to do the right thing, you couldn't make them wrong for seeking clarity.

Heading out of Wallaceburg, back home to Chatham on Highway 40, Del Ray thought if that Bruckner and Stevens were the cream of the crop, DEA, then no wonder the Americans were in so much trouble with the rest of the world. Dressed like a couple square-dancers trying to get to Nashville, real dandies.

Not only that, but now that Del Ray was thinking, did they have their thumbs over their pictures when they badged him? Maybe, but Del Ray had better calm down before he started making big allegations with little evidence. Running into the office, shouting maybe these DEAs who took the girl that hogtied him had thumbs over the pictures. Flashbacks like that—he knew what they'd say. Next time, make a point of asking them to take their thumbs off the pictures. For now, shut up and don't go causing an international incident.

Knowing what they were going to say didn't make Del Ray feel any better. Those DEAs took that Indian girl just when he had her. This was supposed to be his day, after all that shit in *The Chatham Daily News* under the headline, "Mountie bound and gagged during strip probe."

Well, maybe if she was back in town, she'd been asking for her old job back. Didn't make sense, what with the warrant. But Del Ray knew it was one of those things he'd better discretely double-up on, maybe find out what those DEAs liked her for. If they'd been to Walpole looking for her, chances are they stopped at JR's, right?

Olin was back in 1976, reminiscing with Henderson about Fidrych starting the all-star game, winning 19, despite not getting his first start until May 15, and the hearts of the country during its bicentennial summer. Rookie of the year, Olin was saying, then the guy threw his arm out the very next summer. He kept trying to come back, but was never the same. And baseball never quite felt the same after that, not even when the Tigers won the Series in '84

Fidrych was a pig farmer now somewhere in his native Massachusetts, so Henderson figured he probably wanted to get back into baseball. He was saying The Bird would be itching to sell that farm, how bad it must stink, swine, when Di threw Olin's door open, walking into his office waving her arms, something wrong.

Olin couldn't see what could be more pressing than the possibility of The Bird coaching at Tiger Stadium, so he put Di off, holding up an index, one minute. To Henderson, Olin spoke into the mouthpiece, saying they had to ensure Fidrych was attaching his name. Maybe Henderson himself should contact Fidrych, and wouldn't Henderson want to ask The Bird about the time he beat the Yankees on national TV, game of the week?

Di was still waving, a little frantic now. Olin said he'd call Henderson later, strategize. Bird was probably listed, guy's a farmer, right? But yeah, with Di chopping the air, angry, Olin had to go, bye. Placing the phone on his cradle, he looked up, Di whiter than usual. "What?"

"I had them run the GPS, like you said."

"And?" Olin couldn't believe she wouldn't just tell him, the drama. "Where are they?"

It was so bad Di couldn't even say, handing Olin a pink piece of message paper she'd written the information on. Reading it, he looked up, said, "You mean it appears they're near the river?" Then he watched Di shake her head. No, she said, it appeared that they were in the river.

CHAPTER TWENTY-FIVE

With Mitchell prodding, Sadao collected Catori and dropped the Mini off by four. Turned out Budget had an office in the strip-mall up the street. Together in the van now, Sadao at the wheel, they stopped at Esso on Keil Drive to gas up, Sadao poking his head out the window.

"Do you know where they have a clothing-by-the-pound here?"

The attendant scratched his ass, Fruit of the Loom waistband riding high. "A what?"

"A Goodwill," Sadao said. "A Sally Anne, Value Village, something like that."

"Oh." The guy pointed down the street. "We have a Sally Anne. Take a right at Grand Ave., another at Wellington. Can't miss it, right-hand side."

Sadao said thanks, paying for the gas, hitting the ignition, then pulling into traffic. Stopped by the first red light, they waited behind a white Firefly, *The Chatham Daily News* splashed across the hatch. Sadao focused on the red lettering, said, "Look, I'm sorry."

Catori glanced at him. "That it?"

"I'm just sorry." The light turned green, Sadao hitting the gas. "What, do you want an excuse? Like, you know what they did made me talk."

"Did the same thing to me, I didn't say anything. Did the same thing to the drag queen."

"Heard." Sadao looked about nervously at everything and nothing. "I can't believe they goosed Empress, either. Like I told Mitchell, she is the Empress. Can't do that, she's a sacred cow, works for good causes, charities. You and I, we're just doing it for —"

Catori cut him off. "Point is they did it to all of us. None of us turned snitch bitch. What'd they do to you, it was so bad?"

Sadao hit the indicator, right turning on Wellington. "I'm still shitting blood. There blood in your stool?"

Catori shook her head, no.

"Well then I guess they did something to me they didn't do to you, it was so bad. On top of that, I'm here, stepping up, Hosowich calls it, trying to make it right." Nodding at the Sally Anne sign as he pulled into a parking spot. "Taking you shopping. I mean, we all did some stupid shit that got us here, so how much more do I have to pucker up and kiss your ass?"

Del Ray parked his Chevy Cavalier in the shiny black-top lot behind JR's, took the backdoor in. Stepping from sunlight to darkness, his eyes were a little bugged, but soon he could see the candy-apple redhead on stage, lip-synching to "Always On My Mind," the Pet Shop Boys covering Brenda Lee. The redhead repeated the song's refrain as she bent over.

That's what you want to see, Del Ray thought, heading to the bar. There, he asked Pammie for Earl, the manager. Earl had gone for a late lunch, Pammie said, back any time. Del Ray said give him a Steam Whistle. Pammie said sure thing, cracked one open, put it in front of him when the teaser on TV over the bar, News 4, captured Del Ray's attention.

"Law enforcement officials are attempting to pull a vehicle reportedly containing two federal police officers out of the Detroit River, and News 4 is there. Skip Hayes will have the breaking story live within minutes."

Glancing at the Elvis clock above the bar, King's legs ticking, 4:20ish, Del Ray looked back at Pammie pouring a pitcher of Bud. "Catori Jacobs been here?"

Angling, guarding against foam, Pammie fought off a smile. "Like, since the incident?"

"Yeah." Del Ray twitched. "Since the incident."

Pammie shook her head, no, still fighting off a smirk.

Del Ray said, how about today, yesterday? Had anyone been here asking after her recently? Pammie said nope. Was she sure? Pammie said Del Ray should wait, talk to Earl.

"Okay," Del Ray said, biting down, jaw bones showing.

"Because I'm a Mountie, on duty, I ask who I like what I like. And now I'm asking you, are you being uncooperative?"

Pammie looked at the beer in front of him.

Del Ray got that, the girl non-verbally saying she's serving him on duty, free. He reached across the bar, grabbing her JR's T-shirt by the horse's snout. "And just because I am asking you, personally. Now, were there any DEAs in here asking after Catori Jacobs?"

She looked at his hand gathering the orange material. "Nobody's been here asking, no."

"Nobody?"

"Nobody, now you going to let go of my bra, Del Ray?"

At first, Catori found shopping second-hand vaguely depressing, the place musty. But then she found some worked-in 501s, a matching shirt. Also, she came across something for Mitchell, a brown man poncho, white details, XL, same style Clint Eastwood wore in *A Fistful of Dollars*.

By the time she was modeling a cobalt-blue summer dress with green cacti and red Gerbera daisies, she was flirting with Sadao a little, crinkling her nose freckles whenever he tried saying something funny. He was modeling a tan T-shirt from a bar in Hawaii, The Ugly Tuna Saloona, a fish skeleton on the front. And he was asking, had she ever heard the one about the Polish Texan, the Japanese American, and the Canadian Indian?

Catori laughed even though the guy didn't seem ready to deliver a punch-line. Thinking what the hell, maybe she should forgive him. He didn't seem very good at his job. Like, he wasn't that funny, so she kind of felt sorry for him. At least he was trying to make her feel good. Besides, nobody would lie about blood in their stool, so she was happy for the poor man when he found a nice, albeit modest, five-gallon hat for three dollars, plus some jeans that fit for five. Good for him. And Mitchell, the guy would be de-freakin'-lighted with not only the poncho but how much they'd saved.

Olin stood on the banks of the Detroit River, sipping from his green Perrier bottle, watching a crane pull Enid's Jeep from the water. Turning back to Skip Hayes, he said, "They're just bringing my people up, and you mean to tell me News 4 is going live with that the day after the first anniversary of September 11?"

Skip, doe-eyed, said, "Off the record?"

Olin brought a hand over his mouth, nodding.

"It's hardly my call. I was sent. If I don't do it, someone else will be sent. Get it?"

Olin got it. He took in a deep breath, puffing out his cheeks. Inside, he was building an argument as to why Skipper shouldn't do it anyway. Something about how certain images of what happened at the World Trade Center had been censored out of respect for victims, their families, and that News 4 should show the same respect for his operatives, their families. But then Olin was growing hesitant in his old age of taking on fights he couldn't win.

Worse, Skip was asking after names now, pointing at the crane just beginning to swing towards the shore. Who were they?

Soon enough, Olin thought, everyone in the world was going to find out. Still, it seemed prudent to withhold as much as he could for as long as he could.

Sadao handed over two twenties and Catori settled the bill, enough change left for a pair of hardly used red-and-white leather cowboy boots, five bucks, her size, nine. It wasn't quite the vast wardrobe Mitchell promised, but then Chatham didn't have a clothing-by-the-pound, just a thrift shop, so they'd done well, all things considered.

Everything paid for, they went back to the van. Sadao unlocked her side first. Running around the bumper, jumping in the driver's side, he hit the ignition, surfing the tuner.

Catori said, "What're you looking for?"

"Detroit station. Just want to hear the local news, hear how the Tigers did."

Del Ray started to wonder if Earl was coming back at all when the TV over the bar came back from commercial to a shot of a crane lifting a Jeep Cherokee out of the water, Skip Hayes' voice.

"A young boy made a grizzly discovery while fishing on the Detroit River earlier today, snagging a detached body part. After alerting police, a 1999 Jeep Cherokee belonging to the Michigan DEA branch was discovered nearby and is now being pulled from the water."

Camera on him now, Skip paused, the lens widening to reveal an old black dude drinking designer water, Skip saying, "I'm standing here with Assistant DEA Director Olin Blue."

"Assistant deputy director, Michigan." Olin yanked at his tie knot, uncomfortable. "And I don't know where you got that about the boy fishing. That's not right, either."

Del Ray watched Hayes, back on his heels now, asking the guy drinks fancy water, "Okay, can you tell News 4 what led to this discovery?"

The Perrier dink said, "Can't comment on that, pending investigation."

"Do you know how they were killed?"

Olin watched the suspended Jeep getting closer, looking away at what he saw, Fowler and Enid pushed up against the back window. "Too early to say. Right now, we're still trying to retrace their last movements. Going to have dogs sniff up and down this whole industrial park." Sucking his lips in, making himself say it just like the chief director said to say it, the narrative. "I can only say that the agents were investigating links between the local drug trade and organized terror at or about the time of their demise."

"Can you tell us who they are?"

"Names will not be released until we confirm identities and notify next of kin."

That's when Skip came back to the terror link. Was Olin saying this could be the work of al-Qaeda? No, Olin wasn't saying that, just that the officers were investigating links between drugs and terror at or about the time of their demise. Then he wasn't saying anything, putting a hand over the mic, walking out of the frame.

It couldn't be, Del Ray thought, but then what the hell else could it be?

"You okay?" Pammie said.

"Yeah." Del Ray nodded to the screen. "Just a shock when fellow officers go down, no matter the jurisdiction."

Sadao was still surfing stations. Catori said, "Try WJR. It's one of the few comes in clean this far. We're a good hour out."

Sadao switched over to AM, said, "What number's WJR?"

"You're from Detroit, live there."

"I don't listen to AM, mono." Sadao waved at himself. "Just tell me, what number."

Catori said 760.

Sadao tuned in just in time for sports. The Tigers lost 8-0 to Minnesota. Southpaw Mark Redman gave up all eight runs in the first two innings, falling to 8 and 15. Brad Radke got the win, improving to 8 and 4. Torii Hunter led the offence with three RBIs. The Tigers were enjoying a travel day today before opening a three-game series in KC tomorrow, Friday.

Del Ray looked on as News 4 TV cut to a sports break. Mark Redman, ice-pack on his left shoulder, was complaining about a blister on his pitching finger. Del Ray, thinking Redman was being a bitch, drank up, hoofing it out of JR's to his Cavalier. Hitting the ignition, putting it into gear, he headed for Richmond Street, figuring he ought to check the hotels first.

Most everyone coming to this part of the world stayed at Wheels right here in Chatham because of its amenities, the water slide.

But a quick thrice-over of the lot showed no blue van with Michigan plates. Del Ray didn't see the Mini, either, so he parked, went inside to the front desk. Finding no one there, he rang the bell. After he hit it three, four times, a young brown girl, couldn't have been 18, walked out. "May I help you?"

"RCMP." Del Ray badged her. "You see some half-assed pilgrim posse—a cowboy, Indian girl, and an Asian in a yellow hat?"

Smelling beer, the girl pulled back. "That supposed to be a joke?"

Del Ray pointed at the computer. "Check for someone with a van, Michigan plates."

The girl blinked, went on the computer, logged in. By now, two families were standing there, waiting. This was going to take time and these people probably weren't here. Probably hadn't done anything, even if they were, so why should she turn them in to some cop with beer on his breath? Scrolling, feigning attention, she said, no—no vans with Michigan plates. Fine, then Del Ray wanted a list of all vans belonging to registered guests. Closing her eyes, she said there was an acre of minivans parked out there, two U-hauls, a chartreuse microbus, plus a custom 1978 G20 with a rude rendering of Dolly Parton—and for Del Ray to feel free to run the plates on anything he liked. Then she looked over his shoulder to the first couple, waving them over. "Welcome to Wheels Inn. Do you have a reservation?"

Chapter Twenty-Six

Mitchell did some tossing, some turning. But even those little Jack Daniel's from the fridge, probably costing Sadao's credit card a good 10 bucks per, hadn't put him out. Just took the edge off, at least until Mitchell saw Skip Hayes doing that bit with the DEA boss drinks Perrier down by the river. And did News 4 have to show them like that, faces pressed up against the window? Mitchell didn't think so.

It was on CNN now, some high-strung bottle-blonde, had to be speeding, saying the feds should make the hot-seat mandatory for anyone who kills a cop, no questions asked. Now there's an objective comment, Mitchell thought, making a mental yellow sticky to keep Catori and Sadao out of the loop. No sense in riling them. That's why he got himself out of the room when CNN cut to that public service announcement. No sooner than the first kid said he helped murder families, Mitchell clicked the TV off.

Locking up, he walked into the quad, grabbing a putter and a red golf ball. He was ready to cut Catori and Sadao off at the pass, keep them away from the TV, where they'd be showing those dead DEAs all night. Plus, a round of mini golf might keep Mitchell's mind occupied. About 60 feet from their room, he placed the ball on the turf. Wrists firm like that long-ball rebel from Arkansas, John Daly, recommended during that interview at the State Farm Golf Classic, Mitchell stroked the ball through the windmill. It came out hot, Mitchell displaying body English as the red circle burned the cup, saying, "Call the cops."

Sadao in tow, Catori walked over, said, "Did you switch sides —call the freakin' cops?"

"Metaphorical." Mitchell pointed to the hole on the other side of the windmill. "I was robbed, is what I meant." Catching a flash of her red and white shitkickers, he looked up to the cacti on her blue cowgirl dress, clinging. "We're supposed to be incognito and you're dressed up like a double scoop of café latte Häagen-Dazs gonna be the main attraction at the hotel bar." Pointing down the hall. "The Stable Lounge. Yeah, we're bellying down in the bush."

"I keep telling you, I don't think so."

Again, Mitchell said he wasn't hitting on her. Had he ever been fresh? No, she simply looked too nice. It'd even be a compliment— the cacti were in all the right places—if they weren't trying to be stealth.

Mitchell noticed a young boy with Poindexter glasses leering, intense. "You're not inconspicuous, is what I'm saying." Sniffing. "Smell good, too. What's that?" When she didn't answer, he placed the scent, the oil of sage. "Are you using my Burt's Bees deodorant?"

"No."

"Thanks for asking. Anyway, I'm just saying you look too good to be lamming, is all."

Catori looked down at herself. Okay, she did look pretty freakin' alright for 37. And yeah, she probably ought to tone it down, the colors. "Sorry." She patted a plain white plastic bag. "I have quieter stuff for tomorrow. Also, we found something for you."

Mitchell held a hand to his collarbone, him?

"You." She reached into the other bag, pulled out the poncho, presenting it.

Mitchell checked the size, XL, held the garment out for inspection, hardly worn. "Same as Clint in the spaghetti trilogy." He sniffed it, slid it on, head popping out. "How's it look?"

Catori dusted a piece of lint, said it fit, that he looked like Clint, circa *Fistful of Dollars.*

"Now I know you're rodeoing me." Mitchell smiled, sheepish, smoothing the material as he looked up at Sadao, noticing the new hat, new to Sadao anyway. "Nice, what brand?"

Sadao removed it, looked inside. "Bailey Frontier Collection." Putting it back on.

"Quality." Mitchell walked to his ball, bending over his putt, stroking it—dammit, he just missed, again, and that now that red thing was rolling 10 feet by, Mitchell in danger of double bogey. Looking up at Catori, he said, "Something I want to talk to you about."

"Oh good." She rolled her eyes. "Time for wisdom and stuff from stoner white."

"Look, what I have to say is about the killing, that it's something you do because you have to, only when you have to. Even then, you can't drag it out like you did the law lady, made her suffer."

Catori ground her teeth, looking at Mitchell, ungrateful. "You saying I shouldn't have?"

Mitchell said one could build a reasonable argument that Catori had to. Only she shouldn't have used Hasty like that, drawing an innocent critter into it. Plus, he thought Catori was enjoying herself, making art of it, the way she was quoting biblical Johnny Cash shit.

Catori bit her lip, said, aw fuck it, she did enjoy it.

So far as Mitchell was concerned, that was the problem. Sure, it felt good, but it set her karma all wrong.

"And now," he said, "your karma is connected to my karma."

"Which is connected to my karma," Sadao said.

Mitchell looked at Sadao, said shut it. Catori asked Mitchell how she should've done it.

"You had her gun." Mitchell snapped his wrist, made a pistol of his hand. "Should have shot her in the back of the head, bang bang, no suffering, same as if you're euthanizing a sick animal, which is what she was, a sick animal."

"Should I have done you like that?" Catori said. "Bang, bang?"

"Just let's not make performance art of it, is all I'm saying."

"I'll keep that in mind, but why tell me now?"

Mitchell took a breath, said, "Just in case we find ourselves in that position again."

"Meaning you think there might be more killing?"

"Shouldn't come to that. We're not crack people, Phil and I."

"You know he's into coke now, close enough"

"He's getting a chance to make it right. Everyone deserves that." Mitchell looked at her square. "Even you."

"Alright," she said, thinking she does something nice for the guy, and now he's on her again, schooling her. Had he ever killed anything? She didn't think so. "Let's get it all out."

Mitchell rested the putter against his thigh, crossed his arms, let's.

"You want to know why I did what I did?"

Mitchell nodded. "To me."

"Fine." She didn't understand, the guy making her out and say it, again. "You left me twisting in the wind. There was a sign in the road, a sign. That was before Sadao here got fisted, and you still didn't warn me. You didn't warn any of us."

"A sign?" Sadao looked back and forth, settling on Mitchell. "A sign says what?"

Catori, focused on Mitchell, said, "If you think it's dry now, wait 'til November."

Sadao's hand shot up to his face like Elyce had just slapped her Sadao Saffron voodoo doll. "I'm feeling bad all this time for doing what I shouldn't have done—and I still shouldn't have done it—but you didn't say anything." Sadao looked at Catori. "Didn't warn her or me." Back to Mitchell. "That was a sign to all of us to stop doing what we were doing. What did you think it meant?"

Speaking slowly, dropping his head, shame, Mitchell said, "Tell you the same thing I told her. I thought it was metaphorical. I thought the goddamn sign was metaphorical."

"Metaphorical," Catori said. "Was it also metaphorical you fed me pot cabbage rolls?"

"Now wait just a horse-eatin' minute." Mitchell reached out, put his hand on her arm. She jerked away. "Told you right from the start I was joking about that."

She looked up at him through her bangs. "Were you?"

"I done told you—of course."

"Well, it didn't feel like a joke. You put that in my head, made me paranoid."

Made her paranoid—okay, Mitchell had taken the sign too nonchalantly, no question. But she was paranoid because of the situation, point of fact. And even if they did get their wires crossed over a gag gone wrong, that still wasn't reason enough to kill him like that.

When those wannabe DEAs didn't turn up at Wheels, Del Ray pulled into a Dairy Queen lot and parked. Slack in his seat, he thought maybe it was time he called this mess in, at least some of it. But two fake American cops thumbing their headshots and Del Ray still let them go? Just in case they had the badges of the DEAs reported dead—they weren't releasing names yet—Del Ray figured he was better off not mentioning it. Why build a discipline file against himself?

Aside from that, it wasn't like Del Ray could just go ahead and call the DEA, say he needed to know if the names of the dead agents were Stevens and Bruckner. If he did that—and if those really were the dead cops—an invisible helicopter would surely descend in front of him soon thereafter. Did Del Ray want a chopper deployed for him? No, Del Ray didn't want that.

Trying to think what he could reasonably desire, circumstances considered, he opted for a little breaky-break, reaching for his bottle, opening the childproof cap, throwing back a few 222s, grinding them down with his molars, waiting, scanning the tuner, stopping at 92.9, CFCO, when he heard that famous Canadian Jew—Del Ray couldn't remember his name—singing, "You don't really care for music, do you?"

Considering the baffled king's story, feeling the subtle, velvety kick by the time the Jew sang of the broken hallelujah, Del Ray decided to keep doing what he was doing, checking where that pilgrim posse might be staying. Christ, if he could make a bust like this solo, it would make every on-the-job miscue go away. Rooting out DEA killers might even win him a big American award, a movie deal like that Kiki guy. So yeah, Del Ray was going to make something out of nothing here, coming up with new and interesting ways of covering up old mistakes.

If only he could figure out where those fake DEAs were staying.

The more he thought, it shouldn't be tough. Criminals on the road hid in hotels and motels, and there wasn't that many in these parts. After Wheels, Del Ray had checked Comfort Inn on Richmond. No luck, he tried Travelodge on Bloomfield. Same thing, not that it mattered. He was going to check every rent-a-cave in Kent County—two, three times if he had to.

But what if they already did what they came here to do and left? Del Ray backed out of Dairy Queen, steering the Chevy towards Highway 40, Wallaceburg, home of the Super 8.

The way Del Ray saw it, if those fake DEAs had already come and gone, they were never here, so far as he was concerned. Yep, that'd be his story—if it came to that.

But it hadn't, not yet, Del Ray accentuating the positive as he rolled on the never-ending soya landscape. He actually could find them, bring them in. Del Ray stood as good a chance as anyone. As good a chance? Del Ray had the best chance, because he had seen those fake DEAs, talked to them, and, most importantly, Del Ray seemed to be the only one who knew they were here. So why couldn't Del Ray bring them in? There was no reason whatsoever.

Just knowing they were here was a righteous piece of police work. Mind you, if he did bring them in, he'd have to cover himself off for why he'd let them slide. Why—they were carrying DEA ID, that's why, saying the girl had something to do with the Taliban wanting to blow up where the Red Wings play.

In the moment, Del Ray thought he was cooperating, just like head office told him after he told that CSIS dude, blow. But shit, Del Ray couldn't say that. Who was going to believe hockey pissed off the Taliban? No one. In fact, Del Ray himself could list 10 U.S. landmarks off the top of his head that the Taliban would target before where the Red Wings play.

Mitchell, Catori, and Sadao took dinner shortly after six in the hotel restaurant. It was called The Tree Room, twisted Corkscrew Hazelwood branches hovering. Much as the New York steak was calling, Mitchell decided to get back to clean living, ordered fried tofu stuffed with local nuts and twigs. He remained expressionless when Sadao ordered the steak, blue, but couldn't believe Catori had the gall to ask for the veal parmigiana. Cupping an ear, he said, "Pardon?"

As the waitress walked away, Catori tightened the tie of her black halter behind her neck, casual. "You want to order for me now, white man?"

"Done told you, stop calling me that. I'm Polish."

"Polacks aren't white?"

"You say it negatory, Polack, without consideration of the oppression Poles faced from the Nazis, Soviets, and Ukraine Insurgents. Also, I haven't done a thing against the First Persons of Canada. And you, using gender and skin color, again, to detract from the substance of my point. That's an *ad hominem*, so let's just bring it back home, young lady." Mitchell pointed at Catori's place setting. "Do you know what they do to the veals makes 'em so tasty?"

"Yeah, so?"

"So? Bad enough you're a carnivore, but this? Might as well go ahead and eat people meat if you eat veals, the poor things."

"Okay, that's a bit much."

Eyes and mouth pinched, Mitchell pointed, giving it to her. "Don't you ever, ever, tell me how to go about respecting the animals. Making the poor veals stand in one spot their entire lives, can't exercise on account of they want to make them atrophy until they're tasty. Somebody did that to Simmi, made her stand in one spot, I'd put 'em on a spit, jam it right up their ass and say, 'Oh, I'm sorry, just trying to make you tasty, motherfucker . . .'"

Catori covered her smirk, let Mitchell get it all out, the freak. Then she said, tomorrow: What were they doing and how were they doing it?

Mitchell shot his eyes at the waitress approaching, shut it. When everyone was served their drinks, waitress gone, Mitchell took a sip of his draft, ah. "Like I said, I'm giving Phil every chance to make this right, to pay us what we've got coming."

Catori sipped her house white, said, "Sixty-grand, American."

"Fifty," Mitchell said. "Plus exchange on the first 10."

"Same split?"

Mitchell nodded, 33⅓—each.

Catori looked across at him, concerned, said, "And there's still enough left for your dime that way? Twenty K—how's that good enough for you, the grower?"

"It's not." Mitchell took another pull on his draft. "What it is, is a matter of right and wrong. Also, 20K tides me over to spring. Assuming no further hardships, I need that just to get me and the critters through winter, figure out what to do next, maybe hydroponics."

"You said you were getting out."

"The hell am I supposed to do? I'm 52, no skills, none legal."

Catori thought about it until she actually felt bad for Mitchell. What was he going to do? And okay, maybe the guy hadn't consciously screwed her over. He was being fair on the split, and that was after she left him for dead, so to speak. But all this might be moot, she thought, asking, "Do you actually think Phil's just going to give you the money?"

Mitchell said he was trying to avoid pre-judging.

"Why even give him the chance?" Catori said. "He already cheated me."

Mitchell nodded, said yeah. Then again, Phil had only cheated Catori after she left him, Mitchell, for dead. Mitchell gave her a second chance. As such—like maybe Phil was protecting Mitchell—Phil deserved the benefit of the doubt, for now.

Sadao held up his bottle of Blue. "I don't know much about drug people, but—"

"Don't know?" Mitchell said. "You've been selling for me how many years? Seven?"

"Nine," Sadao said. "Point is, we're not like a lot of drug people. And at this level—like, I don't know this level from Cheech and Chong—it just seems to me that he has your dope. In his head, he probably thinks he's paid for it, so what do we when he says piss off?"

"Then we just take the money, smash-and-grab." Mitchell looked into his pint glass, almost empty, wondering where's the waitress? "Phil's always saying people ask him, 'Phil, where do you get your money?' Then Phil says, 'When I want some money, I just go and get some.'" Looking at Catori. "So where does he get it?"

She smiled, relieved that Mitchell was getting past just asking. "He keeps it in this martyr icon in his office. Key lock. His key is on the chain attached to his belt-loop."

Mitchell said, "Thought Mennonites weren't supposed to have belts."

"They're not, but loops are okay. I think."

"Also thought Mennonites weren't supposed to have icons, idols."

"Again, they're not, only this one's special," Catori said. "Dirk Something. Phil said Dirk stopped his escape from prison to save a guard who fell through the ice chasing him. Then the guard turned around, burned this Dirk at the stake, martyred him."

"Seems they have a lot of exceptions," Mitchell said. "Good news is there won't be many plain people because Phil's crop wouldn't have been harvested yet, no need. I'll give everyone jobs when we see the layout, where everyone's positioned. Shouldn't be tough for the three of us, armed, if it comes to it."

Catori, held her wine glass up, almost toasting. "I counted two guns between you."

Mitchell said his varmint gun was hidden in the wallpaper rolls in the van, that it would be Catori's piece, powerful at close range. He had more shells in the toolbox.

Agitated again, Catori looked at him. "You mean I also smuggled arms?"

Mitchell held up an index. "Just one."

"You're freakin' lucky I made it, and it was close."

Mitchell turned his head, made a *pft* sound.

Catori put her glass on the table, closed her eyes. "I'm telling you I barely got through."

That did it. "Look," Mitchell said, "I'm trying to be civil on account of it's in our best interests." Pointing at Sadao, Catori, then himself. "But you can't (A) leave me for dead, then (B) complain I didn't properly position you to get away. That's called sucking and blowing at the same time, can't do it, so can we just put that part on the shelf for now? We're not going to forget, can discuss it later, but could we, for now, put it on the shelf?"

Catori nodded, yeah, okay, she could put it on the shelf. Sadao, too.

"Okay," Mitchell said. "Now do tell what Phil's using for a gun these days."

Catori, recalling the newfangled Credit Card Shotgun, described its shape. It looked like a TV remote more than a credit card, and it was a muzzle-loader.

Mitchell pulled back, said that was inconvenient.

Yes, Catori said, but that's why they were able to make them so small. Mitchell said a gun like that couldn't have much pop. Oh, it could put a nice whole in someone at close range, Phil had told Catori. Well, Mitchell said, the important thing was that they knew what to look for, and did Sadao hear that? Yeah, Sadao heard. This Phil has a gun looks like a TV remote.

"Anyway." Catori looked back and forth at them. "If we have to smash and grab, I still say we up the ante, take everything after what that man put us through."

"No, I said." Mitchell smiled, trying to be patient. "Me, I wouldn't mind scooping his alleged Diego Rivera original, donate it to a gallery simply on account of Phil the Philistine can't appreciate it. But I won't take anything for myself moneywise that I'm not owed because of the same thing I've been trying to school you on, the Paul Newman character in *Hud*, greed."

Catori grimaced, the guy still throwing *Hud* at her. Well, fine. She knew the film. "Totally different thing," she said. "In *Hud*, Paul Newman's his own worst enemy, screwing over his family. Here, you're sliding Phil a break, allowing him to simply pay what he said. But if he makes us take it from him—if it comes down to that—why wouldn't we take everything?"

Last time, Mitchell said, it was his money, and he was taking what he was owed, another 50-grand American, plus exchange on the first 10, no more. Did anyone have problem with that?

Sadao and Catori looked at each other. No, they didn't have a problem.

A few more good questions aside, it was settled by the time dinner arrived, everyone ordering another round. Mitchell dug into his fried tofu stuffed with local nuts and twigs. Couple bites in, he looked to Sadao, asking how's the steak? Nice, Sadao said, want a bite?

Mitchell held his thumb and index an inch apart, said, "Just a taste."

CHAPTER TWENTY-SEVEN

First Olin had to go to the Detroit morgue at the City County building, ID the bodies. Given Enid and Fowler had been dead a short time, it didn't take but a couple good looks. Why had they dragged her? What sort of medieval instrument had they used on Fowler? And what were they doing down by the river?

Neither had said anything about the Boblo dock, and nobody seemed to know better, least of all Olin. Embarrassed, he was back in boardroom five, trying to piece it together for the local Homicide and FBI honchos, both of whom made it clear that they were leading what was now being called a joint investigation. The Homicide guy, Wes Spungen, didn't want Olin talking to reporters, and did he have to make Skip Hayes wrong two times? No way. All media inquiries would go through Spungen's office, and was that crystal?

Olin thought about saying Jerome had cleared him for that interview to run interference, get the narrative out. But Jerome wasn't saying anything, so Olin looked at the table top and waited for Spungen's next question.

"You don't have an idea what your people were up to, their interest in the dock?"

Last thing they'd mentioned, Olin said, was this farmer out in the green ghetto. Olin told them not to go at night. Would Fowler have gone along with that? Olin didn't think so. Even if he had, that wouldn't explain how they ended up in the river, eight or ten miles away. Olin thought it unlikely they'd been transported that far in a vehicle without a trunk, their vehicle.

"Procedurally speaking," Olin said. "The farm is something that has to be checked and crossed off. Procedurally, a lot of things, people, need to be looked at, crossed off."

Also, Fowler had been living in a residence suite at the Ansonia Hotel on Cass until he could move into his condo. Ansonia was swish, marble lobby, historical, but Olin said it had poor security. Enid was supposed to be taking Fowler there last night, as directed.

Was Olin suggesting, Spungen wanted to know, that they were taken from the Ansonia? Olin said it was just something else that needed to be checked, procedurally. He didn't think it likely that the killer or killers transported them from Cass all the way to the dock, either.

"It's true," Spungen added. "People who kill people in Detroit, they don't tend to move their victims. They get the hell out of there, run."

The central point of interest to all parties was the industrial park itself, as well as the Boblo dock. Maybe Enid and Fowler were checking out intel she'd been withholding, an E lab. She was protective of her cases, so it was agreed that the focus should be down by the river, to keep K-9 sniffing, to look for people in the vicinity, any people, to question.

As a secondary focus, Olin brought the conversation back to Enid's conduct. Speaking to Danny Grier, the FBI guy, Olin mentioned the brouhahas at the KISS show and the Noir Leather party, illustrating that this was an agent making enemies. Her recent movements had to be checked, again, as a matter of procedure, the idea being to find people she'd maybe used excessive force on, something that might've come to a head at the dock. It would seem they'd crashed the gate in their vehicle, met their demise after. Was it something they happened onto? Was it something they followed? Were they chased? The deaths were brutal, vengeful. Enid's neck was broken, so they should be looking at people motivated from that point of view.

"She dirty, you're telling us?" Spungen said. "Brought it on herself?"

Now hold on, Olin said, raising a hand, ballpoint between his fingers. Objectively, all he was saying was that Enid was loaded for panda on this drugs-meets-terror thing, running roughshod over people, and the investigation needed to consider the same.

Grier said, "And following the lead of your own head office puts her in the wrong, how?"

Olin looked down at the stack of folders in front of him. "Just that she was maybe going too hard on the wrong person, persons."

Grier nodded to Olin's papers. "Can you give us a record where she's been?"

"Partial." Olin plucked a folder from the pile, opened it. "One of the last things they did on record was attend The Motown Hoedown. Country bar doubles as a strip joint on Joy near Unassumed Road, where urban Detroit meets prairie. Checked a dancer yesterday, Gina the Ballerina. Took her coat, found like an eighth later in a secret zipper when they returned here."

Spungen made a note of it, but where the hell did Joy meet—was it, Unassumed Road? Olin said it would be listed in old city maps, back when it was still serviced, as Medland Estates, eight or ten miles northwest of Briggs. Good enough, Spungen would find it.

"While you're there, engage this farmer." Olin looked into his folder, turning pages. "Name of Hosowich, Mitchell P. Lives on Unassumed Road."

"Thought you said they weren't going there."

Olin said he told them not to go there at night. Given where Enid and Fowler ended up, Olin couldn't see how Hosowich was the guy. Fowler hadn't made the farmer for more than a redneck slacker. So, keeping K-9 working down by the river should obviously be the focus. Same time, anyone the agents had recent contact with should be engaged. Speaking of which, there was a comedian, Sadao Saffron at The Gentlemen's Choice Burlesque, Olin wanted checked, again, as a matter of procedure.

"Procedure? You the lead now?" Grier laughed, looking to Spungen. "Guy loses not one, but two agents, thinks he's point man." Looking back at Olin. "How long since you had to carry out procedure, in the field, Mr. Point Man?"

Here we go, Olin thought, putting an elbow on the table. He looked at the Wesclox, past eight, 24 hours since Enid and Fowler were last seen, and they were nowhere. "Just giving you my informed opinion, as a stakeholder. Means we also attend the Booby Trap, Michigan Avenue, look for Wyndi. Then, at The Black Orchid Cabaret on Livernois, ask for Champagne."

"Strippers," Spungen said, "that all you people do?"

Olin knew how it looked, like he wasn't directing his people, letting them go wherever they picked up a scent, and, well, at this point, that was partially true. So rather than get into another fight he couldn't win, he just kept going. "Also, they attended Menjo's on West McNichols, Highland Park. There, you want a drag-queen bingo caller, Empress Envy. Hair changes from blue to red, depending on the light, Fowler's notes say."

Alright, Spungen would do it, but what linked all these degens?

Olin folded his hands. He didn't want to say this next part. It sounded conspiratorial. But he went ahead anyway, explaining how Enid was after a bunch of people selling dope wearing jackets with Sandinistas on the label. She said Sandinistas meant it was political.

"This Fowler," Spungen said, "what'd he say?"

Olin took a sip from his green bottle. "That they were chasing small timers."

"And what do you say?"

Olin figured Fowler was right. Enid was chasing dime baggers, at best, hoping against hope that it would lead to something bigger, terror. Only reasons Olin mentioned any of this were procedure and disclosure. He didn't want anyone saying he was holding back in case a small thing became a big thing. Reality was that they'd had a problem with Enid for a while now.

Grier, trying to read Olin's notes upside down, said, "So now you're saying it's a drag-queen did your agents?"

Again, Olin said Envy was simply among the last people engaged by the agents. As such, she, too, had to be re-engaged, procedurally.

"Their computers." Spungen pointed down the hall. "When can we have access?"

For the first time, Jerome spoke. "Can't. Classified."

"Classified?" Spungen said. "You have two operatives, dead, and you're withholding?"

"Anything relevant on their hard drives, it's yours, hard copy." Jerome nodded to Olin. "Assistant Deputy Director Blue is at your disposal, will see that you get it."

"You know we can get it all ourselves," Spungen said. "That

we can get a court order."

"And, due respect, you know that I can get it quietly quashed." Jerome leaned forward. "We'll handle that part, fine-toothing their computers, DEA property."

Spungen and Grier looked at each other then got up and walked out. From the elevators, Olin and Jerome heard Spungen say, "Fuck 'em."

Catori was watching the TV on mute. Mitchell had turned in early and managed to get some shut-eye in his cot until the girl started whispering, was Mitchell up? She'd been riled by something on MTV, apparently.

"What?" Mitchell said, quietly so as not to wake Sadao. "They playing Shania?"

"I was channel-surfing earlier," Catori whispered. "They found those DEAs, showing their pictures on CNN, flashing their names across the screen."

"Well, we knew that was going to happen." Mitchell glanced at the bedside digital, 8:37 P.M. "Lucky we bought ourselves as much time as we did, and they still don't know what put those agents in the water."

"But it's a great big freakin' national story now, terror and drugs."

Mitchell closed his eyes, said he knew, that he'd seen them pull the bodies out on News 4 earlier, didn't want to upset her. She didn't know what to do with that, saying only would he hold her? Hold you? Mitchell said. Hold me, she told him.

Hesitating, he said okay, just holding, sitting up on his cot. Just holding, she said, reading the words printed across his threadbare nightshirt, "The Flesh Columns, Ban Nestle Products." He said okay, and walked over, awkwardly lying next to her, asking how? When she sighed, he said, okay, political correct, how did she want to be held? She said, "Spoon me."

Detroit Homicide hit the street before nine, looking for the freaks who come out at night, Spungen said, just like the Whodini song. Starting on the edges of town in Highland Park, two-man teams covered exits at Menjo's. Inside, Spungen found the roughed-up waiter. He had two black eyes, a split lip, and he wanted ID before answering questions. Satisfied at Spungen's shield, he said go ahead.

Spungen held a pen to his notebook. "Name?"

"Lucier, Richard Lucier."

"Okay, Mr. Lucier," Spungen said, jotting it down. "I'm looking for a drag queen."

Lucier scanned the room, a good dozen men dressed like ladies, boas, big hair. "Appears you've come to the right place, detective."

"Specific." Spungen flipped through his notebook. "Envy, calls bingo."

Lucier nodded, said she hadn't been in, missed today's shift.

"Any idea why?"

Yeah, Lucier had an idea, saying that this DEA lady came in Wednesday, yesterday, heel-punched him like it was nothing, then went out back, caught Envy smoking a jay, pushed her against the garbage. Envy said they looked up her whoopsie-daisy. Get caught with a jay and have your back door opened, what was that?

"You into it, drugs?" Spungen said. "Can feel for her?"

Lucier said he'd been clean and sober for three years, four in January.

"You know where this Envy's gone?"

Lucier said he didn't want to know. Okay, did he know where she was from? Guatemala, Lucier said, and if she was smart, after what that DEA did, she was going to stop plucking her brow and go back there to be a dude, blend. Spungen wanted to know her male name. Lucier couldn't help, saying she came to Menjo's as Envy Arroyo last year, won the Empress crown, had been Empress Envy ever since.

"Don't you have employment papers. A social security number?"

Lucier said Envy called bingo for the Detroit PWA, a non-paying gig. The detective could talk to the manager, but why would

Menjo's have her papers, her social security? And why would anyone ask her for a male name? That would've been impolite.

"She ever hurt anyone? Have violent tendencies?"

"No, do you actually think she killed those cops?"

Spungen didn't want to put it like that, but okay, he could cut to the chase. Could she?

Under the right circumstances, Lucier said anyone could do anything. But he didn't see it. Envy raised money for charity, not exactly rough trade.

"Then why's she AWOL?"

"Because she's scared," Lucier said. "I told you what they did to her. People on the fringes know to run after something like that. They will not be believed."

Scared, Spungen thought. Two dead DEAs and this Lucier's worried about a pouf dresses like a pro. Also, Spungen was figuring maybe Lucier knew where she was hiding when the interview concluded. Giving Lucier his card, Spungen told him if this girl, or whatever, showed, that Lucier was to call him, Spungen, first and fast.

Lucier said yeah, okay, he'd call.

Spungen didn't believe him, heading out through the back where one of his men, Barnes, was covering off the exit.

"Anything?" Barnes said.

"Maybe, maybe not." Spungen wiggled his fingers. "Get Mr. Point Man on the phone."

Back at 431 Howard, Olin was snooping through Enid Bruckner's computer. He'd found some documents that were password protected, flagging them, sending them to systems to get cracked, when he heard his phone ring. Up from Enid's desk, he broke into a slow run to his office, picking up, answering with his last name, Blue.

"Mr. Point Man, it's Wes, Wes Spungen, how're you doing?"

Still with the point man shit, huh? Olin took a swig of Perrier.

"Fucking mint."

"Me too, but we may have something."

That was quick, Olin thought. "Okay?"

"Drag queen calls bingo at Menjo's," Spungen said. "She's gone, AWOL."

"And," Olin added, "innocents tend to stand their ground, stay put."

"Same as I'm thinking, but we can't get his/her real name. You have it?"

Olin held his head in his free hand, said no.

"That's what I was afraid of. They only know her as female, have no alleged record or recollection of the queen's male name. She's not a Menjo's employee. Waiter here implied she has a male identity she can slide into. Makes IDing a problem. If anything like that pops up in a file, let me know. I'll call back when we have more. Going to call Grier, get him to put out an APB, national. See if we can get John Walsh to put Envy's picture on TV."

John Walsh? Olin thought Spungen was getting ahead of himself, but Envy, given that she was AWOL, was as good a lead as any.

"You been to the farm yet?" Olin said. "Strip joint on Joy Road?"

"We're getting there," said Spungen. "Working our way back from Highland Park. You find anything on the computers?"

"Still working on it."

"I'm keeping you posted," Spungen said, "you keep me posted."

Mitchell was doing like he was told, spooning Catori, thinking he'd been holding her like this for an hour now. All the while, he'd been hoping and praying that Phil was just going to hand over that money tomorrow.

Bad as it was getting—terror linked to everything—Mitchell never thought the whole thing was going to hit him so personally. Now he's trying not to get excited while he's spooning this girl yonder in Canada like some draft-dodging desperado trying to recoup 33⅓ percent. His dime, huh? Well, it really wasn't worth it anymore, not hardly. Wasn't time to process what it all meant, either. If Mitchell finagled his way through, there'd be time to rehash when the law-breaking was done. There was just no sense in getting all psychoanalytical before he did what he had to do to put himself in a position of being able to start over.

Asides, much as he had done something to bring all this on—okay, he had ignored that sign, fine—Mitchell figured he grew a little bit a dope, so what? Not only didn't he eat critters, most of the time. But he didn't rip people off, either, selling both quantity and quality at reasonable prices with an eye towards long-term gain, loyalties and royalties.

He wasn't exactly pushing whales back in the water. But if growing a little pot, in and of itself, was dishonorable, well, at least Mitchell produced something that, for the most part, made people feel good, nonviolent. So let's just say he was ready to be judged, if there really was a big boneyard in the sky, especially the way he was lying here with this sweet thing, just holding her, warm, no matter what thoughts crossed.

Push had come to shove when that Federale came around with her stink glove. Catori, Sadao, the Empress, Wyndi, Champagne—none of them deserved that. Asides, those DEAs put it to his animals, and that wasn't right, either. It was one thing to confront a man on his own land, quite another to denigrate him for kicks, shoot his critters. And how was Simmi doing? Mitchell was worried. By now, he was also somewhat convinced that Phil intended to profit off a fellow farmer's hardships. If true, the man had crossed a line, simple. There was no way Mitchell could let that stand. And that's the thing that finally lulled him to sleep, knowing he was, at worst, less wrong than all that. Plus, he hadn't killed anyone. Had that going for him, too.

Spungen walked back into the rows of cars parked in the Menjo's parking lot as Barnes came trotting over, a little excited, holding another cellphone out.

"It's Grier," Barnes said. "Looks like we're wasting our time."

"Wasting our time?" Spungen pointed at Menjo's back door. "I have a he-bitch AWOL had a run-in here with both deceased on 11 September, yesterday."

"It's the dogs," Barnes said. "Fucking dogs down at the industrial park found a grow-op in an old bakery down there, huge. They're still counting plants, but it's in the thousands. Can't be a quarter mile from where they found the bodies."

"I'll call Olin Blue again." Spungen went for his phone, flipped it open.

Barnes reached out, covering it. "Don't."

"Don't?" Spungen couldn't figure Barnes. "Why not?"

"Because," Barnes said, "it's our investigation now."

CHAPTER TWENTY-EIGHT

Del Ray's clock radio went off at 5:30 Friday morning. He thought he'd heard the WJR news reader say something about those dead DEAs. Of course, Del Ray wasn't awake yet, not entirely. Shuffling through the kitchen, wondering whether he'd crap, damn 222s, he fired up the electric stove to heat his kettle. He was on his way to the living room when he aimed his remote at his new "state-of-the-art"—the hell did that mean anyway?—Sony plasma TV on the wall.

Sitting, seeing that hot bitch with high cheek bones, same as her twin, also a CNN news reader, Del Ray ran a hand into his blue-plaid night shorts, Old Navy on the waistband. His morning chubaroo felt hmm, hmm, good, and he was thinking about giving it a spank, therapeutic, when he heard the girl has high cheekbones suggest that the two dead Detroit DEAs could be connected to a big box grow-op they'd found overnight. Also, for those just tuning in, CNN had learned the identities of the dead agents: Fowler Dean Stevens and Enid Kay Bruckner.

Del Ray looked back and forth to make sure he was alone. Jesus, sitting there like that, little Del Ray in hand, he figured that by tomorrow they'd be talking about him same as that cop let the pig farmer slide killed all those prostitutes in B.C.

The kettle whistled.

It was official now. Del Ray had the DEA killers—he had them—and he let them go.

Mitchell remained under his sheets while Sadao and Catori had their respective morning toilets. Each bathed and said they'd see him in The Tree Room. Alone, Mitchell took a long shower. Singing "Home on the Range," he soaped down with complimentary gel, putting his day off. He felt his grizzle and would have liked a shave, if only he'd remembered his Burt's Bees Shaving Bar. He hadn't.

Instead, he toweled dry, dressed, put on a fresh pair of Tommy's, a couple patches, a clean white T-shirt beneath the poncho Catori bought him.

He looked in the mirror, told himself that while he was dressed like Clint, he hadn't done anything truly violent in his 52 years. Nonetheless, he watched himself tuck the Glock into his pants, letting the front of his poncho fall over it, no bulge. Taking a last look, ready, he walked into the room, sat on the edge of a bed, aiming the remote, hitting power. It was on MTV, Bob Marley. The sound was muted, but Mitchell could read Bob's lips, "I Shot the Sheriff."

Again, Mitchell reminded himself that he hadn't shot anyone, even if he couldn't help but find another song he admired negatory just now, time and place. Aiming the remote again, he switched to the News 4 morning program, and suet, there was Skip Hayes, tie undone, looking like he'd been up all night, reporting from the banks of the Detroit River.

Noting the words BREAKING NEWS in the lower left-hand corner, Mitchell unmuted, Skip saying: "Local and federal police, armed with drug-sniffing dogs, have discovered a massive marijuana grow-op consisting of some 3,000 plants less than 800-yards from where two DEA agents were found executed yesterday."

Mitchell reckoned the chill running down his back was of both relief and regret. One hand, he wasn't going to take joy in the hardships of a fellow farmer, no matter the bounty. Soon as the law caught up with this indoor rancher, the dude was going to the big pasture for sure. Other hand, what was the guy thinking bringing up 3,000 plants? That was Paul Newman in *Hud* times a hundred, greed, and now the farmer faced a year a plant.

Skip described a "sophisticated hydroponic hothouse," likely, Mitchell thought, DEA gobbledygook jammed in his pie hole. Located in the former flagship of a popular regional chain specializing in baked Greek goods, Pappa's Bakery was the ideal set-up, coming with work and sleep stations for staff, along with a lab where genetically mutated strains were bred.

"Interestingly, the innovative growers retrofitted massive dough-beating vats to perform as incubators to nurture seedlings and clones at optimum temperature and humidity."

This, police were telling Skip, allowed growers to produce powerful pot that commanded a higher price, and a lot of it.

Into the back-story now, Skip said the former bakery was re-built in the '80s after a suspicious fire took the life of Pappa's founder Georgios Pappadoupolis, a case that closed by the time the family moved to Eastern Market in 1999. While the former headquarters was rented out the same year, police and family spokesman Nick Pappadoupolis were not releasing the identity of the tenant who was now being sought.

For now, six people manning the plant were in custody on a variety of cultivation and trafficking charges. Further charges could be expected if or when police establish links between the facility and two DEA agents found executed less than 800 yards away.

Suet, Mitchell didn't know anything about climate-controlled environments, incubators, and genetics. He'd just put the seeds in the ground, cull the boys, give the girls some African Violet Mix, then harvest the batch, following some of the steps from a handwritten manual by a dude that went by Alexander Sumach, *Grow Yer Own Stone*. The whole deal was about as complicated as growing basil. In fact, it was easier on account of cannabis needed a little dehydration by late-summer to encourage blooming, so proper care actually included neglect.

But was this the future of growing, having a dope factory? If it was, it looked big and complicated, and if Mitchell was going to need all those gadgets, he'd just rather not.

As for this Greek renting out his dead daddy's bakery, Mitchell figured he was into some serious enough *guano* with just the tenant growing 3,000 plants. And the Greek didn't know? Right, Mitchell thought. By the time this was done, they were going to connect the poor guy with religious Commies aiming on blowing up the Ambassador Bridge for sure. As much as Mitchell wasn't going to have a heehaw at the expense of a farmer in that situation, he had to thank thee for this blessing, a distraction bomb that bought more time.

From Chatham to Wallaceburg, Wallaceburg to Dresden, Dresden to Blenheim, Blenheim to Tilbury, Del Ray had re-checked every hotel and motel in Kent Country—nothing. By now, he thought maybe they had gone back to the States or deeper into Canada, east, rural Quebec.

Man, with what they were saying on the radio and TV, naming names, if they ever found out Del Ray let those pilgrims flashing dead DEA badges go . . . Well, let's just say *The Chatham Daily News* was going to make a reality show of it, Del Ray knew it. That's why he'd been retracing his footsteps ever since he heard the CNN lady with the high cheek bones, trying to make the situation right before anyone found out he'd made it wrong.

By 8:41 a.m., according his dash, Del Ray was back in Chatham, pulling up to Wheels Inn, again. It wasn't that Del Ray missed something yesterday. He'd given the lot a good thrice-over, and the van surely wasn't there. But then it also could have been that the pilgrims hadn't checked in yet. Or, maybe they were out. That's why Del Ray was back, persistent.

Fact was, if they hadn't fled, Del Ray would have bet dollars to 222s they were somewhere at Wheels, still rated the top family hotel in the county because of the amenities, everything families could need.

Driving around the side, he didn't see it right away, but then he wasn't exactly looking out front. Alright, so it took a couple passes, but parked in the back, in the middle of a clique of rigs, there it was, the blue Dodge Ram, plates from The Great Lakes State. Yeah, Del Ray had that pilgrim posse. Only now that he did, what was his best move? Was he going to play it safe, just sit here, wait? Del Ray could keep it simple as bread and butter, get 'em on the way out.

Mitchell felt numb when he joined Catori and Sadao in The Tree Room. Neither had much to say over the din of the dead garden, quiet with thoughts of how the stars and the sun had aligned. As for that bit on the TV, again, Mitchell thought mentioning it would rile them, even if there was good news. Shoveling raisin bran and soya milk into his mouth, he watched Catori pick at her bacon. Next to her, Sadao was cutting on sausage.

"Hey, funny boy," Mitchell said, eyes on Sadao's plate, making like he was carving phantom meat. "How 'bout a little taste?"

"Sure thing." Sadao took one more bite, pushing his plate to Mitchell. "Can't eat anymore. Feel like we're about to storm Pearl Harbor, sick." Pointing to the lobby. "I'm going to get some Pepto from the machine, go back to the room, call Elyce."

Mitchell said thanks, pulled the plate over. "Think it's a good idea? Calling from here?"

"Way you put it, I'm the only one you know they're not looking for." Sadao relaxed his shoulders. "Only one who hasn't done anything anyway."

"Other than impersonating a dead DEA."

"Yeah," Sadao said, impatient, "other than that. Besides, I think it's safe to say the Mountie bought it, you fooled him."

Mitchell thought on it, said, "Alright, but let's you use a payphone, stop on the way."

Del Ray drummed fingers on the steering wheel to "Gypsies, Tramps and Thieves" on WJR, Cher before she fixed her nose, her teeth, visceral like that Catori girl. Shortlisting his options, Del Ray thought maybe he should barge into Wheels, catch 'em flatfooted, take 'em down in their rooms. But then he risked losing one out a side door, something like that, maybe shooting someone's kid by mistake. After letting them go, Del Ray felt he needed to collar all of them, without shooting someone's kid, just to make yesterday a wash.

Besides, he thought, crunching some 222s in his molars, if the pilgrims had those dead DEAs badges, they likely had their guns, so going in could get someone killed, namely Del Ray.

No, raiding the place wasn't necessary.

Also in a situation like this, high risk, it was best to keep it straightforward. Oh yeah, Del Ray told himself to go back to his instinctual first reaction. He'd hide, wait. They had to return to the van, just had to, so Del Ray was certain that they would pretty much come to him. Right fucking on, this was some *Art of War* shit Del Ray be doing. And when they eventually did come to him, the more Del Ray thought about it, maybe he should continue to give 'em enough rope. Shit, if he hung back, followed, he could get the whole pilgrim posse on whatever they were here for, plus killing those DEAs, and find time to settle a little something up with that girl.

Three cop killers, plus whatever they were here for? Yeah, Del Ray was going to hang back, get his. And game on. They were up and about, Del Ray watching the cowboy says he won that Kiki award two times walking out to the maze of trucks, disappearing briefly. Pulling out, he reappeared behind the wheel of the van, parking near the lobby then sliding over to the passenger side. Del Ray took note of the little dude taking over as driver. That Indian girl was out there, too, running around in double denim and red boots. But did she get in on the other side or did she go back into Wheels? Were they splitting up? Del Ray couldn't tell, this angle. Main thing, with the girl no longer in cuffs, free, it was clear that these pilgrims weren't who they said they were.

Just look at the little guy wearing a big, black five-gallon today. Yeah, Del Ray thought, that was a DEA man. Maybe a man trick or treating as a DEA. What was he, five-seven? Probably didn't even meet the height requirements.

Chapter Twenty-Nine

Sadao noted the little Jack Daniel's on his receipt, time and dated 9:18 a.m., Friday, September 13, 2002. Catori met him in the lobby before they joined Mitchell in the idling van. Sitting on the passenger side, he told Catori to ride shotgun in the back. She opened the sliding side door facing the lobby, climbed in with her knapsack. Mitchell thumbed his map even though this was Catori's country. Sadao took the wheel. First, Catori instructed him to hang a right outside the lot, another at the second light, following Keil Drive to Highway 40, north. Past McDonald's, Walmart, there wasn't a lot out this way other than clear-cut farmer's fields, soya.

When Sadao saw the sign, Country View Golf & Country Club, he figured they had a payphone, asked was it okay if he stopped to make his call.

Mitchell pissed and moaned, oh, he didn't know. Sadao hit the indicator, saying he was being polite. Like, they were about to take down a Mennonite drug cult, excellent—he was entitled to a phone call. In fact, Mitchell was going to owe him, Sadao, after this. Also, Sadao wasn't happy about the bill. What were all those little Jack Daniel's, $12 each? Even so, Sadao was being a sport, but he was making his phone call first.

Mitchell covered his smile as Sadao parked near the pro shop, getting out. "And Sadao?"

He stopped. "Yeah?"

"Don't go telling her where you are or what you're doing, hear?"

Sadao nodded, said, "Hear."

A quarter mile back, Del Ray pulled over on the gravel, reached for his binoculars. The hell were those dirty pilgrims doing at the golf course now? Was someone at Country View involved? Del Ray was on the verge of finding out. He was going to find out everything. In his next breath, 222s taking hold, he was arguing with himself, the battle of two Del Rays, one telling the other that maybe waiting to see where they were going might not be such a good idea. If he just stomped on it and took them down now, Del Ray could corner them at Country View.

Other than some golfers milling about, there wasn't anyone around, and who's side would the golfers take? Except for that Tom Watson, golfers were conservative, felt better around cops. Plus, with cop killers, you could do anything apprehending a suspect, take liberties. Meaning, Del Ray could just beat it out of them, wherever they were going, get them on everything without going to all the trouble. Conspiracy, if worse came to worse.

Yep, taking down this pilgrim posse could have been one-stop shopping if only the two Del Rays weren't divided, holding the big man back, making him unsure of his next move.

What was seizing him up? Fear? Maybe, but if he did take them down at the golf course, he was committing himself to acting alone when maybe he should be calling for back-up.

Call in, good Del Ray counseled. Keep 'em in your crosshairs until the cavalry arrives.

But then if Del Ray used back-up, he wouldn't be solely in control, and if there was one thing he wanted, it was to control this DEA-killing posse into the ground.

Flashing badges of dead cops—if they were badging him with dead cops' IDs, that meant they were involved in the killings. Also meant they had an interest in that grow-up on CNN, probably made them terrorists, at least yoked with terrorists. And man, if Del Ray could take down someone even loosely associated with the boxcutters, he'd run Kent County.

Back-up, he thought, back-up was for fags.

Sadao held an offset Ping-Zing putter, cradling the phone tight to his ear. "Come again?"

On the other end, back in Detroit, Elyce wasn't crying but Sadao could hear the fracture in her voice. "The Gentlemen's Choice is closed," she said. "That deal with the citizen's committee finally went through. We're done. It was in the paper."

Feeling something inside go slack, Sadao was relieved that he made it this far. So much so he couldn't find the right way to put it, and that was a problem because Elyce didn't get it.

"You think this is a good thing?" she said.

"Don't you see?" Sadao waited for an answer. When he didn't get one, he said, "We did it, honey. We were the last of the buffalo."

"Yeah, well we have to clear out. We're going to need jobs. You back today?"

Sadao thought about it, said he'd try to try to be back today.

"What does that mean, you'll try to try?"

"Means I'll try to try," Sadao said, returning the putter to its display case. "And honey?"

"Yeah?"

Sadao waited a beat, said, "You sure were something in *Weekend at Bernie's II.*"

He blushed at what she was calling him, no sacred cows, slamming her receiver in his ear. Hanging up, turning, some guy with a gator shirt, maybe the pro, was looking at Sadao. That T-shirt, Ugly Tuna Saloona, hanging over Sadao's worn jeans, and a cowboy hat in the pro shop. Really? Gator shirt guy said, "Unless you're Shingo Katayama, there's a dress code, sir."

"Don't worry." Sadao said, already starting to the door. "Was just using the phone."

Outside, crossing the gravel lot with a little skip in his step, he was smiling when he climbed into the van, mind free.

"You're so chipper." Mitchell looked sideways, suspicious. "Why?"

"The burlesque, it's over, closed. The deal with the city went through."

"And that's good news for you?" Mitchell said. "How?"

From the back, Catori said, "I keep telling you, watch it with that how shit."

"Not everything's about you." Mitchell shot a dirty look over his shoulder. "But fine, political correct." Looking at Sadao. "How is that good news? You, out of work."

"I thought a cowboy would appreciate it." Sadao put the van into drive, hit the gas. "We were the last of the buffalo—Elyce and I, a few others."

"Ah." Mitchell nodded, watching Sadao point the van north on 40. "All this time, I was worried about you finding out."

Sadao, picking up speed, said, "You knew?"

"Was in The Freeps yesterday, Thursday, local section. Didn't want to go upsetting you."

"Anything else you're holding back?"

It was about now, re-thinking strategy yet again—how many times had he gone back and forth?—Del Ray realized he still didn't have a plan he could stick with. That meant he pretty much didn't have one, not good. Sure, he still wanted to bust the pilgrims on the Detroit thing, plus whatever they were doing here. That's why he'd gone against submarining them at the hotel then the golf course, both easy-peasy collars.

But now that they were rolling on Highway 40 again, Del Ray didn't know if simply tailing them was the way to go anymore. When they hung a right onto Baseline Road, he thought maybe they knew they were being tailed, leading him up into the hills. Hills, shit. Everything here was cleared, sectioned off, flat. It was the goddamn prairie, depressing, and that's why Del Ray needed the 222s. Without the 222s, who could take it, the sameness?

Okay, so maybe the pilgrims knew Del Ray had a bead on them, taking him to a bad place, an ambush. Maybe that's what the little dude had been doing at the golf course, calling for their own back-up. And wouldn't they have cellphones if they were DEAs? A lot of people had cellphones now, most certainly DEAs. Pretty much everyone except drug people, because drug people used payphones, the anonymity.

Sure, they looked dumb, but seeing as how it was logical at this point that they'd offed two DEAs, Del Ray couldn't underestimate them.

The further this went into the county, the better chance Del Ray stood of losing them, somehow. A blown tire, a dead animal on the road, a deer, someone lying in wait, a rollover . . . Things could go wrong out here on a lonely two-lane highway, no one around. So yeah, Del Ray was just going to get it over with, do it now.

Passing Bobby Jean Mortimore Farms, Del Ray reached for the portable siren between his seats and rested it in his lap. He removed the cigarette lighter, missing when he tried to plug the chord in, dropping it.

Mitchell pressed play, and suet, if he found that Clash number negatory, this was worse. Johnny Cash was singing about tying this girl, name of Delia, to a chair. Much as Mitchell liked Johnny, the message was wrong—cowboys who needed to reshape their attitudes, instead hearing this and doing their women like Delia got done. Talking about the first time he shot her, taunting her—this was some sick shit to be going on about, even for Johnny, regretful in the way Mitchell could tell how the man was terrified of dying, being judged.

Mitchell hit eject, deposited the disc in its case, put it in the glove box. He retrieved another CD and slid the platter into the player. Sitting back, he joined in with Neil Young, note for note, welling up a little when he got to the part about the deer and the antelope. He looked out the window, and thought how the flat Kent County landscape was getting to him. Seemed like every damn farmer was growing soya. At first, it was beautiful, lush. But more and more, it seemed like a cartoon on a budget reusing the same background.

Back in the green ghetto, Mitchell had his colorful herbs, something to keep him interested. Yeah, there was that creepy house with eyes that said don't burn me, negatory in its own right.

But it rated favorably against this, the nowhere capital of nowhere on the way to nowhere. Blinking, Mitchell switched his eyes to the sideview. Goddammit, didn't he tell Catori to ride shotgun? Yeah. Well, Mitchell said, ride shotgun meant keep a lookout. Catori said she thought it meant to ride in the back holding the shotgun in case she was called upon to blow someone's freakin' head off. Why? What was Mitchell getting at? He nodded at the sideview.

Shit, Catori could see him through the back tinting. "Del Ray freakin' James."

"Looks like it," Mitchell said, "Same car, cow-patty brown Cavalier. Now just you stay low back there, beneath the window, beneath Sadao." Eyeballing in the sideview. "Double suet."

"Now what?"

"He done just magnetized a gumball machine to his roof. Means pull over, us."

Sadao reached out the window, adjusting his sideview.

"Goddamn you," Mitchell said. "Don't look at him like that, giving him the fisheye."

"Fisheye, that supposed to be some kind of Asian crack?"

Mitchell leaned closer, speaking slowly. "Pull the goddamn car over, now."

"It's a van."

"Be that as it may." Mitchell reached, hit the indicator himself. "Pull over." Grabbing Sadao's shoulder. "And you're going to hold the sarcasm when we get to talking."

Mitchell hit the power button on the stereo, off.

At Ike Parent Farms, one of the few tobacco fields that hadn't been converted, Del Ray pulled the blue Dodge Ram van over. Stepping onto the gravel, reminding himself that these pilgrims probably punched out DEAs, some kind of hillbilly terrorists, he told himself not to do anything fancy, smiling, polite, as he drew his Glock, approaching the driver's side.

"Will you gentlemen kindly step out of the car?"

Sadao looked at the guy, deadpan. "It's a van."

"A van, huh?" Del Ray frowned, pissed already. If the pilgrim wanted to be a smartass, circumstances considered, Del Ray would treat him as such. Reaching through the open window, he grabbed Sadao by the front of his Ugly Tuna Saloona shirt. "Then get out of it."

"Whoa." Mitchell had his hands up. "Done told you yesterday, I'm a two-time winner—"

"Two-time killer more likely." Del Ray let go of Sadao, casting his eyes about. Yep, he figured, they left the girl back at Wheels. "Cops on your badges are dead, on the news." Moving his head from side to side. "But then you probably already know that, so just please make this easy on yourself and step out of the car."

"I keep telling everyone," Sadao said. "It's a van."

"And I keep telling you." Del Ray had his piece on Sadao now, in his face. "Step out of the—" He stopped, seeing Mitchell get out of the passenger side, rounding the front bumper with his hands in his poncho. Pointing his gun at Mitchell, then Sadao, not sure who to keep it on when Mitchell chin-nodded over Del Ray's shoulder.

"What?" Del Ray said.

Mitchell put his head down, taking his eyes off Del Ray, disrespect, grinding a foothold in the gravel with his right boot. Without looking up, he calmly out and told the young Mountie that when a man teaches ethics from the book of infliction, the student learns to respond in kind.

Open-mouthed, confused, Del Ray had his eyes on the chief pilgrim when he felt something poke him in the back. "I hope that's just a pickle in the pocket of a very tall man."

Catori, reading the brand off the barrel, said, "Remington M700 Varmint-Synthetic."

Del Ray looked over his shoulder, the Indian girl holding an old shotgun. "Does that thing even work? It's from before the war."

Maintaining eye-contact, Catori pumped, loading a shell, pointing it in the air, firing. As the report echoed, fading, she racked it again, telling Del Ray to drop his weapon.

Del Ray—seeing Mitchell pointing a Glock of his own now, the Asian guy, a Les Baer—dropped his piece in the gravel. Yeah, he'd managed to fuck this up again.

"Now you," Catori said. "Down."

Del Ray had his hands up, saying wait a minute, he was RCMP, when Catori pressed the hardware to the side of his head. Telling him down, all the way, before she took his freakin' hair.

Down, okay, Del Ray was doing as he was told, see. Now maybe they could talk this out. They didn't want to make it any worse, probably wanted in Detroit, right? But looking over his shoulder, Del Ray saw detached rage in the girl's golden-brown eyes, dead, and goddammit, he thought she was going to do it, too, right here, right now.

While the cowboy was trying to make her back off, the girl had Del Ray in her crosshairs, even if there was no reason, this range, talking crazy Four Horsemen shit. She eased off only when the cowboy pushed the barrel away, saying no to the girl, to just put the Mountie in the back, cuff him to the side bar, and collect his gun, another Glock, that the girl could have it.

CHAPTER THIRTY

Back in boardroom five, Olin sat next to Jerome Dumont, listening to Danny Grier explain how the FBI had all but nabbed the killer or killers. If it wasn't the Arab-sounding guys working the hothouse—they all requested lawyers, uncooperative—it was the landlord of the former bakery, Nick Pappadoupolis, who was investigated when the original place was fire-bombed in 1986, killing his dad.

Wes Spungen picked it up from there. He'd checked the files. Not enough evidence to prosecute Nick Pappadoupolis, yet, but enough to build on the theory that he had his old man burnt so he could get his hands on the deed to the Pappa's chain for this explicit purpose—cultivating to fund terror.

"Except Greeks are targets," Olin said, "infidels in that they practically invented sodomy, why it's called Greek in escort ads today." Scanning the faces across the table, uncomfortable. "What I'm saying is, what's a Greek got to do with it, terror?"

"That we don't know," Spungen said. "What we do know is if a guy could do that to his old man, burn him, imagine what he could do to cops found out he was running a big-box grow-op. Worst case, even if the guy's telling the truth that he didn't know, we're for sure going to get the guy leased the place in November 1999, one Yosef Atta."

Grier said, "Same surname as the guy blowed up the World Trade Center, Mohammed Atta. Both born in Cairo, so maybe next time you'll learn to back your agents when they say they find the link between drugs and terror in Michigan."

Man, much as Olin didn't take kindly to eating FBI dookie, he wanted to believe the grow-op was connected to Enid and Fowler. Aside from providing a tidy resolution, being that it was 800 yards from the bodies, it seemed like rounding up this Yosef Atta and getting just one of his cronies to turn state's was all there was to it.

Granted, it felt easy. As such, Olin was doing his best to avoid getting excited or discouraged, especially after last night.

For a while, he'd allowed Spungen to get him wound-up over the AWOL drag queen, both men thinking they had a solid lead. And yeah, Spungen had confirmed that Enid and Fowler attended Menjo's on the 11th, Enid checking the queen for keister stash.

That seemed promising, like maybe Olin wasn't crazy after all. Who would run but someone with a reason? It wasn't that he thought the queen had acted alone, but maybe someone connected to the queen, like a boyfriend or pimp. The same logic followed when Spungen's underlings attended the Black Orchid, Champagne missing. At The Motown Hoedown, Gina the Ballerina was gone as well. But they couldn't find any farm out there, not at night, and where was it again? As for the burlesque, Spungen's boys couldn't get in, no one there.

Rounding them up for interrogation seemed automatic to Olin. Now, however, the only thing that mattered was finding this Atta before six o' clock. Olin thought they would've had him in custody by now if it wasn't already on News 4. Who told Skip Hayes?

You could change the music, but Olin was hearing the same old song, the media running hard with it before the case gelled. Once they started, of course this Yosef Atta was in hiding, about to be convicted in the kangaroo court of pop culture.

Maybe Olin was getting too skeptical during this, the autumn of his tenure. After all, name on the lease was Atta, same surname as that guy masterminded 9/11, probably a bad dude in his own right. But Olin still didn't want to see a one-dimensional investigation. That's why he'd spent the night working on his dead agents' computers, trying to find something, anything.

As Olin prefaced his report, the complicated matter emerging was that Enid had so many enemies. All cops did, no doubt, but there was documentation after documentation of threats made against Enid over the years. And yes, while the grow-up down by the river seemed to be a promising lead, the investigation also had to consider dozens of people Enid may or may not have defiled.

Like Spungen and Grier, Jerome wasn't keen to see Olin go off point but knew well enough to hear the man out.

"Could be someone had them killed from inside?" Jerome said.

"That the thing?"

"Not saying it is, just one of the things it could be." Olin pulled loose sheets from a folder, passing them around. "Could be a lot of people. Could be Webb Robinson Enid put away in June 2000 on a five-year bit for his part in a Hillbilly Heroin ring. As the marshals took Webb, he said he was going to drown her and rape her and drown her again."

Grier said, "You got the autopsy report back?"

Olin reached for the bottle of Perrier in front of him. "No."

"Then what makes you think it's a case of rape, point man?"

Olin gave Grier the stink eye, Grier calling him point man, again. "It's the drowning I deem key, her in water." Olin looked back in the files. "Also Syd Pope, threatened he was going to tie her to his trailer hitch, drag her clear down Woodward Avenue after he gets three years on his second cultivation rap, a year for each plant." Bringing the green bottle to his mouth, taking a sip. "The dragging part being key here, Grier."

There was more, but those were the closest matches of threats to what actually happened. Again, all Olin was saying was that these were among the people who had to be checked and crossed off, procedurally.

"And I'm sure they will be, procedurally," Spungen said. "But don't you think we're losing momentum going anywhere but the grow-op, time being? Guy's name is Atta, same as the guy blew up New York. The link between drugs and terror—same as your agent told you."

"Again," Olin said, "could be. Only I'm just as interested in what I found on Fowler's computer." Olin looked at Grier, Spungen. "This is information given out on a need-to-know basis, so I'm lowering the cone of silence." When both nodded, Olin looked back to Jerome. He also nodded, okay. Olin said, "Appears that young Fowler was building a file on Enid."

"I knew it." Spungen laughed, looked at Grier as he spoke. "This is the part where we speak ill of the hero agent, spin it so she brought it on herself."

Olin cut his eyes, said, "Gentlemen, if I may, we need to have a mature discussion about power as it pertains to its use against marginalized peoples. Fowler's reports indicate Enid actually liked checking for keister stash. While he was right to document it, truly disturbing, young Fowler missed the key point. Enid didn't get off on looking up people's asses. She got off on the power that came with the license to look. According to Fowler, she was exercising that power, regularly deploying excessive force."

Quoting Fowler's computer printouts directly, Olin said, "September 10, they attend the burlesque. Agent Bruckner breaks down a door, no warrant, uses latex gloves on one Sadao Saffron, nothing, pistol whips him. Next day, September 11, she confiscates dish gloves to check a stripper when they attend The Motown Hoedown. The incident with the drag queen bingo caller at Menjo's was no exception. There's more." Holding loose pages up. "Kid's notes are detailed—times, dates, places, names. Uses the word 'abuse' over and over. Only thing is—and this is why we have to expand the investigation—not once does Fowler mention an Atta or another Arab name."

Spungen said, "How long you say Fowler was working with her?"

"August 19, his first day."

Spungen did the math, less than a month, said maybe they ought to talk to her partner before that, see if Yosef Atta came up. Sure, Olin said, only she had been operating without a partner for five months, and there was nothing on her computer about Atta. Olin checked.

"She worked alone before this?" Spungen said. "How come?"

Olin looked at Jerome. When the state director nodded, go ahead, Olin said, "Because nobody wanted to work with her."

That did it. Spungen was up from the table, pointing at Olin, saying his agent was dead, and Olin still wasn't backing her. Bringing unsubstantiated allegations the day after a fellow agent dies—what was that? Did Olin want this to get out to the press, the agent's family? And how demoralizing would that be to cops on their way to the funeral from all over the world?

Olin glanced at the eight-by-ten of Junior—this was all his fault.

Grier was saying this Enid lady was a hero, that she had made Olin wrong, got herself killed to do it. And if Olin had listened to what she was telling him, instead of trying to change an uncomfortable narrative, maybe he would be able see that she'd found a link between drugs and terror, if not the link, right here in Detroit, Michigan.

The meeting ended, Jerome following Grier and Spungen out. Waiting until he heard the elevator ring, Jerome shut the door, saying, "Why can't you work with it, the narrative?"

Now just a minute, Olin said, not one but two of his operatives had gone down. Being they were under Olin's command, he wanted to ensure the investigation was comprehensive, procedurally, that they got the right people. Then he pointed into the hallway, said, "How come those two keep getting hot, walking out?"

Jerome, eyes wide with disbelief, said, "Because you're not playing ball."

"And you think I should?"

"It'd be the politic thing for a man seven months short of retirement."

"Well." Olin picked up his files, holding them out to Jerome. "Don't you think we should have all these people tracked, checked, and sweated?"

"Sure, and if it was our call, I'd say go for it."

Olin slid the file down the board table. "I'm fighting Enid, saying don't go out to that farm in the dark. Next day, they wind up dead, and you know she's insubordinate. Still, nobody's gone out to the green ghetto, that farm."

"Thought you said it was impossible the cowboy did it." Jerome closed his eyes, tired. "Him so far away from the bodies."

"Unlikely that he transported their vehicle and bodies all that way, is what I said. I also said he's someone that ought to be engaged, like the rest." Olin looked at Jerome, square. "And you know I'm right, procedurally."

Only thing Jerome knew was that they were under stress, and had Olin managed to get any sleep since this came down?

Olin said, "You know I haven't. Not much."

Jerome stood, picking up his papers, fluffing the edges on the table to organize them into a neat pile. "Why don't you take a little relax, a little nappy?"

"A little nappy, chief state director?"

"A little nappy," Jerome said. "No nappy, no happy."

CHAPTER THIRTY-ONE

Charlene Legace stood alongside Aurelio in Phil's field smearing compost on the soil, preparing the plants with one final blast before harvest. "This is its flaw," she said. "Probably the only flaw. Unlike most other plants, not much can kill it. Also unlike most plants, cannabis doesn't give back to the earth, just takes, takes, takes."

"*Si*," Aurelio said, shoveling compost from the wheelbarrow, dumping it. "Is why they call it weed." Looking back, seeing Phil on the patio taking his morning tea, smoking already. "He really thought I think he grows the cotton batten?"

Charlene smiled without looking up, said, "At first."

Aurelio nodded in Phil's direction. "Mr. Phil is doing, how you say?"

Charlene turned, seeing Phil with that stupid pipe. "We call that a wake and bake."

Aurelio dumped another shovelfull onto the soil. "We call it too early." Stopping, looking at Charlene. "But that is my culture. My culture also decides that I do not judge. I mean no offense, even if Mr. Phil is paranoid."

Charlene ran her eyes over Aurelio, his arms thick with his sleeves rolled up, muscles tensing as he dropped another shovelfull. "None taken."

Aurelio stopped working, put a hand to his heart, earnest. "Maybe again tonight you would like to *viva* my Guadalajara?"

"Maybe." Charlene watched Phil, taking another hit. "He would kill you if he knew."

Aurelio patted his boot. "Is why you gift me the Browning Hi-Power BDA. That happens, I kill him."

Charlene said only if it came to that. If they were careful, it shouldn't, at least not until Aurelio's paperwork came through. If something happened before that, it might look like they were so anxious to kill Phil they couldn't wait.

From the passenger side, Mitchell read another sign in the road, speaking over his shoulder to Catori in the back of the van. "What's that, Uncle Tom's Cabin?"

Catori said it honored founder Josiah Henson and the pipeline of slaves fleeing to Canada. Did she mean the Underground Railroad? Yes, she said, that was the route to Uncle Tom's, sanctuary.

Mitchell said, "They get grant money for that?"

Catori said she used to catch headlines in the local weeklies. Uncle Tom's Cabin gets a restoration grant, a summer student project, promotion, road signs. Now that she thought of it, those little grants added up. Funny though. When you got there, it was just a log cabin, a shack. Wasn't so much what you saw. It was being there, standing where Josiah stood.

Mitchell said, "Huh," pausing as Sadao drifted onto the gravel, bringing the van back. "Where's your government on legalization now, pot?"

"It gets talked about, political noise, polls, but it's years away, decades. Why?"

"Done right, the proceeds could solve a lot of problems for a lot of people. Hell, if your government was serious about reconsideration, they'd legalize, cut the First Persons in."

Catori figured Mitchell meant reconciliation, but maybe the government could reconsider allowing chemical valley upstream from Walpole. Also, maybe the community could reconsider the clean-water pipeline, what with the wealth-distribution balloon Mitchell was floating. Thinking maybe someday, she knelt next to Del Ray, face down on the van floor, cuffed to the sidebar, taking every bump as they made Dresden.

"You know we have to kill him." She trained the varmint gun on him. "Bang, bang."

Mitchell flicked his wrist, said it wouldn't come to that. Maybe they'd bribe the cop, make Phil pay, something like that.

Catori jammed the rifle against Del Ray's ear, grinding it. "He's not going to talk if we give him hush money? He'll take our money, turn on us, say, 'What money?' We'll have a bit of a credibility issue at that point."

"We already have a credibility issue," Mitchell said, thinking yeah, Del Ray probably had to go to the big boneyard. Mitchell wasn't going to do it until he thought it through. Wasn't no sense in riling the narc during the interim, so Mitchell spoke quickly to Catori, glossing over key points. "Sometimes you get and sometimes you get got. And today, your old friend here got got, so just enjoy that, young lady. Later, we'll figure a way to use persuasion." Thinking about it, then deciding to share. "Like Castro."

"Fine," Catori said. "Only telling a man to bugger off and him actually buggering off are two different tricks entirely."

"Point taken." Mitchell turned to look at Del Ray, Catori letting him feel the varmint gun. "Don't be pointing a weapon in a moving car."

"It's a van, I keep telling everyone," Sadao said. "A van."

Mitchell told Sadao to shut up and drive, that Catori was going to shoot the Mountie by accident in his vehicle, all these bumps. That would be another choice situation, Mountie blood everywhere. Asides, they had a job to do, and they were now turning onto Phil's private road, passing the sign out front, Dresden Mennonite Harvest. Beyond lush evergreens lining the property, Mitchell could see a couple of the plain people in traditional garb—probably one of them being Charlene, yeah that was her—working the field, giving it the fall treatment.

Whatever Mitchell was growing next summer, he was going to have to give his field the treatment, too, compost. Damn dope didn't give anything back. Then, as Sadao guided the van up the long driveway, Mitchell said, "We do what I say. Everyone has jobs."

Sadao brought the van to a stop alongside the house, everyone lurching. "Now that we have visuals, I want to hear you say it, spell it out for me, what you want me to do."

"Simple as the date, September 13, 2002," said Mitchell, pointing his hat at the house.

"I noticed on the bill at Wheels. It's a Friday the 13th."

"I left the day out, purposefully, on account of I knew you'd take it that way, superstitious." Mitchell was peeved, the comedian looking for an issue. "So let's just you put that aside and do it like I said. I'm going in, all non-threatening, tell Phil, diplomatic, make this right, kindly pay me my money."

"And if he doesn't?" Catori said. "You know he won't."

At this point Mitchell didn't know *guano* from Jell-O, which is why he felt obliged, no compelled, to just ask for the money. If you don't ask, you don't get. Same time, if either of those plain people in the field came in behind Mitchell, Catori and Sadao were to follow his path. Catori would go into the study and Sadao would take the study window from outside. And both had better be prepared to come heavy.

Sadao said, "You want us to have a good snack?"

Mitchell pointed at Sadao, said they'd already eaten. Heavy meant guns. Alright, Sadao knew. He was just trying to keep everyone loose, but he knew what come heavy meant. When Catori asked if Sadao knew how to use his gun, he said point and shoot, simple.

"How about you," Catori said, looking at Mitchell.

Mitchell nodded, confident. "Just took down a rabid fox hanging around the chickens no more than a month back—bang, bang—on account of I really, really had to. Mission of mercy. Not my first mission, either."

"Yeah," Catori said, "only this is not a mission of mercy."

"I know," Mitchell said, "I know."

That settled, Mitchell said godspeed, non-denominational, as he stepped down from the passenger side. Starting to the house, he saw pansies of every color planted for fall in clay pots, one of them broken, dirt scattered. Just beyond that arrangement sat Phil, sipping tea.

"Mitchell." Phil hit his corncob. "Last I heard, you were no longer of this world."

Out in the field, Charlene cupped her hands around her eyes. Even out this far, she could recognize Mitchell Hosowich. The way he dragged his spurs—who even had spurs anymore?—put his hands on his hips. Bad enough the cowboy was alive, his crop undercut. But now he was probably mad as a wet hen, wanting his money, and Charlene figured he had every right.

She knew Phil was going to grind this into a circular semantical discussion until Mitchell either pulled a gun or walked. And if he walked, he was going to go home, stew, probably come back with some dudes from the D. Right now, he was just asking, but she knew Phil was about to turn this into a trifling matter.

Charlene, pointing to Mitchell's van at the side of the house, told Aurelio there could be someone else. Who knew what that First Nations girl was up to, coming here, saying Mitchell's dead—why had she said that? For all Charlene knew, she was running a game on Phil.

"*Sí*," Aurelio said, "but what does this mean?"

"Means we protect our investment, is what it means." Charlene looked at the van again, studying it, back at Aurelio. "Also means you keep doing what you're doing, working the soil with an eye on that van. I don't like his tinted windows. Anyone comes out, follows me, you follow them. You follow?"

"*Sí*, but is a lot of following. You think is safe?"

"Not so much. I'm worried this time, Aurelio."

"Why do you do it for Mr. Phil? Talks down to you, like me. Why do you protect him?"

She put a pinky to the corner of her mouth, said, "So that I may continue to *viva* your Guadalajara while maintaining the lifestyle to which I'm accustomed."

Aurelio dumped a load of compost onto the ground. "Just be careful, for me, us."

She nodded, pretending to examine different patches of the field, slowly moving out of sight from the van until she was safely behind the barn.

Man, she told Phil how many times? What did he think happened to bookies that didn't pay? Yeah, well the same thing happened to drug families that ripped off other drug families.

"No longer of this world, huh?" Mitchell looked out to the field, saw that big Mennonite kid out yonder, but where was Charlene? Looking back at Phil. "Well, as you can see, reports of my demise have been greatly exaggerated. Means we have to talk, Phil."

"Sure." Phil offered the pipe, peace. Mitchell shook it off. Phil, taking one more hit, led Mitchell inside to his office. Phil sat behind his desk, next to his Dirk Willems icon. "Now how may I do you a personal favor?"

"How." Mitchell, sitting on the other side, tapped the desk with his index. "You know damn well how, Phil."

Phil held a hand out, "Say it."

Mitchell couldn't believe the Mennonite-masquerading prick talking bad from the get-go, making him say it. "You have to pay me my money, goddammit."

Phil made a rectangle with the thumb and middle finger of each hand, looked through it. "First, you had dope to sell, you said. Then you were dead, Catori said. That is all I knew. Meantime, I made another deal with Catori. My money is committed, spent. Then you"—breaking the rectangle—"come here saying you and I have something to settle. Now this is me asking you, what?"

"You owe me same as the 76ers in '94, indexed favorably."

"Do you have product?" Phil looked at the van's front bumper sticking out from beside the house. "Are you holding product in your van?"

Mitchell bit into his cheek, steady. "You know I'm not, old buddy."

"Then that is your problem." Phil swatted at a mosquito, missed.

"No Phil, my problem is that you paid about 50-grand less for it, got it off Catori—no, you took it from her—for a measly 10, Canadian."

Phil pointed at the desk. "Do you know why?"

Mitchell licked his lips, dry, listening. Phil said it was worth less because it was dirty, tainted dope that had been hard-fought-and-won in a battle against DEA agents. Glorious though it may be, it was a shipment Phil had to move fast before he found himself at the center of something larger than selling the most dope in Kent County. So, Phil was doing Mitchell a personal favor by taking it at all. And in case there was any confusion, Phil had already taken it. It was his dope now.

On top of that, Phil had sampled Mitchell's product, not exactly Anaconda Mamba, the way it was grown old-fashioned, seeds, carrying the unbearable stench of dirt. Mitchell said it was a slow-creeper. Phil blew that off. Said Mitchell had not dried or separated the fruit, devaluing the harvest again, because Phil now had to take Charlene and Aurelio off other tasks to hang everything. They would then be taken off other tasks going forward to do the trimming, the sweating, the curing.

In addition, because it was packed before being dried, Charlene and Aurelio had discovered mold in the airtights. And, to paraphrase the government man in *Hud*, something Phil knew Mitchell would understand, mold was the worst thing a dope man could have.

CHAPTER THIRTY-TWO

Inside the van, Sadao hefted the Les Baer Prowler III. He couldn't remember how many bullets were left. What had Mitchell said? Five? Six? Sadao recalled Clint Eastwood having a similar dilemma. Unlike Clint, Sadao had time to check, except he was afraid to open his gun in case he couldn't close it again. Open it? Sadao didn't even know how to do that. But maybe, just maybe, if he stopped fucking around with it, he really could just point and shoot—bang, bang.

A gun, good. Sadao was coming heavy, and what did he know about that? Just a couple days ago, he was a pot-selling, third-rate comedian shacked up with a hot, if not aging, hipster girl, relatively satisfied. Had he become all he could? No, but then he wasn't holding a gun, either. Now here he was, accessory to two DEA killings, babysitting a kidnapped Mountie, and backing up this Hamtramck cowboy boosting his dope money from drug Mennonites in a foreign land. Like, how did he get to this particular time and place?

Looking at the piece in his hands, Sadao decided it was what it was. He was here now, and well, that had to mean something. Then he heard Catori say, "Look-it."

Sadao followed the line of Catori's finger. From around the barn they saw an attractive woman, wholesome, until she hiked her long work dress, reaching to her inner thigh, drawing something that looked like a TV remote from her garter.

"That's her gun," Catori said. "One of those Credit Card Shotguns I was talking about. They must both have one."

"See," Sadao said, "and I always thought Mennonite's were nonviolent, pacifists."

"Stereotype," Catori said over his shoulder. "Not supposed to have electricity, but look, power lines."

"Also, they're not supposed to have zippers. If they're not supposed to have zippers, they're definitely not supposed to have garters. Garters are burlesque." Sadao closed his eyes. It felt nice, her warm breath on him, contact. "And if they're not supposed to have garters, I'm thinking these particular Mennonites don't care what they're not supposed to have."

"They're not real Mennonites," Catori said, watching the woman work her way towards the house. "You are aware of that?"

Yeah, Sadao knew, he was just saying how yellow it was of them to be hiding behind those costumes, full-grown people shielding themselves with religion. Yellow? Catori thought Sadao gave Mitchell PC shit for calling him yellow for chickenshit. Of course, Sadao said, but it was okay for him, Sadao, to talk like that, him being Asian. Catori said she didn't think it was okay to say Asian anymore, that there was another word now. Well, Sadao said, then maybe everyone should just choose their own words and leave each other the fuck alone. Like, just imagine who Sadao could've been if there really were no sacred cows.

"Mold." Mitchell shook his head. "Shee-it, Phil. First off, Hud's daddy's problem was hoof and mouth, cattle. Two, it wasn't enough time for mold to set. Three, as for you doing me a personal favor, your metaphorical boots aren't on the ground, good buddy."

"Be that as it may, I am in control." Phil drummed his fingers on the desk. "What I paid is as good as you are getting for moldy dope that has not been dried, cut, sweated, or cured, and at the same time must be moved quickly in that it is connected to something bigger, terror."

Alright, Mitchell had done the right thing thus far, affording Phil every chance. Deeming it time to speak to the man in another language, Mitchell pulled up his poncho, rubbing his tummy above the butt of his Glock. Yeah, he'd about heard enough, out and out telling Phil it was time for money to exchange hands. Amused, Phil said, "And if I do not do as you say, what are you going to do? Strike up a committee?"

Goddammit, Mitchell was honestly telling his quasi-friend how it had to be, showing him the Glock, and Phil was still trying to figure a way of not coughing up those greenbacks. Reverting to plan B, all the way now, Mitchell drew the gun and said, "Phil, you know how you say when you need some money, you just go get some?"

Phil hesitated. "Yes."

"Well, go get some."

Phil cleared his throat in his fist, let a smile creep out. "If I do not?"

Mitchell ran a hand over his face, noticing Phil's very cherry papers. "Phil, I have affection for you, and, until today, I respected you. But if you don't give me what I'm honestly owed, taking advantage of a fellow farmer's hardship, I'm a going to shoot you like that rabid fox I done did trying to get my chickens."

Phil wrinkled his nose, confused. "You shot a living thing?"

"No more than a month back, had to. Really, really had to. Mission of mercy."

"Fine," Phil said. "I'm impressed, very impressed, except for one thing."

Mitchell said, "Except what?"

"This is not a mission of mercy."

Mitchell fought off a laugh, said, "Actually, Phil it kind of is."

"How So?"

"You can't see it." Mitchell leaned forward, looked at Phil earnestly. "But I'm still trying to do you a personal favor, old buddy."

Catori watched the Mennonite woman angling herself against the house, looking in through the office window. Holding her rectangle gun like a cop, both hands, she stayed tight to the clay bricks, stepping lightly to the porch.

"She's going inside," Catori said, looking over Sadao's shoulder. "You ready?"

Sadao thought about it, said, yeah, he was ready.

"I'm following her in," Catori said. "You wait, keep an eye on that guy in the field. If he goes in the house, you let him, then take the office window, same window she was looking into, and back Mitchell and I up from the outside. Otherwise, stay here."

Sadao figured inside the house was more dangerous than inside the van, that it should be him going in, not the girl. "Why don't I do it, you take the outside?"

"That's so sweet, Sadao." Catori loaded a second shell into the varmint gun, racking it, putting four shells in her front pocket. Checking Del Ray's Glock in her waistband, secure, she said, "I've been here, know the inside layout. You just take the office window from outside if that guy in the field goes in the house, simple." She pointed out the office window, again, just so they were clear, then said, "And hey, you ever fire a gun or not?"

"I get the general drill." Sadao let the piece fall to his lap. "Aim and shoot, right?"

"Right, aim and shoot." Catori watched Sadao trying to figure it out, the poor guy. Poor guy—all this meant was that the dirty work would fall to her. "Okay, again, I'm going in. You cover us, simple." And simple? He'd be lucky if he didn't shoot his freakin' eye out.

Sadao nodded, watching Catori quietly open and shut the back, inching around to the house. Looking around, Sadao didn't see anyone, except for the dark-skinned guy, still way out in the cabbage patch. Turning, speaking over his shoulder to Del Ray chained in the back, Sadao said, "What'd you do made her this way?"

Del Ray sat up as much as the cuffs would let him, sore. "I'm just a Mountie laying down law I'm sworn to lay down. I don't get a say on law in the House of Commons, but it's my job."

"To lay it down," Sadao said, "right?"

Del Ray pulled the cuffs against the sidebar, no use. He looked out the tinted window, someone to shout out to, help. "Hey," Del Ray said, "can you do something for me?"

Sadao, slightly surprised, said, "You can ask."

"I got a condition, medicine in my shirt pocket. Would you please put a few of those medicines my mouth?"

"What kind of condition?"

Del Ray thought of saying he had a slipped disk, but how could he be a on active duty with a slipped disk? Then he thought, fuck it, said, "I got, like, the problem, 222s, and may I please have three?"

"What's a 222?" Sadao said.

"Aspirin with codeine. Nothing serious, over-the-counter."

"Over-the-counter? My girl takes it for migraines. Needs a prescription."

"You're American," Del Ray said. "Here, Canada, it's over-the-counter."

"Tell you what." Sadao closed his eyes. "Tell me what you did to that girl that made her this way, I'll give you as many as you want."

"Can't I just have my medicines first? It's not like I'm saying put a spike in my arm, send me to the moon. It's just oral medicines."

"You're answering my question with a request." Sadao reached over to the glove box. Inside a plastic Farmer Jack bag, he found a collection of bootleg country CDs, mostly Johnny Cash, Xeroxed liner notes with library stamps, bar codes. Carefully removing them from the bag, putting the CDs in the glove compartment, Sadao closed the box. Thinking he'd given Del Ray ample time, Sadao said, "I asked, what did you do to make her this way?"

Man, Del Ray thought this was it. Give him some 222s—they weren't just going to kill him. No, they were going to do something bad, make it hurt. His mouth was parched. For a few seconds, he felt ill, physically, like he was about to hurl. The birds changed that, little sparrows singing near the van's window, instrumental nothingness, a white space that left him with that song on the radio from yesterday. He remembered most of the lyrics until he came to the song's last quarter, then he blanked. Why, oh why hadn't Del Ray taken the time to hear the song out? Maybe it meant to say something. Was Del Ray the baffled king?

Thinking maybe this was the that part that came after the broken hallelujah, Del Ray found himself trying to explain, recalling how he'd been tipped off to a dope-selling dancer at JR's. He broke into her room above the place after her show, what was it, seven weeks back? Despite what she was up to, selling, Del Ray had it in mind to do her a deal, keep her out of the system while still letting her know what she was doing was wrong, negative reinforcement. Yeah, Del Ray couldn't help but smile, the way that half-breed girl was so hot to trot.

"Hot to trot?" Sadao blew air into the plastic bag, closing it at one end.

"That's what all the signals said, wet little tongue flickering my left nipple. That's my button, she knew it."

Sadao put pressure on bag, testing it for holes. "Except how is it you ended up tied wrists to ankles, she wanted it so bad?"

"Thought it was kinkiness she wanted."

"Kinkiness?" Sadao turned, looking over his shoulder. "You see any tape back there?"

Del Ray looked, said yeah, there was a roll of silver duct-tape sitting right there in the open tool box, now could he have those medicines? Sadao said he didn't think so. Why, Del Ray wanted to know. He'd made good on his end, now why couldn't he have some 222s?

"You didn't answer the question," Sadao said, stepping low around the driver's seat holding the Farmer Jack bag. "What did you do to her made her this way?" When Del Ray didn't answer, again, Sadao said, "Like, you're describing something, sketchy, but you're still not answering. Besides, if you were me, would you help you?"

Del Ray thought about it, said yeah.

"No, you wouldn't," Sadao said. "You'd lay down the law."

CHAPTER THIRTY-THREE

Shifting his weight behind his desk, Phil pointed at Mitchell then himself, said, "You are not taking one thing from me, from us."

Mitchell tightened his grip on the Glock. "Come again?"

"My beautiful wife." Phil motioned over Mitchell's chair. "She has the prototype Credit Card Shotgun on you. We bartered for them through a source that has a source that has a relationship with another source that robbed Koscielski's Guns and Ammo. Koscielski makes them right there, by hand, in Minneapolis— Murderapolis, Koscielski calls it. By 2004, they will be all over the market, $99.99 each, but Charlene has one now, and it is on you."

Mitchell kept his gun trained between Phil's eyes, said, "I done heard her come in, Phil, and you don't think I counted on this? There's a reason I got those windows in my van tinted. Did the job myself, $29.99 for a kit at People's Auto Parts. See, I done struck a committee while you wasn't looking, and we're already warm, practiced up to bring some Detroit-style shit down if you don't kindly pay me my money."

From behind, Charlene said, "Mitchell, you and Phil have known each other a long time."

"Indeedy." Mitchell nodded, eyes on Phil. "*High Times* convention, Cobo Hall, 1989."

"Good, so let's all just cool down, settle this without gunplay, be friends again."

Mitchell said, "That's exactly what I came here honestly aiming for."

Charlene poked him with the Credit Card Shotgun. "Then how come you're aiming that plastic pistol at my husband?"

"On account of I done asked nice I don't know how many times, and he still hasn't paid me my money." Mitchell was going to leave it there, then he heard the faint sound of his van door beeping. Thinking goddamn Sadao, leaving the keys in the ignition and opening the driver's side, again, Mitchell spoke to the Diego Rivera original above Phil's head, the peasant working under the watchful eye of his boss, socio-political. Mitchell said he was pretty sure it was painted in the '30s. By the '50s, hand-painted reproductions were everywhere. Did Phil have it authenticated? No, well then Mitchell, was just curious, what happened to the guy paid Phil with a stolen Diego Rivera original? Maybe he could provide provenance.

"Can't eat it." Phil looked up at the painting. "Lost its value, so that was it for him."

Sadao crawled back to the driver's seat. If he didn't hear Del Ray beating his head on the wall, it was because he, Sadao, couldn't see the brown-skinned dude in the field anymore. Shit, Sadao should've been covering the office window by now. He planned to leave the door open, but the van was beeping as soon as he opened the driver side. Double shit, he'd put the keys back in the ignition, so he just left the door unlocked, shutting it gently, then shimmying along the house. He looked sideways through the window.

Inside, he saw Mitchell holding the Glock on the guy Sadao figured for Phil, both of them sitting. In turn, that nice-looking Mennonite woman, kind of like Kelly McGillis in *Witness*, had her gun—it really did look like a TV remote—on Mitchell. Behind her, just coming into the room, Catori was aiming the varmint gun at the Kelly McGillis woman.

Great, Sadao thought. Three cops dead now, and they were going to plug a couple plain people. They were really going to have to do it, too, because the guy Sadao made for Phil had a free hand under his desk and behind his back, slowly reaching into the back of his trousers. With the guy's vest riding high, Sadao could see it now, the gray of a gun that looked like a TV remote, same as the Kelly McGillis woman was holding. Like, was there a sale?

Mitchell said that if he was half a man, he'd take the Diego Rivera, too, send it to a gallery where other people could appreciate it. Phil cut him off, saying, "You, a hardcore vegan, going to kill for it? Can't even eat a slider and you're going to shoot me, a human, for art?"

"Look Phil." Mitchell kept his gun cocked. "Despite the fact I just fell off the wagon—"

"Ate meat?"

"Broke down." Mitchell closed his eyes, the shame. "Had the Farmer's Cholesterol Explosion Burger Deluxe Combo up at the Big Chief yesterday. Still, it's always been my goal to get out of this without putting a lead plum into no person." Speaking over his shoulder. "Especially Charlene here, finest looking of the plain people I ever saw—healthy, substantial."

She tried to make light, poked him in the back. "Should've stopped while you were ahead, Mitchell—substantial."

"Sturdy, is what I'm saying. Nice child-bearing hips."

"Hey."

"Meant no offence. Wholesome, like that girl played Harrison Ford's wife in *Witness*."

Charlene said, "Kelly McGillis?"

"That's the one," Mitchell said. "By the by, Phil said you dealt with my dope, how is it?"

"Nice," she said. "It's a slow creeper."

"Any mold?"

Phil was telling Charlene she didn't have to answer that, legally, but she spoke over him anyway. "There wasn't any mold, no."

Mitchell, speaking directly to Phil now, serious, said, "Mendacity aside, Phil, I've had such a goddamn 48 hours, not even. I'm getting out of this business. Thinking about maybe getting a grant, turn the place into a fine, upstanding tourist trap."

Phil shook his head. "No." He didn't believe it. What was the stupid cowboy going to do? Sell more veggies from that highway cut-off?

"It's so," Mitchell said. "Was just telling Sadao, I got like five hairs in the butter. So just kindly pay me my money and it'll be nice knowing you, old buddy."

Phil said nothing, thinking, Sadao? Who was this Sadao? Probably one of Mitchell's barnyard friends, one of his chickens. And where did Charlene get off putting in her opinion? It was up to Phil to speak for the business. Further weakening his position, now she was pointing at his icon, Dirk Willems, saying, "God sakes, Phil. Just get the money, have it done."

Phil told her she was out of line, to just back him up. Oh yeah, well, if Charlene was man enough to hold this newfangled gun on Mitchell, then she was man enough to tell Phil what to do— especially when he was making it worse by sticking to a bad position. "Just reach into Dirk and get Mitchell his money, before this turns into a trifling matter."

Phil was mad at Charlene's disloyalty, madder for her saying where the money was, and he was saying so. At least until Mitchell said he already knew on account of Phil had to show it off in front of Catori, making a big deal of reaching into the big head and pulling out 10-grand, when Mitchell knew Phil had the whole kit and caboodle in there.

The Dresden sun was working towards 11, warm, like Catori's breath, Sadao thought, shielding his eyes from the glare off the window. One last time, he had to be sure he was seeing this right, that he wasn't going off half-cocked when maybe this could still be talked out. Yes, there it was behind the back of that Phil guy. Wiggling his ass in his chair, Phil had his fingers on the little newfangled gun now. Clearly, from Mitchell's angle, he wouldn't see it.

Sadao thought maybe Mitchell was distracted by the woman who looked like Kelly McGillis. She still had her gun on Mitchell. But for now, Sadao was the only one who could see that Phil also had a gun, that he was angling to use it. Maybe the woman playing his wife had a sense of what was going on, which was why she wasn't shooting anybody. She had to know Phil had the gun. Now that he was raising it bit by bit, it was up to Sadao to hit first, before the guy shot Mitchell under the desk.

Like, without Mitchell, what was Sadao going to do? Sadao didn't even know the way back to the highway from here, so there wasn't much left to consider when he took aim, forcing himself to go slow, using his left to steady the piece in his right. He took care to squeeze the trigger gently, not pull, as he had learned during a Martin Lawrence movie.

First time he fired there was no click, nothing. Sadao inspected his gun, found what appeared to be the safety. He switched it off. Thinking nobody told him about that, he aimed again, waiting another beat, squeezing off three quick rounds—bang, bang, bang.

Soon as Sadao heard the reports, a cloud of broken glass exploded in his face. He clawed at his eyes, turning in circles. His eyes, his eyes—Sadao couldn't fucking see. He could only feel tiny knives of glass stabbing whenever he rubbed, blinked. He heard footsteps before the rapid report of another gun at close range. It came from behind, a number of shots, hammering Sadao through the window, taking his gun and pieces of glass inside.

Mitchell was sprawled out on the floor. First thing he saw was Charlene crawling to her gun while Catori ripped at Charlene's hair, pulling her back. Reaching out, Mitchell slapped Charlene's piece away, sending it spiraling. He held his Glock on her while Catori let go of the woman's hair and retrieved the varmint gun as well as Charlene's Credit Card Shotgun, then Phil's matching piece.

Seeing Phil spitting up blood, Sadao trying to push the insides of his stomach back in place, Mitchell looked around for—what was it now? A second shooter. Man, Mitchell's ears were ringing, but he could hear someone barging through the front, coming down the hall, footsteps heavy. That poor Hispanic boy from the field must have shot Sadao. He was making noises that sounded like curses, even if he formed few actual words other than Charlene, Charlene . . .

Mitchell had his gun trained on the open office doorway but needn't have bothered. Catori was one-handing Charlene's Credit Card Shotgun in her right, firing off two shots when the boy may as well have run up Hamburger Hill, in Mitchell's estimation. The kid knew he was going to die, but he came no matter. Now that was love.

Charlene was crying out his name now. "Aurelio, no. N-O-O-O." He managed to get of an errant shot off that hit Phil in the face, but Catori had already hit Aurelio twice. He was wobbling when Catori switched pieces and gave him the varmint gun full on, blowing him back against the wall, an instant red splash setting behind him as he slid to the floor.

Charlene pounced on Catori who started screaming out for Mitchell to shoot this Kelly McGillis-looking bitch.

Mitchell had his Glock on them, trying to lock onto Charlene. But dammit, he couldn't do it the way they were rolling over top of each other, Catori losing Del Ray's Glock as it skittered across the floor.

For a split-second, Mitchell had a clean shot, but he hesitated and then Charlene was on top, holding Catori down hand to hand. Mitchell feared any shot would go through Charlene, kill both. There was nothing he could do until Charlene took a knee to her groin, rolling over and holding herself when she saw the Les Baer sitting on the floor. Again, Mitchell was ready to shoot, no matter how fine a woman Charlene was. Just about to do so, stopping when Charlene lurched and put the gun in her mouth. "No," he heard himself say. "No more."

Charlene was laughing, saying *el corazón*, fellating the piece when it went off, the kick knocking her back into the corner, behind the ottoman where Mitchell couldn't see her. That would have been just as well, but he had to go over, respectful.

"What's that mean?" Catori said, "*El corazón*?"

"My heart." Mitchell closed his eyes. "Hispanic for my heart."

Seeing Charlene like that, hole blown from her mouth through the top of her head, Mitchell looked away, saying Phil couldn't have done it so long without her. Plus, Phil would have still been in business, alive, if only he would have been man enough to take a smart woman's advice. Otherwise, Mitchell told her lifeless body he was sorry, just so sorry.

Behind him, Catori already had Phil's keychain and was into the Dirk Willems icon, loading the money into her knapsack, saying there must be 200-grand here, more.

Mitchell said, "Yeah, but you know that's not what we came here for, not all ours."

Catori waved bundles of cash. "These are 10-grand each, sure, but it's—"

"Never mind." Mitchell said, cutting her off. "We don't take all of it, that buggers the cops on motive. Further we put them off motive, further we get. There's also karma to consider. Just you take what we're owed, no more."

"What about Sadao?" Catori looked at the comedian blinking blindly, right hand trembling as he unfolded a creased picture.

"Sadao's going to be fine," Mitchell said. "Now just take five of those stacks, plus exchange on the first 10-thou."

"I still don't see why we don't take all of it, especially when you consider—"

"No, I said." Mitchell shook his head, moving over to Sadao.

"You won't even listen."

Mitchell waved her off. Kneeling next to Sadao, searching for words, Mitchell didn't know what to tell the poor guy. Sadao was a goner, that much was sure. Blinded by the glass, he looked blankly in the direction of the creased-up picture he held in one hand, his intestines in another. "Elyce's cinema card from *Weekend at Bernie's II*, tell me what you see."

Mitchell took it, said he saw a woman getting her top snatched off by a dead guy.

"Beautiful." Sadao said. "Funny too."

Mitchell looked at the cinema card. "Yeah, give you both those things."

"Just do something for me," Sadao said. "Tell her something."

"Why don't you wait, tell her yourself?"

"Kind of you to say, but look at me," Sadao said. "You have to tell her for me."

Mitchell began to nod, then said alright, listening. First, Sadao said, Mitchell needed to get Sadao's share, plus his wallet, to Elyce.

Secondly, and more importantly, Mitchell was to wait a beat, then tell Elyce that she sure was something in *Weekend at Bernie's II*.

CHAPTER THIRTY-FOUR

Olin sat as his desk sipping Perrier, re-reading the autopsy reports, just in from the coroner. Accordingly, it seemed Fowler took the worst of it, suffered the most. Report said he'd been stabbed repeatedly with a dull object, something like a homemade tool or an animal tusk. What was that? Some kind of medieval ritual?

These people, Olin thought, when they got around to killing a DEA, they did it up right. Right back to Kiki Camarena, it was some sick shit—cattle-prods, drowning operatives in dirty toilet water, branding them, scarring cryptic messages into their flesh, cutting their bits off a little at a time until they died.

The thing that made even less sense was the accompanying ballistics report indicating that Fowler had been shot in the neck with Enid's gun. In and of itself, that wouldn't have been hard to cover off, the logical explanation being that the drug-lord terrorist people had stripped Enid of her Les Baer, turned it on Fowler. But that didn't explain the residue burns on Enid's hands, indicating she'd fired her piece, and that was one inconvenient truth. As for her, it appeared she'd been tied to the back of the Jeep, dragged to death and hanged at once, road rash all over. Cause of death: Asphyxiation.

It was late morning, Olin expecting to hear from National Director Herbert Baker any time now. And what was Olin supposed to say? He hadn't wanted to put Fowler with Enid in the first place, said so. But then Jerome didn't want to break up productive teams, and, again, no one wanted to switch off for Enid. That being the case, Olin held his nose, went along with it.

Now, with the whole thing focused on that former bakery, even Olin had to admit that it was beginning to look like everything had gone down there, simple. Mostly because of the dragging. Couldn't prove that though, what with the storm washing away any tracks leading to the crime scene. Proof or not, it was hard for Olin to deny at least the appearance of a link between Michigan marijuana and terror.

Checking the time on his phone, 11:34 a.m., Olin was wondering whether Herbert Baker was still calling when he, Olin, picked up his remote, aiming it at the TV. A blip of colors materialized, Skip Hayes interviewing Danny Grier, the FBI guy.

They were standing in front of the grow-op as coppers in Hazmats hustled the plants out in the background. Grier was saying that while local and federal police sources had yet to confirm whether Yosef Atta was a relation of Mohammed Atta, the same sources were advising the FBI that the pair had attended an al-Qaeda training camp in Afghanistan in the early '90s.

It appeared that Yosef Atta had entered Canada as a visa student in 1998, attending few of his Economics classes at the University of Western Ontario. By the time he'd flunked out late that year, it was believed he was already living in Detroit illegally.

As for Atta's Detroit landlord, Skip Hayes told Grier that unnamed sources had been telling News 4 that Yosef Atta had been paying the Pappadoupolis family in cash, something the family was not claiming for taxation purposes, declaring the building vacant. Was that so?

Grier said he couldn't comment on that. Back on point, he added that, given the apparent links, Yosef Atta had been placed on top of the FBI's Most Wanted list, behind only bin Laden and people close to bin Laden. As for the owners, Grier confirmed that Detroit Homicide was re-opening an investigation into a 1986 firebombing in which the principal of the Pappa's chain, Georgios Pappadoupolis, was killed, and that the FBI would be assisting in that probe.

"So," Hayes said, "What does this mean?"

Grier brought his lower lip over the top one. "Means all around, we expect numerous additional charges. That's what it means."

Knapsack on her shoulder, Catori climbed into the passenger side of Mitchell's van. "I forgot about freakin' Del Ray. What do we do?"

"What with all the killings, I done forgot myself." Mitchell slid the Diego Rivera original behind his seat, dumping a mess of guns on the floor, climbing in, hitting the ignition, putting the tranny into drive and making a circle in the driveway. Then, on Phil's private road out, he said, "Guess we better think fast." Looking over his shoulder, Del Ray, limp with a plastic bag over his head. "Goddamn you, Catori."

"Goddamn me, why?"

"Why." Mitchell jerked the van to the side of Phil's road, stopping. "Del Ray's wearing a bag, and he's not moving. Del Ray's dead. That's goddamn why."

Catori turned, looked in the back. What was this now? She didn't freakin' know.

"You don't know?" Mitchell gripped the wheel, tight. "There's a Farmer Jack bag taped over his head, your signature all over it—asphyxiation, more sick thrill-kill shit. Creative, just like I told you not to do. You made him suffer, goddammit."

Catori, biting her lip, said, "Sadao must have done it."

"Sadao, right. Only when you bite your lip that's when I know you're stringing me a whizzer." Mitchell looked up the road, then in the sideview. Clear, he cut the ignition, taking his keys as he crawled into the back. "This is so you. Same thing you did to me, only better."

Catori shrugged. Again, it really wasn't her. Had to be Sadao, the sweetheart.

"Convenience on account the dead don't speak." Mitchell, selected the skeleton key, uncuffed Del Ray from the side bar, peeling the tape, pulling the bag away. Then he opened the back door, stepped out, grabbed Del Ray's feet, pulled him out. His torso fell onto the gravel with a grunt. Mitchell dropped the Mountie's feet, looking at Catori. "You hear that?"

"Didn't want to, but yes, I heard."

"Now what?"

Catori put her hands in the air, said, sorry, they had to shoot him for sure now, bang-bang. Mitchell turned abruptly and started walking.

"Where you going?"

"For a walk, young lady," Mitchell said, still moving away from her. "Figure things out."

"Yeah, well don't take too long figuring."

Mitchell waved behind his back, mad, walking along the evergreens. Seeing the two-lane highway in the distance, a provincial copper passing in a hurry, he had to admit the girl was right, time to giddy. Turning, he started back. Ten steps from the van, he pulled the Glock, telling himself to do his figuring later. Closer now, Del Ray was coming around. Wasn't exactly up and about, but there was movement, recognition of Mitchell aiming that gun, DEA issue. Catori abruptly stepped in between them, leveling the Mountie's own Glock. "It's me who should do it," she said, "with his own gun." Squeezing of a round, bang, she punched a hole through Del Ray's forehead, then bang, another, teeth everywhere.

As Catori stepped away, Mitchell looked down at the Mountie, dead for sure this time. "Okay, we got to burn the breeze, now."

Catori said, "D'ya think?"

When Olin's private line finally rang, he answered with his last name, Blue, finding that the national director wasn't half the hard-on Jerome made him for. No, Herbert Baker wasn't pleased, what with two dead agents missing shields and guns, but he wasn't going out of his way to make Olin wrong, either. Baker was just making it clear that he'd been briefed on the autopsy report. Now he wanted to know everything officially unofficial.

Olin took a pull on his Perrier bottle, said, "What do you think, national director?"

"Name's Herbert, and I already know what I think. I want to know what you think."

"Truth?"

"No, no." The national director was more than a little sarcastic now. "Genuflect."

"Look, national director—"

"Herbert, I told you. I want to know what you think, Olin."

"Fine, Herbert, it's just my thinking doesn't necessarily put the DEA in the right."

"I know. This Fowler shot with the lady agent's gun, cordite burns on her hands. Now tell me."

Olin took a breath, said, "Enid was doing some bad things out in the field, young Fowler already building a case on her. So, one theory is—and that's only if this Atta business doesn't pan—it could very well be sources and/or suspects who turned on her. Worst case, somebody she abused along the line. Somebody still out there, likely marginalized."

The national director said that he and Olin were on roughly the same page, unofficially. It was the ways they were killed that had the national director coming around to Olin's way of theorizing. Bad enough what they did to Agent Bruckner, dragged her, but where would they get some ancient biblical instrument to gore Stevens? Whoever did it, they were mad.

Okay then, Olin wanted to know what the national director wanted him to do about it.

"Just keep doing what you're doing, assistant deputy director."

"But." Olin stopped, careful. "I'm not doing anything, sir, that's the problem."

"And, officially, that's what I want you to continue doing," Herbert said. "It's an FBI-Detroit Homicide investigation, and there's a reason why we're doing it that way."

Here we go, Olin thought, covering his eyes. "And that is?"

Appearances, Herbert said. The DEA had to appear not to be investigating itself. Best way to do that was to let the Fibbies and the locals tell the DEA how it is, all very procedural.

"But procedurally," Olin said, "they're not doing anything to rule anyone else out. That's the problem. It's not procedural."

"Procedure?" Herbert said. "When's the last time you carried out procedure, in the field, assistant deputy director?"

This again. Olin had come up through the ranks, been shot at, kicked and punched, spit upon, and paid his dues. But whenever he cornered someone, it was never about the gist of his argument, no. It was something unrelated they could use to discredit and disrespect him.

Seven months, Olin thought, just another seven goddamn months. And yeah, maybe Jerome was right about the national director after all, the prick.

How long since Olin was in the field—why did the national director say it like that?

CHAPTER THIRTY-FIVE

Mitchell didn't speak, driving past a rickety white structure with a hand-painted sign, U-Pick-It-Apples. The only interaction was his nodding in affirmation of Catori's directions. Taking Highway 15 over the Kent Bridge, passing McKay's Corners, he felt relieved to be getting through the most important part, the getting away part, merging onto Highway 401 west towards Windsor, where he'd take the bridge back to Detroit.

As much as Mitchell didn't know what he was walking into at home, he still couldn't worry that far ahead. That's what brought him this far—never minding the second hurdle until he'd jumped the first. He had to get rid of some evidence before crossing. Also, he had to get free and clear of Catori. Free and clear—he didn't mean it like that.

"It's just," he told her, passing a sign, WINDSOR 44 KM. "Who knows who remembers a cowboy wearing the same poncho as Clint and a First Person of Canada girl in a blue van, Michigan plates. It's not a matter of getting free of you as it is removing fractions from the equation—us from each other."

Catori didn't want to be alone for this next part, but she knew it was better to keep moving separately. She didn't want to go back to the green ghetto where they could find Mitchell. If they found him, that'd be it for her. She didn't want to try her luck at the border again, either. No, they had to split.

"It's okay," she said, running fingers over her brow. "You're right, I know."

Mitchell reached back for her knapsack, tossed it on her lap. "Time to count, accurate."

Catori pretty much knew the numbers but undid the drawstring anyway. Silently counting out the bound stacks, she told Mitchell to shush when he said c'mon, how much? Finally, she said, "Seems to be 10,000 each brick, like we thought."

Mitchell pulled his lips tight, hitting the indicator, drifting into the right lane.

Catori sensed something wrong, said, "What?"

"Goddammit, you know what. I put a question, you answer sideways, evasive, impolite." Mitchell poked himself in the chest. "You know I'm asking 10,000 times what, young lady."

Catori smirked, said, "Don't worry, Hosowich. I have everything you said, plus."

Mitchell looked into the sideview, nothing behind him for a good half mile. "Plus?"

"Plus, relax."

Suet, if there was one thing Mitchell couldn't stand, it was people saying relax just when he's getting rightly riled. Relax, huh? He wasn't quite losing it, but you bet he was smiling about as tight as Dan Quayle's arse when he hit that indicator again, slowing, pulling onto the gravel shoulder. Slowing some more so as not to slide, bringing the van to a stop near a flashing sign, ROAD WORK AHEAD, EXPECT DELAYS.

Catori said, "What?"

"We're so close." Mitchell grit his teeth. "And you just buggered our karma—greed, just like Paul Newman in *Hud*, again."

She held up her hand. "Get back on the road." Blinking. "We can't just be sitting out here, all this money."

Mitchell turned off the ignition, crossed his arms.

She looked at him, guns behind his seat, then into the oncoming eastbound lane, cars everywhere. Seeing a white woman pass, talking on her cellphone, Catori said, "We have to keep moving, now." Looking in her sideview. "And check this out, perfect."

Mitchell looked in his mirror, a Canucklehead gumball machine coming on.

"Okay." Catori watched the provincial copper getting bigger in the mirror. "I took a few bundles too much, an accounting situation, but—"

"Accounting situation, indeed." Mitchell felt sweat on his back. Still, he wasn't going to let the girl see it. No, he was going to learn her good, no matter that copper coming on too fast to be for them. "What, like a $30,000 accounting situation, our favor?"

Catori looked into the knapsack. "Looks like a quarter million, total."

Mitchell didn't even glance when the OPP blew by. "Two-hundred thou, plus our 50?"

"Look, I know what you think—"

"Yeah," Mitchell said. "That you buggered our karma."

Point made, he hit the ignition, pumping the gas when it didn't catch. Smiling tight again, looking ahead, he said, "She gets fussy sometimes." Giving it another shot, same thing. After the third and fourth tries, Catori said stop. He was going to fry the battery, flood the engine. And not to worry, she was sure it was the plugs, for Mitchell to pop the hood.

Seeing as she was calm, Mitchell did his best not to show his gold chopper, watching the girl disappear under the hood. He glanced away at the clear-cut field up the highway, more soya, thinking what the hell had he done now? The girl said try it, so he hit the ignition—nada. Whatever she thought she knew, it wasn't helping. She waved him off, fiddled some more. Backing away, she said she had it this time, loose plugs, like she said, try again.

Mitchell gave it shot, feeling the ignition catch, ah. The girl dropped the hood, tested it, shut, then rounded the front, climbing into the passenger side.

"Nice work." Mitchell put the van into gear, eyeballing the sideview. He hit the indicator as he gained speed on the gravel, easing into traffic.

"Tell you what." He looked into the sideview again, not another black-and-white in sight. "You don't say I told you so, neither will I."

She scowled, punched him on the shoulder, hard.

"The fuck was that for?"

She groaned in her seat. "Don't even."

"Look." Mitchell made a peace-V, two fingers. "We're both wrong."

Catori shut her eyes, tight. "I kept trying to tell you. You wouldn't listen. I took it all because it was in Canadian, worth like 60 percent."

Mitchell let out a breath, read a sign, FATIGUE KILLS, TAKE A BREAK. "Still shouldn't have taken it all."

Catori wanted to let it slide, but couldn't. "There's blood everywhere, five dead, and you want me to stop, do the math? If I did that, we'd still be back there making change for the cops."

Mitchell took a few seconds to think, said okay, fine.

"Okay, fine," she said, spitting his words back. "Just you take the lesson for a change."

Resigning himself to the girl's logic, this time, he said, "I'm sorry."

"Okay."

Then he said, "Now you."

She hit him in the arm, harder. Stupid white man.

Olin was doing exactly as he was told, nothing, when Di walked into his office saying he had media calls from the *Free Press*, *The News*, as well as the local TV stations—2, 4, and 7. Olin looked at his desk, papers everywhere. He hadn't any sleep in 36 hours, couldn't have looked good, knew he didn't smell any better, stale. "Refer them to the offices of Spungen and Grier."

"But they want to talk to the assistant deputy director, you," Di said. "They already have comment from the FBI and Homicide. It's you they want."

"Yeah, well they aren't going to get me because I'm not allowed."

"You?" Di looked around, huffed. "What do you mean, not allowed, you?"

"That's right, Di, not allowed, me. I'm only to advise the investigation, not be part of it, not comment on it. Otherwise, unless it's important—and I mean really fucking important—hold all calls. Especially hold Ruby's sister."

Di cringed. "She phoned again."

Olin buried his face in his hands. "Just hold all calls, okay?"

"What are you going to do?"

"Nothing." Olin cracked open a fresh bottle of Perrier, saying,

"Like I've been told." Nodding to his black-leather couch. "Also, I've been ordered to take a nap."

"Ordered?"

"That's right, ordered. No nappy, no happy, Jerome said."

Watching Di lower the blinds then leave, Olin took off his tie and grabbed a textbook off his shelf, *Detroit's Role In The War of 1812*. Curling up on his couch, he read up on that war fort the butchers tore down over at what was supposed to be Medland Estates.

On the next page was a forensic architect's rendition of what they thought the thing looked like when it was first built; a canvass roof, power hungry would-be Canadians shooting off cannons from little holes, sharpshooters up top.

Olin still couldn't believe they tore it down. Developers, ruining everything, leaving nothing. He had to keep telling himself that, in just seven months, he was going to dedicate all his time to making sure something like this never happened again. Or, at least, not as often.

Thinking like that now, of the audacity, the short-sightedness of governments, all governments, Olin couldn't turn himself off. The sleep deprivation mixed with adrenaline and frustration—it was the wrong combination—so he went over to his desk, tapped a tiny pastel-blue pill out of a plastic white bottle, washed it down with a swish of Perrier.

Replacing the bottle, he looked at a framed picture of Ruby and him holding hands and removed it from the drawer. Ruby had always wanted to go to Montreal, because that's where Leonard Cohen was from and she wanted to see where he wrote poetry. The picture was taken at Bagels Etc. Ruby had read that Leonard used to mooch free coffees there, and presumably, write poetry. Even near the end, bald, Ruby was proud, beautiful, and just happy to be with Olin in some dirty, old town where culture was made. She'd be gone a year next month.

Noticing a bump in the picture, Olin picked it up. He tried to smooth it out by pressing the frame together, but could he feel something in there? Opening the frame, he found a piece of paper, unfolding a poem reprinted in Ruby's hand, "As The Mist Leaves No Scar." Olin read it aloud, Ruby underscoring the last two lines: "So we will endure / When one has gone far."

Despite warnings of delays, there were none. At 1:27 P.M., according to the dash, Mitchell and Catori passed the sign, Welcome To The Rose City, Windsor, Population 209,000. Mitchell drove by the never-ending mini-mall on Dougall Avenue, which led to Ouellette, the tri-phallic Renaissance Center visible when they reached the peak of the Jackson Park overpass. Detroit's richer skyline came into view before Mitchell took a right on University, pulling up to the Windsor bus station, putting the van in park, looking sideways. "You take your cut?"

Catori patted her knapsack. "Canadian, 83-grand." Looking over her shoulder. "The rest, 167-thou is in your overnight bag. I put the guns in there, too. Would you like to do a count?"

Mitchell said he hoped he didn't have to because they had no choice but to trust each other now. "But it's still a fragile trust. Can't be tested." Tipping his hat. "You understand?"

She closed her eyes, said she understood. And again, she was sorry about before.

Mitchell looked at his lap, thinking, sorry for leaving him for dead, like it's a mishap? But he didn't open it up this time. Instead, he said, "Accepted. Just no matter what happens, we're on the same side. There can be no fuckery between us."

She smiled, sad. "Okay, but what are you doing with the extra third?"

"Sadao."

"Sadao's dead."

"His estate," Mitchell said. "His girl, Elyce, does what you do, only old-style, pasties, at the last burlesque in Detroit. At least she did. Place's closed. She can use Sadao's money."

"How do I know you'll give it to her?"

C'mon, Mitchell said, he'd done some pothead things, missed

the sign, underestimated the risks, but had he crossed Catori? Even Phil, had Mitchell crossed anybody? He didn't think so. He'd made poor decisions, as opposed to vindictive decisions. Nonetheless, rest assured that Mitchell felt shame for the hell he'd brought on his people, her, Sadao, and his critters.

"Okay," Catori said. "I believe you, no bad blood."

Looking at her, a little girl now, he could see she didn't know what to do next. Like him, she had been taking this whole deal one step at a time. Now there was only one thing for her to do, to get on the bus, to pick somewhere and go, somewhere she might blend. Mitchell, he didn't know where, either, not until he took off his hat, reading the gold lettering inside—CALGARY TOURISM AND CONVENTION BUREAU.

And so it was, Mitchell telling her to go west and never contact him, at least for a couple years. Even then, she should make sure this whole deal was filed.

Catori would be downright lonely at first. But suet, Calgary was the right place, booming. For a girl with her natural farm skills, there would be under-the-table work on the rodeo circuit. Plus, Calgary had the greatest show on earth, and the Stampede could use a girl like Catori, too.

She could start over, become a totally different person. So much cream in her coffee, yeah, even if worse came to worse, what would they say? That they were looking for a First Person of Canada girl looked Italian? Mitchell didn't think they could even say it like that, politically incorrect. Otherwise, he told her not to take this the wrong way, but it'd probably be a good time to find a boyfriend, maybe a roommate, then move into an established address. That way, she wouldn't have to sign a lease, invisible.

"What?" She looked at him, playfully astonished. "You're ruling it out? Don't want to belly down in the bush with me ever, old timer?"

Mitchell put his hat back on. Shucks, he knew when he was being teased. Same time, he earnestly thanked her for doing it. Just one question before she left.

She nodded, okay.

Mitchell said, "I need to know, one time, did you put that Farmer Jack bag on Del Ray?"

She blinked, said no, watching him lick his lips. "Do you believe me?"

"Yeah." Through the windshield, he saw kids waiting under a sign, 5B Dominion. "I do."

"Why?"

Mitchell looked over. She had her feet up on the seat now, holding herself. "I just think maybe too many people fucked with Sadao. He took a lot of shit at the burlesque." Hesitating, closing his eyes. "And he took a lot of shit from me." Looking at her, nodding once. "Got to Del Ray, I think Sadao found out what Del Ray did to you, enough anyway, and he probably thought we had to kill him anyway, wanted to make himself useful."

"I never told him," Catori said. "Del Ray never said anything, at least not in front of me."

"It was implied," Mitchell said. "Implied." Then he said, "Just one more question."

"You already said that, white man."

Mitchell smiled, said he was going to cheat, especially now that she was giving him shit for his skin color again, just one more thing he had to know.

"Okay, what?"

"Why'd you step in front of me back at Phil's, shoot Del Ray before I could?"

Catori thought on it briefly, said, "Three reasons." Rocking in her seat. "One, I wanted him to die by his own gun, like I said. Two—and don't get all offended—but it didn't sit right, having a white man save me from him, again. And three, I did it for you and everyone else."

Mitchell watched her hide behind her knees. "What do you mean, me, everyone else?"

"You haven't shot anyone."

Mitchell said, "Meaning you didn't think I'd step up?"

"Oh, I think you can do it, if you have to, mission of mercy," she said, looking away. "You're just not compromised that way.

You don't need that in you. The world doesn't need that in you, one less American shooting off his big gun."

Mitchell welled up a little, flashing to that line about the deer and the antelope, then said, "One more question."

Catori said Mitchell had used up his questions, but she had one. He nodded. She smiled, cocky, like she had something on him. "That Diego Rivera, what are you going to do with it?"

Mitchell put a hand on his chin. "That's a very good question."

"I know, right?"

"Fair enough, young lady, but my ambitions there are largely community-minded." Mitchell looked in the direction of Detroit. "I'm going to hang it on my wall and leave it there until the morning I fail to notice it."

"Then what?"

"I'll to pack it a big, brown envelope and send it to the Detroit Institute of Arts, anonymously. If it's authentic, they'll know what to do. DIA has a whole room dedicated to Diego, The Detroit Industry Murals, Diego's favorite works."

CHAPTER THIRTY-SIX

Mitchell took Riverside Drive west, stealing looks across the water—the Fisher Building, still one of the best pieces of corporate architecture in the world, Cobo Hall, Joe Louis Arena . . .

Passing beneath the Ambassador Bridge, he stopped at the Home Hardware near the motel he'd stayed at with Sadao, bought a hibachi, a small propane tank, some fishing gear. He made a note of the thrift shop, Second Time Around, doubling back to Wally's Baits where he bought jelly night crawlers—no sense killing real things when decoys were just as effective—and a fishing license, drove to the Mill Street Dock a half block away, and set up.

Working his pre-strung rod and open-faced reel, he cast his line, resting his gear against a green fence. Back to the van, he assembled the barbecue, had it going within minutes, even if he hadn't used all the parts. Seeing the rod fluttering, jerking, a bite, he reeled in a baby pickerel, illegal, released it and recast.

Retrieving the DEA IDs, he slid them under the grill. As they caught, he went to the van for the guns, walking to the dock's edge. He thought about just dropping them, plop, but figured this part of the river was dragged from time to time, that he better give 'em a toss. He looked around, imagining people everywhere, but were they watching? Mitchell didn't think so. He gave the first three pieces one discus-style throw, both Glocks, then the Les Baer, breaking water.

He went back for the varmint gun and the Credit Card Shotguns, then tossed them one-by-one in different directions—*splash*, *splash*, *splash*.

Mitchell noticed that he was roughly across the river from the Boblo dock. Squinting, he could make out shapes, stick people walking stick dogs. They didn't seem interested in whatever was over here, Windsor.

Back to the barby, the DEA IDs were ash, just metal parts remaining. Mitchell killed the gas, putting on a pair of gloves, shaking the stars out, picking them up, and throwing each one sidearm, the skidding action taking them further than the guns.

Job complete, he saw his rod bending, another bite. He noticed more fight in this one, a sheepshead, reeling it in, releasing it, recasting, letting the westerly current take the slack. Sitting on the breaker with his rod and reel, Mitchell wanted to get gone, go home. Same time, he figured he'd better slow down, again, in case he had to account for himself later. Considering remaining loose ends, he caught two more baby pickerel, releasing them, poor things. When were they going to make this water clean again?

Looking up at the Detroit skyline, Mitchell still had to pull a rabbit out of his Stetson to get through Customs with 167-grand, even if it was Canadian. This was going to be a moment of truth, if not *the* moment, the way they were checking on the American side.

Sure, it was tough over there, but Mitchell didn't think the Canuckleheads were much nicer, despite the media always saying they were polite. Law officers on both sides had been trying to get a hold on that girl when they had more urgent matters, like how many slickers were murdered in Detroit this year alone? No, it wasn't 714 like in '74, but Motown was still a shoot-out capital, on pace for another 400-plus.

Dysfunctional as Detroit was, Mitchell loved that city like it still was Paris of the Midwest. And even if his dope-growing days were done, he was thinking that just maybe he could go home again when he felt another bite, the rod bouncing in his hands. Likely a sheepshead on account of the fight. Those pickerels were like pulling in a dead log, just give up. And yeah, reeling slowly, he could see it, another sheepshead.

When the silver fish surfaced, Mitchell lifted it out of the water, removing the hook, leaning over the dock, gently rocking the fish back and forth until it took off. He stood up, rubbing that sheepshead juice on his shirt and neck. He was fishing, smelled like fish, and who was to say how long he was dipping his stick? Okay, Mitchell was going home. Just one more thing. Suet, there was always one more thing.

Packing up his gear, loading it, climbing in, Mitchell started the van, headed to Sandwich Street, turned right and parked across the street from that thrift joint, Second Time Around. Inside, he bought the first two paintings he saw, leaving the one he liked least, a cosmopolitan street scene, near the curb. He packed the other, gold-blue flowers in a vase, in the garbage bag it came in along with the Diego Rivera original, tucking both behind his seat. Slipping the receipt into his shirt pocket, he climbed into the driver's chair, hit the ignition, and let that van roll, 10-4.

He made a U-turn on Sandwich, a right on Huron Church, then a left on University to the Ambassador Bridge. Digging in his ashtray for change, $2.75, paying the toll, he drove upwards, surfing his tuner. On CJAM 91.5 FM, DJ Alex Très Baked was having way too much fun with the big bust at the Detroit bakery, playing "Marijuana Motherfucker" by D.O.A., Joey Shithead singing the refrain, "they'll bust your fucking ass if they want to." Mitchell didn't think you could drop that many F-bombs on radio, even in Canada. Still, he made the center of the bridge believing Sadao would've had something to say about the song being played at this very point in time.

Winding down, glancing at the river below, Mitchell dial surfed again. Finding Detroit's only country station, Dixie Chicks singing about a guy had to die, Mitchell listened as the song faded. Linda Lau came in, saying she was at a hastily arranged news conference at police headquarters. According to sources, the FBI, in conjunction with Detroit Homicide, was about to announce an arrest connected to the deaths of two Michigan DEA agents.

So far, Mitchell felt his luck was holding. He slowed as he approached Customs, coming to a stop, waiting behind a silver Jag. Reaching for his wallet, he removed his birth certificate, placing his wallet in the drink holder. When he looked up, the light turned from red to green. He switched the radio off, pulling up to the kiosk, tipping his hat at the woman inside. "Howdy, ma'am." With his free hand, he passed the officer his birth certificate.

She took it, made eye contact, then looked to the passenger side. "How long out of the U.S.?"

"Less than 48 hours."

She glanced at his birth certificate, handed it back. "Purpose of your trip?"

"Fishing."

The woman sniffed, said, "I can smell it. How many of what are you bringing back?"

"None, I'm on the catch-and-release program, officer."

She seemed relieved, said, "Good boy. Did you do anything else while you were over?"

"Some gambling. I'll admit it."

"And how'd you do?"

"About usual. Got beat out of some groceries."

Smiling, a little sad, she asked if Mitchell bought or received anything?

Mitchell didn't mention the fishing gear or the barbecue, already used, but there was something he wanted to declare. "Two paintings I bought yonder in Sandwich Town for my mancave," he said, withdrawing the receipt from his shirt, handing it over.

She took it, studied it, said, "Two paintings for $9.98?"

Mitchell nodded, yes.

Waving at herself, the officer said, "I have to see these paintings."

"Behind me," Mitchell said. "Take a gander. The sliding door is unlocked."

The agent rounded the van from the rear, slid the sliding door, looked in the back, seeing fishing gear, a hibachi, one piece of luggage. Putting one knee inside the van, she reached behind Mitchell, half opening the garbage bag. She read the signature on one painting, said, not bad, who's Diego Rivera? Likely a pseudonym, Mitchell said, for a starving artist. Whatever, the Customs lady was really taken with the gold-blue flowers, even if the piece wasn't signed. Nice frame, too. Sliding the door shut, she rounded the van back to Mitchell and said that must be a hell of a mancave, good taste, then asked to see the van's paperwork.

Mitchell reached into the glove compartment, digging under his bootleg CDs for his ownership and insurance in the City Bank Pouch, handing it over.

Reading each document, she said, "So you're a farmer, Mitchell P. Hosowich Farms?"

"That's me." Mitchell pushed his hat back. "Also do renovating in the off season."

Closing the pouch, handing it back, she said, "Mr. Hosowich, you're good to go, but you'll need a passport going forward. We're advising everyone."

Mitchell said to consider him advised, thank you, kindly, then nudged the gas.

He was through.

At Michigan Avenue, he hung a right, heading east when he flicked the radio on, Linda Lau saying the press conference would start momentarily and that WYCD would carry it live. Looking in his sideview, Mitchell hit the indicator, pulling into the lot at Bill's Blue Disco Lounge, cranking the volume.

Olin figured he'd been asleep less than an hour when he heard the knock at his door. Thinking it was Di, he shouted fuck off. Jerome Dumont barged in shooting Olin a look, asking if he talked to Di that way. Olin said no. Then, Jerome asked, why was Olin talking to him that way? Olin said he was taking a nap, as ordered, and now that he was finally able to sleep, why was Jerome waking him? That was cruel and unusual. Jerome said turn on News 4.

Olin remained lying there, jacket pulled up to his chin like a blankie. Jerome went for the remote, aiming it at the 14-inch Sony on a stand in the corner. The screen bounced to Danny Grier and Wes Spungen sharing a podium at Detroit Police headquarters.

Reading from a prepared statement, Grier was telling the live audience that FBI agents, working in conjunction with Detroit Homicide, had captured and arrested one Yosef Atta at an undisclosed location earlier this afternoon. In addition, Grier reaffirmed that Atta was the chief operator behind the covert marijuana grow-op located in an industrial park west of the Ambassador Bridge. Grier also reaffirmed that Yosef Atta logged time in the '90s at an al-Qaeda training camp with Mohammed Atta, believed to be the mastermind behind the 9/11 attacks.

Background dispensed with, Grier said that Yosef Atta was using his grow-op to finance local terror cells in a bid to declare Jihad against U.S. interests in and around the greater Detroit area, primarily the two border crossings as well as key Big Three plants.

"And it appears," Grier said, "that DEA agents Enid Kay Bruckner and Fowler Dean Stevens had discovered not only the operation, but Yosef Atta's intentions, shortly before meeting a watery grave less than 800 yards from the massive grow-op."

For now, Grier said Yosef Atta was charged with various offenses connected to cultivation of an illicit substance, intent to traffic, tax evasion, and living in the country illegally. Charges connected to the deaths of agents Bruckner and Stevens were pending.

As the press conference moved along to the question and answer portion, Jerome hit the mute button and turned to Olin. "Satisfied?"

Olin, still bundled, said, "Wish I could be."

"Look, I know there's egg on your face here. Mine, too, but how could it be anyone else? They find a grow-op not 800 yards from where our operatives die. Enid said she'd found a link between drugs and terror in Michigan, the grow-op's run by a guy wants to pull a local 9/11, yet you still want to zig when the smart money's on zagging."

Olin stood, walking to the window, looking down at a guard talking to someone in a silver Miata near the blockade, pointing the driver away from the building. Seeing a young lady, no more than 25, marching through a red light, brief case in hand, Olin told Jerome there were lots of grow-ops out there, thousands. If they bothered looking, that industrial park was as good a place as any. Spend a couple more days with the dogs and they'd find an E-lab, someone making crystal meth, maybe even people making people sausages. Who knew what went on down there?

Impatient, Jerome said, and the point is?

Olin closed his eyes. "Point is, you ever see *Jaws*?"

"Once, on TV. Never felt right in open water again. Doesn't even have to be salt water."

"Good," Olin said.

"And how's it good *Jaws* made me afraid of the Detroit River?"

Olin cracked a smile. "It's just good that you'll recall the part where a mob of yahoos goes out in boats with dynamite, guns to hunt the shark. Sure enough, they caught a Tiger Shark, posed for pictures, got the wire services to pick up the story, the mayor swimming again."

"Yes, and this is germane to our situation how?"

"Problem was, they got the wrong shark." Olin looked at the TV, a still of Yosef Atta filling the screen. He was wearing one of those scarfs same as Arafat, evildoer. "I'm not saying this guy's got the same last name as the dude blowed up the World Trade Center isn't important. Clearly, we want him for a bunch of things, growing way too much weed included, so it's just as well we got him. But so far, all we have is a super grow-up and a cop killing in the vicinity of each other in one of the worst parts of America's murder capital. No more, no less. Also saying we have a dead agent who was making enemies, giving lots of people motive."

"That all?"

"No, because in addition, I'm saying we had all better be correct. Otherwise, we've just given DEA killers a two-day head start. And you remember what happened when we zigged the wrong way on the Kiki Camarena case in the '80s?"

"The '80s now." Jerome picked up Olin's empty Perrier bottle, sniffed it.

Jihad on Detroit—Mitchell couldn't see how the state's top FBI guy could out and say it if it wasn't so. This wasn't some government spot where they could fudge the identity of the dope man, show him financing some vague religious Commies. No, they were personalizing it, putting a face on the guy who attended some kind of terror workshop yonder in Afghanistan for real. And dogs, it was peculiar that the dude was tripped up by dogs on account of Mitchell had heard al-Qaeda definitely didn't like canines, or even pictures of canines, like the two pit-bulls on each side of Johnny on his first *American Recordings* platter, dark and light.

From Bill's Blue Disco Lounge, Mitchell pulled onto Michigan Avenue. Taking it east while the FBI guy on Detroit's only country station started on about how several countries—the U.S., Canada, and Great Britain included—had been following up on a UN motion to shut down the offices of several charities with alleged links to al-Qaeda. As a result, seized documents showed that Yosef Atta had made donations totaling almost $3-million since January of 1999 to four organizations listed by the UN.

Mitchell, thinking shit, he'd sure opened up something, turned the radio off. Passing the old Tiger Stadium, abandoned, he couldn't see as how the combined intelligence of the DEA, FBI, and local Homicide could completely miss him.

At least one federal officer had been going on about how maybe Mitchell was financing some kind of rabble rousers gonna blow up something, and she was dead, so they had to get around to talking to Mitchell. Unless, of course, they really weren't supposed to be there in the first place. Maybe they decided to raid Mitchell on the fly, hadn't told anyone, because Mitchell most definitely heard Fowler screaming that deputy someone or other told them not to go at night, something about the animals, good advice.

Hanging a left at Woodward, past the new baseball and football complexes, Mitchell still figured that some popcorn kernel or another would lead back to his spread. Didn't they run his plates? Of course they did, and there'd probably be paper on that. Plus, Mitchell was on the rat list from Gall's Hardware. That alone seemed to merit a visit.

Deciding again that was it for the dope business, no matter, he parked in a meter spot in front of a box building advertising $99 apartments. Getting out of the van, he looked across the street at the Gentlemen's Choice Burlesque Revue and Show Bar, some guy on a ladder putting one word on the marquee, CLOSED, a spotter below making sure the ladder didn't shift.

Inserting some Canucklehead change, the meter took it, thanks, but gave Mitchell no time. He rooted around for some Yankee quarters then told himself he'd pay the ticket, if it came to that. He looked both ways, heading for the front entrance. He found the doors unlocked, running into a young skinhead girl, a cigarette behind her ear. She said, "You see the sign? Says closed. Closed means closed."

"Whoa." Mitchell held his hands high. He was going to be amiable. "Take no prisoners young lady. I'm not here to leer. Just looking to have speaks with Elyce Ecstasy."

"Of course you are." Watching the cowboy put his hand over his heart, shaking his head, innocent, she said, "You know her real name?"

"Just kindly advise her Sadao's friend is here, means no harm."

"Everyone's clearing out today—go tell her yourself." The skinhead girl nodded at Mitchell then the red leopard doors into the theatre. "Through there, behind the stage, up the stairs. First room to the right."

"Much obliged." Mitchell tipped his hat, patting his jacket. Yeah, the money was there.

Through the doors, the scent of perfume, sticky-sweet, hit him as he walked down the aisle. Behind the oxblood curtain, up the steps, first door to the right, he found a woman taking her unmentionables down from framed pictures. He cleared his throat, said, "Elyce Ecstasy?"

She turned, looked at him, piercing blue eyes wide and unnatural. "Yes, and you are?"

"Sadao's friend."

"Sadao's friend, who?"

"Just Sadao's friend."

She looked him up and down, the cowboy wearing that poncho in the city, cheap white straw hat with a blue feather, spurs. Mitchell Hosowich was pretty much as Sadao described him. "Just tell me, he's dead right? That's why you're here, not him."

"Sadao didn't make it, no." Mitchell took his hat off, placing it over his heart. "But if it makes any difference, he died with honor, and he died thinking of you."

She sank into her chair, heartsick, even though she knew there was no tomorrow with Sadao. She remembered how he used to call her the Exemplary Elyce Ecstasy, the Exquisite Elyce Ecstasy. Then she said, "Whatever you guys were doing, I don't want to know."

"I think that's best." Mitchell crouched so as to meet the lady at eye level. "I'm here to give you something of his, something he wanted you to have." Reaching into his jacket, placing eight stacks on her lap, loose bills on top. "His share, $83,000."

Elyce fondled the stacks. "His share of what?"

Mitchell itched the stubble under his chin. "Thought we agreed it's best you don't know."

"Right." She picked up a stack, looking at it, holding it in front of him. "It's Canadian."

"Worth about 50-grand-plus here, 83 over yonder, Canada." Mitchell waited for her to say something. When she didn't, he said Sadao wanted her to have his wallet, placing it on top of the stacks. Then he said, "Just one more thing."

"What?"

"Sadao's last words were to you."

"To me?"

"Point of fact, first he asked that I give his share to you, plus his wallet." Mitchell nodded at the stacks in her lap. "And there you have it, done."

"Then what'd Sadao say?"

Mitchell waited a beat, as per Sadao's dying words, then said, "You sure were something in *Weekend at Bernie's II.*"

Elyce's hand shot up, slapping him, the stacks falling on the floor.

Mouth open, surprised, Mitchell rubbed his cheek. "The hell's that for?"

"He knew how much that bugged me." She pointed to Sadao's shot on the wall, Sadao holding the mic close. "Him."

"Yeah." Mitchell was still rubbing his face. "Well, you hit me."

"It was just a gag," she said. "A routine, ours."

CHAPTER THIRTY-SEVEN

The press conference was over when Jerome Dumont hit mute again, restoring audio. Skip Hayes was interviewing a terror expert from Wayne State University, the professor explaining how so-called charities allegedly laundered money Yosef Atta and others had given them.

"They might as well funnel money to bin Laden himself," the good doctor was saying. When he mentioned records showing donations directed to unnamed U.S. politicians from both parties, Jerome said, "Talk about burying the lede." Aiming the remote at the TV, he shot it, making the screen black-green again, turning to Olin. "Look, I should have listened to you about Enid a long time ago. Is that what you want to hear?"

"Would have been tough if you did," Olin said. "She got results, and as much as I disagreed, I always try to understand the other point of view. Now I'm trying to make you see the same thing—the other point of view, mine. Here we have an agent busts a kid making bad E killed a Cass Tech kid at a dance. Makes him drop his pants in front of everyone, finds the E in a secret pocket sewn into his tighty-whities. One point of view is you got to take that kid out by any means necessary, which she did."

"That's very objective of you, Olin, but what's the other point of view?"

"That Enid made too many sworn enemies." Olin picked up Fowler's notes. "Tuesday, September 10, she breaks down the locked door of a burlesque comic, checks him for keister stash. Doesn't find anything. Next day, Wednesday, September 11, she lasso bullwhips a stripper at the Motown Hoedown, advises Fowler to advise customers the stripper's working with the Taliban, uses dish gloves on her. She was abusive in the field, making enemies. Still, nobody's checking that part. As for the farmer, they haven't even been to his place, say they can't find it."

Jerome said, "Probably because they know you told Enid not to go."

"Doesn't mean she listened."

"Doesn't mean she didn't. Nothing I see says they disobeyed your directive, especially with Fowler building a case. Why would Enid, a vet, give him, a rookie, leverage?"

"So we just don't follow?" Olin stood, smoothing himself out. "You're the one says check all angles as a matter of course, so why aren't we doing like the chief director says?"

Jerome dropped his head. "So you now think . . ." Walking to the old city map on Olin's wall, pointing at Medland Estates. "They got killed there, driven downtown, to the Boblo dock, then dumped?" Sliding his hand down to the waterfront, the industrial park. "Because this's where they found Enid and Fowler." Now pointing back and forth between Medland, Unassumed Road, and the Detroit River. "That's eight, ten miles, like you said. Long way to transport two bodies in a vehicle without a trunk, also like you said."

"Unlikely." Olin said. "And yes, I did say so myself, give you that. I also said it's possible, needs to be checked, procedurally. So, you give me that, Jerome."

"Oh, it's possible." Again, Jerome ran his finger back and forth between Medland and the dock. "I just don't see a farmer driving a DEA Jeep that far with two agents, dead or alive."

"All I've been saying is that he's someone else who should be engaged, procedurally, as a possible contact in the final hours of the lives of our agents." Olin held each hand to his collarbone. "Just like the comic, the strippers, the drag queen. You check all possible angles, case like this. I don't know, you don't know, and that's the trouble. Can't rule anyone out or in until someone engages them, watches their response."

Olin stood from the couch, picked up a sheet of paper, said, "Sadao Saffron, no priors unless you count a speeding ticket in '97. Driving down Woodward at 62."

"Pretty fast," Jerome said. "Still a long way from killing cops. I make him for a joy boy."

"Doesn't mean he didn't do it," Olin said. "You do that to enough people, violate them, sooner or later you pick on the wrong one on the wrong day."

"Okay, okay. U.S. dollars to the Canadian Peso, I say this Saffron and the rest of these characters didn't do it. Still, I see what you're saying, to a point. But I'm going to tell you, Olin, you're not the last word on it, procedure, nor am I. You want people checked, speak to Spungen and Grier, have them do it. Just speak softly, because this is a wrap far as Washington's concerned, state funerals, maybe a movie of the week. And Olin?"

"Yeah?"

"I know you're down on the advertising campaign, the way it's turning some people, hard. Just don't be afraid to admit when there's a ring of truth to the narrative."

"I know," Olin said, looking at his lap. "I know."

"Yeah, you know alright." Jerome dropped into the seat behind Olin's desk. Something caught his attention in an open drawer. Reaching inside, next to the framed picture of Olin and Ruby, he took a white bottle out, looking at Olin, haggard, unshaven, back to the container. "You taking this shit at work, Nytol?"

"Yeah."

"Yeah—well, it doesn't look good, optics."

"I haven't slept, and I'm tired, Jerome. Besides, you're the one told me, sleep. No nappy, no happy. Remember?"

"I didn't say do drugs working at the DEA. Sure you don't maybe have the problem?"

"The problem." Olin was pissed. "Ever known me to have more than a few beers?"

Olin waited for Jerome to shake his head. Instead, Jerome said that it was no wonder Olin couldn't have but a few, what with all the Nytols in his system.

"Look," Olin said. "I maybe had a few Nytols when I end up working late, sleeping on the couch, uncomfortable. Aside from that, I've had the same bottle in my desk going on four years, I take so little."

"And how do I know that?" Jerome said. "That you've had the same bottle four years?"

Olin shook his head, mouth open. "You know that because the

bottle's expired, it's been in my desk so long. If I was hooked, it would be a brand-new bottle, all times."

Jerome, turning the bottle sideways, said, "Expiry: March, 2000." Holding the bottle next to his ear, shaking it, pills rattling. "The hell are you doing taking shit's expired. We have benefits, man."

"It's over-the-counter, Jerome, not covered."

Jerome dropped the container in Olin's drawer, standing, crossing the room. At the door, he pointed at Olin then his desk. "Before you leave, I want you to sleep that shit off."

Olin waved at him. "Yeah, yeah, yeah."

Jerome said, "Don't you yeah, yeah me. Senior DEA operative taking expired shit at work." Giving Olin a good thrice over. "Look like shit." Sniffing. "Smell about as good." Pointing to the desk. "And taking expired prescriptions."

"Again," Olin said, "It's over-the-counter."

"And you can't afford a fresh bottle, your salary?" When Olin didn't answer, Jerome said, "Just see me before you leave. And Olin?"

"Yes, Jerome."

"Don't you get any ideas about going out to that farm. This is a FBI-Detroit Homicide investigation. I am directed to stay out of it, and you—you are directed to stay out of it."

Mitchell's cheek stopped stinging at 4:48 P.M., according to the dash. He was taking the long way home to pick up some farming essentials. He spent some time stewing in traffic, wondering whether anyone would be waiting for him back at the farm, before stopping at the 76 Station on Joy Road to fill-up on account of he was now officially boycotting Mickey Joseph's Service Station. Mitchell also bought a plastic can and fueled it for the tractor. Yeah, maybe Mitchell was patronizing a franchise, but at least he was saving.

Paid, he took Joy to Gall's Hardware. Slowed by a Scout selling apples out front, Mitchell pulled behind the Yummy Party Store to weigh the merits of burning Gall's down. He went so far as to eyeball the gas can. But suet, he couldn't exactly torch the place with a Scout out front. And well, Mitchell had enough problems without an arson rap. Nonetheless, he was bent on sending a message to Mr. Gall and young Ivan.

Punching the van into drive, turning around, Mitchell parked in front of Gall's, told the Scout he'd buy an apple or three on the flipside and walked in. The door set off a bell mounted above. Tyler Gall and Ivan were behind the counter.

"Why hello there, Mitchell," Ivan said.

Mitchell, tipped his hat, said it was Mr. Hosowich to young Ivan, please and thank you. Steering a cart to the back, Mitchell returned with two bags of dried mealworm and two bags of African Violet Mix, placing them on the counter. "Going try to get another bloom out of my nutmeg thyme, weather permitting."

Ivan looked at his dad, smirking. "That's a lot of nutmeg thyme, Mr. Hosowich."

"Indeed." Mitchell hitched his drawers. "On account of nutmeg thyme accounts for my entire lawn, front and back, young Ivan. Now, are you going to ring up my farming essentials, or do I need to purchase another 10-pound bag of fuck-around? Because, if it's another 10-pound bag of fuck-around, I can buy this here shit on the Internet, have it home delivered, save on gas."

Mr. Gall held his hands out, said to kindly cut the cussing in front of Ivan, and what was Mitchell meaning by that anyway—a 10-pound bag of it?

Mitchell said he reckoned Gall knew, paying his bill of $9.17 with a Canadian twenty, moseying. When Gall said he didn't accept Canadian, Mitchell said a Canucklehead twenty was still worth more than $9.17 American, and if Gall didn't like it, maybe he should call the cops.

Outside, Mitchell bought three apples from the Scout—poor kid going pre-military so early, probably already had a Daisy Red Ryder—and climbed in the van.

Taking Joy to Unassumed Road, he polished one of the apples

on his poncho. Biting in, grinding, swallowing, he passed Enid's sign flat on the ground, someone else taking offense, then the dandelion patch. For a change, Mickey Joseph was working, filling up a silver SUV, probably some slicker made the wrong turn. Mickey recognized the van, waving. Mitchell, he channeled his best John R. Cash and flipped Mickey the bird. Yeah, Mitchell was boycotting the place for sure now, political.

Further, as the Mitchell P. Hosowich Farms sign came into view, he allowed himself a smile when he saw his thyme lawn already blooming for a third time. Likely, he told himself, pulling around back, on account the last installment of African Violet Mix. See, it really was for other flowering plants, like the bag said, so on what basis had the Galls brought this on? Telling himself leave it alone, Mitchell put the van into park. The adrenaline was wearing thin, and it was everything he could do to take a few more bites of his apple, dump the core in the composter and check on the critters. He'd been gone less than two days, so the animals, other than the chickens who'd returned to their pen, weren't too riled.

Speaking of the chickens, he spread some mealworm to put an end to the squawking. Checked on Simmi next, no evidence of infection. Still, he thought it best to douse more vinegar on the poor thing's wound, just to be safe. Noticing specs of blood on her third horn, Mitchell wiped all three down. The cow was testy, but she was alive, healing. Once the new dressing was applied, Simmi simmered, ate some hay, moo.

In the opposite barn, Hasty Kiss had been cooped up too long, so Mitchell took her to the pasture and left her there to jog her ya-yas out. On his way to the house, he saw a V-formation of geese heading south beneath a blackening sky. Yeah, another rain was coming, and, to Mitchell, that was poetry, for whatever evidence hadn't been washed away already would surely become run off with another good storm.

Inside, after a brief shower, hot, he grabbed the two apples and went outside. It took some doing to call Hasty back in. Poor thing probably thought it'd be another 48 hours until she exercised again. But Mitchell just kept talking nice, like a human, and eventually the filly came for the apple, cooperating as he fed her, then guided her to her stall.

Outside the barn, he made a fuss over Lou, poor thing didn't know what to do without her friend Wolfie. But Mitchell couldn't give more than a few minutes of love, feeding her, telling the dog that was it, stop licking, time for old Mitchell to get some shut-eye, then Lou ran off.

Walking to the house, dragging his spurs, yeah, he was loving on his diggers when he saw it. Right there in front of him, it was true, maybe even a sign of peace. No more than 25 feet away, that white-tailed deer the bureaucrats were chasing was standing there, twitching her little nose so cute that Mitchell thought a Santa character had to be hiding somewhere, filming the whole thing.

Mitchell knew right away he wasn't going to tell anyone on account of last thing the doe needed in her life was more government. She was wild, man, wild.

Reaching for the last apple in his pocket, he breathed on it, polishing the skin on his shirt, calling out to her like a human. A baby human, but a human nonetheless.

He held out the apple as far away from himself as he could, making it clear that he wasn't intending harm while still saying she could to take the fruit from his hand, if she wanted.

Mitchell saw it as a test. Maybe he didn't kill anyone, but he didn't see as how that made him pure, either. Suet, he'd done a whole lot of compromisin' and so he probably needed to be judged. It's time, he thought, and if that deer would just take the apple from his hand, maybe it was going to mean something about him, personal—as if that there animal could sense a decent man with more accuracy than law enforcement agencies answering to conflicted politicians. That was Mother Nature, arming the vulnerable to sniff out those intending infliction.

Stutter step by stutter step, she shuffled over, looking Mitchell in the eye as she reached out with her little mouth. Allowing himself a giggle, Mitchell wondered how she was going to wrap her mouth around the fruit when she opened wide and took it, scurrying a few steps away. And the poor thing—she was bobbing her head up and down, unable to break so much as the fruit's skin, no leverage, the apple was so big.

Oh God, it was stuck, and Mitchell was pretty sure the little deer was about to choke. He was wondering if his Civil War medical book had a chapter on this when the animal managed to work her teeth through, grinding the apple into sauce, swallowing. A few seconds later, she scampered through a lavender patch, some trees, bushes. Then she was gone.

Much as Mitchell wanted to ponder the moment, reflect, he was getting over the shock of almost choking the poor thing. What was he doing feeding her an apple whole? Maybe, he thought, he should jump in bed, pull the sheets over his head before anything else went wrong.

Inside, he stopped at the fridge. Removing a Tupperware, he ate the last of the tofu cabbage rolls, washing them down with a bottle of Atwater Block Lager, ah.

Somewhat sated, he brushed his pegs, flossed, gargled, and shuffled off to bed singing "Home on the Range." He was lying on his side, alone, feeling a tear run across his face when he got to the part about the deer and the antelope.

Olin woke on his couch with a crick in his neck. Crick—he might as well have nail-gunned his head to his shoulder, stiff. Walking to his desk, the time on his phone was 7:52 P.M. Out the door, he saw a stack of messages on Di's desk. Most were from news people, pissed the DEA wasn't commenting. Also, that cowboy had been to Gall's Hardware to buy more African Violet Mix. Mr. Gall had left a message complaining that the cowboy paid in Canadian, and what was the DEA going to do about that? Plus, there was yet another message from Ruby's sister, and that set Olin off. Ruby's sister was calling about the memorial, making sure Olin was still in mourning, just like her, and if there was one thing Olin wanted, it was to move on from the mourning phase. That's why he was doubling down on local history, something to obsess over, a distraction. Olin knew what Ruby would say—live your life. That's basically what that poem hidden in the picture said. But Ruby's sister was a different person entirely, and she wouldn't be happy until she made Olin cry. On top of all that was a note from Jerome repeating that he wanted to see Olin before he left the building.

Thinking again how he was seven months short of clearing out, Olin inwardly said fuck Jerome Dumont, heading down the hall to take a whore's bath in the washroom. And yeah, Olin was a bit funky, so he scrubbed up, washed his face. Job done as well as it could be in a sink where you had to press a button for water every 15 seconds, efficiencies, Olin was paper toweling his face dry when he heard a toilet flush in a stall behind him. In the mirror, he watched the door open and Jerome emerge, saying, "Are you getting ready for a date?"

Olin looked at him, odd, said, "You know I haven't gone on one since Ruby passed."

"Sorry." Jerome took a step closer. "Where you off to then?"

Alright, if Jerome wanted to play it like this, top to bottom, Olin could play.

"Just coming to see you after cleaning up, like the note on Di's desk says. And do you know what I wanted to see you about?"

Jerome smiled, took a step back, waiting.

"I was coming to see why you're angling to use the expired Nytols against me."

"Now Olin." Jerome was open, hands out. "If there's a problem, I was looking to help, maybe get you in the employee assistance program."

Olin laughed. "Seven months out and you're looking to help by putting me in the EAP. Thanks, man, thanks. But you know what I think?"

Jerome shook his head, no.

"I think we wouldn't be talking about the EAP if I was down with the narrative. All these years we worked together, you do this now?"

Jerome extended his right hand, said he really was only trying to help, shake on it.

Olin looked at Jerome's hand, said, "I don't think so."

"You won't shake my hand?"

"Not after you come out the stall without washing."

Jerome laughed, embarrassed, said he was just thinking big thoughts in there.

"Then why did you flush?"

Hesitating, holding eye contact, Jerome said, "Out of habit."

"Yeah," Olin said, "only how come I smell shit?"

"Come again?"

Olin looked at Jerome, shook his head, and said, "For the first time since we started working together, March, 1989, I don't believe you."

With Jerome calling after Olin, telling him not to go poking around that farm, Olin walked out. He grabbed a bottle of Perrier from the communal fridge, thinking he could smell something in there, also bad, then took the elevator to the basement lot, stepped into his BMW Wagon.

Up the ramp, outside, Olin passed the guards, the barricades, heading southwest on Howard toward First Street. From there, he took a right onto the John C. Lodge Freeway, merging onto I-94 West, passing the old Joshua Doore billboard.

Veering right onto Livernois, the light turned green as Olin approached and he took it, hanging another right at Warren. Then he took a series of lefts and rights, turning north on Unassumed Road.

The rain started when Olin passed the MEDLAND ESTATES sign, hitting the wipers as lightning spider-webbed the sky. There were no streetlights so Olin flicked on the high-beams, picking up the burnt-out house with eyes on the front door, STOP HALLOWEEN ARSON.

Looking back to the road, he said shit, locking up his brakes when he saw it, briefly spinning out on the gravel. Pumping his brakes, regaining control, he thought, was that a deer? No way, probably just a shadow of something else they had here. Or maybe Jerome was right. Maybe Olin had been taking too many of those expired Nytols and now he was seeing things, doing the exact thing he'd been told not to do. It wasn't just the thing he'd been told not to do, no, it was the thing he told Enid and Fowler not to do.

Further north, he slowed as he drove by the pasture, stopping completely to read the lawn sign in his headlights, Mitchell P. Hosowich Farms.

With the barns and pasture, it sure looked like the guy was just a regular farmer. But how was that possible? This was still Detroit, so he couldn't be making it out here as a regular farmer, and if he couldn't make a living as a farmer, then how was this Hosowich making it work?

The rain was coming harder, so Olin cranked his wiper speed to full. Through the windshield, he saw the blue Ram van out back, meaning the guy wasn't on the run. Given that, Olin figured he'd best take his own advice, come back this way when it was light.

There was a reason Olin had told Fowler and Enid not to come out here late, because, well, it was pretty dark. Even in the confines of his BMW Wagon, DEA-issued bullet-resistant windows, Olin didn't feel right. He'd seen too many movies where a cop gets it just before retirement. They even had a word for it now, retirony, a device Hollywood used to elicit sympathy for a bit-part player about to be killed off. Disrespected and frozen-out at work, widowed, Ruby's sister chasing him like a collection agent—Olin didn't want to serve as an example, no way.

And back there, was that a deer or something else?

Now that Olin had a chance to slow down, think, he still didn't see as how it could be a deer. But if it wasn't a deer, what was it? His high-beams playing tricks, tuning a prairie dog into the shadow of some kind of black-people-eating Sasquatch thing? Yeah, well if that shit was happening, hallucinations, Olin was getting the hell out of this part of town. That was the other reason he told Fowler and Enid not to come here at night, wild animals. Olin didn't know all what was out there, and he wasn't getting out of the car while they were feeding.

Chapter Thirty-Eight

Waking in his own bed, cozy, Mitchell had foggy memories of light coming through the drapes. Blinking the sleep out, he wrote it off to dreams, lightning, lost slickers, maybe a UFO. Up and about, surveying his property by seven, giving his critters some pasture time, he was enjoying his java until he spied his blood-stained clothes beneath the porch. At that, he fired up the barby.

As the clothes burned, Lou followed her big sugar around his spread. Mitchell looked for teeth, fragments, buttons, anything incriminating. Finding nothing, likely on account of the rains, he knew, no matter how hard Mother Nature scrubbed, something would always be out there.

Vague or tangible, he said, dragging his diggers to his van, hitting the ignition. He drove to the self-serve *Free Press* box in front Mickey Joseph's Service Station, closed, which was just as well because Mitchell didn't want to be seen caving on the boycott.

On the way home, Detroit's only country station played an Elvis gospel number, "So High," followed by a station ID at eight, then the news. Linda Lau repeated that the FBI, in conjunction with Detroit Police, had arrested Yosef Atta. After listing off the charges announced yesterday, Linda said additional charges were expected. Given that the anticipated charges could be connected to the deaths of federal officers, federal murder charges could be laid, meaning it could become a death-penalty case, even though Michigan didn't have capital punishment.

As for Fowler Dean Stevens and Enid Kay Bruckner, state funerals were in the works, Linda Lau saying 10,000 officers were expected from around the world. Also, unnamed sources within the DEA were telling a national cable news service, likely CNN, Mitchell thought, that Fowler and Enid were being fast-tracked as posthumous recipients of the Kiki Camarena Award.

Mitchell couldn't believe that last part, cynical by the time he pulled into his driveway. Linda was saying police had found a map of Michigan with notes in a dead language on yellow stickies posted to various landmarks, including the border crossings, the Renaissance Center, the Joe Louis Area, and several automotive plants. For now, they'd called in a language expert.

Making a mental yellow sticky of his own to call Detroit's only country station, say play a record, Mitchell killed the ignition. He went inside, poured cold coffee into his tin then walked to the porch, sitting up in his hammock and unfolding the *Free Press*.

FULL STATE FUNERAL FOR SLAIN DEA PARTNERS

Mitchell wasn't even curious, thinking the less he knew from here on in, the better.

Asides, Mitchell had lived it. Now came time to decide what to do next. He didn't have to have a clear notion, but he definitely had to start thinking on it, and goddamn if there wasn't a story in the bottom right-hand corner setting his antennae off like a Nevada Geiger counter.

AGRI-TOURISM GRANTS TO SAVE MICHIGAN FARMLAND

LANSING—The Michigan Department of Agriculture (MDA) is issuing a call for proposals from farmers, farmers markets, U-pick-it operations, petting zoos, historical sites, and other Agri-tourism businesses that could qualify for a portion of $40-million in aid under a new federal-state program.

Announced here at the state capital Friday, the federal government pledged to match MDA funding dollar for dollar in a bid to save Michigan's dwindling farmland by helping farmers convert to economically viable farm-based ventures.

Mitchell ran inside. Back with a pink highlighter, he sat, highlighting key points, such as the part about how "the economic upturn of Agri-destinations would bolster the fortunes of struggling farmers as well as the state economy."

Yep, this could be good for everyone, he thought. Looking out at his critters, Simmi chewing cud as Hasty ran vague figure-eights in the pasture, his exotic herbs, the legal kind, shades of yellow, purple, white, and red everywhere.

Just like Glen Campbell said, there'd be a load of compromisin'.

But maybe Mitchell could make a convincing argument. Getting tourists to visit, logic followed that they'd want to chow down, vegan-style, buy souvenirs. And maybe, he'd get a fair price for his corn and tomatoes by using terms like "craft" and "small batch." Sundry gobbledygook could carry, and if it did, he'd qualify for a free listing in the *Agri-Tourism Guide*, which aimed to "help visitors identify and locate Agri-Tourism entities appealing to their families."

Hook of it was Michigan had been "losing farmland at a rate greater than any other state in the Great Lakes region." *Free Press* said that, too, and by finding "creative solutions to keep the farming community in business"—suet, Mitchell was beginning to speak bureaucratese—the state believed "the independent Michigan farm could be viable again." Yee-haw.

Easiest way to make it viable was to work it so farmers could convert to cannabis, even if only for rope, fabric, fuel. Short of that—and Mitchell didn't see it happening in his lifetime—he pictured a petting zoo, tourists plunking down greenbacks to pluck lavender. Much as he bristled a bit at the idea of handsy out-of-towners grabbing his herbs, he figured he could keep everything hopped up on African Violet Mix, replenishing. He was still going to keep them away from the nutmeg thyme. That was his lawn, and no self-respecting American was going to stand for strangers picking at his lawn.

The stone formations yonder behind the barns could be another way in. If Mitchell could find some half-baked proof that the arrangement was the least bit historical, he might be able to get a hand in this here state cookie jar on that account, too.

Same time, as he pawed his shirt pocket for his soft pack, extracting and firing up a Camel, Mitchell was thinking how he couldn't see Hasty Kiss going for the petting zoo aspect, nippy, when a newfangled station wagon—yes, it was a Beamer—pulled up, parking near the house. Mitchell watched an old black dude step out. Double yes, it was that Federale making Skip Hayes wrong on the TV. What was his name again? Blue something?

Ah, Mitchell started thinking that his experience with that little doe hadn't meant a damn thing after all. They had come for him, again. Goddammit to hell, just when Mitchell dared to think that maybe all this *guano* was over, here was the government man walking over, smiling, flashing a badge. For sure this was the DEA from the TV.

"Olin Blue," the dude said, holding his green bottle of Perrier in his right hand, transferring it to his left, then extending the right.

Slick move, Mitchell thought, standing, shaking the man's hand. "Mitchell Hosowich."

Olin pointed over his shoulder, said, "Saw a big bandage on your cow, what happened?"

"Drive by." Mitchell hung his head. "Damn gang-bangers. Not enough to do a little cow-tipping, mischief. No, they had to shoot poor Simmi, the cold-hearted devils."

Olin said, "I assume you reported it?"

Mitchell shook his head, no.

Olin couldn't believe it. A drive by and the farmer doesn't call it in? Olin took a step forward, said, "Why didn't you phone 9-1-1?"

Mitchell didn't like it, this Olin invading his space while he was smoking. Okay, if he wanted to play it aggressive, Mitchell would just take another hit, exhaling, the plume creating boundaries. "9-1-1 gonna to pay for Simmi's doctorin'?"

Olin, taking a step back, said, no, 9-1-1 wouldn't pay.

"Well then a lot of good calling 9-1-1 does." Mitchell looked over at Simmi grazing, big patch on her side. "The poor thing—I had to do the operatin' myself."

Frowning, thinking, maybe that made sense, or not, this being the green ghetto, Olin was now standing at a civil distance. "Listen, we're trying to retrace the steps of two of my operatives. Has anybody been here?"

And there it was, the question Mitchell had wished away.

Much as Mitchell wanted to deny, deny, deny—and it seemed a plausible strategy, given he'd heard Fowler scream they weren't supposed to be here—complete denial was the quickest way to step into the lie-trap. Mitchell decided to go with this part, saying,

"Indeed." Taking a hit off his cigarette, exhaling. "Had a visit Wednesday, nine-ish. Why, something happen?"

"Dead, murdered." Olin looked at the paper the guy was holding. "You didn't know?"

"Suet." Mitchell unfolded the *Free Press*. "Didn't recognize them, make the connection." Pointing at their headshots. "Dude had big clunky glasses when he was here, not in this picture. And the lady, she's had some work done since this."

Olin nodded, right, explaining how a nearby hardware store gave his agents Mitchell's plates, said he'd been buying excessive amounts of African Violet Mix. Then, last light, Olin got a message saying Mitchell bought more, paid in Canadian, and was that true?

"True." Mitchell looked at his cigarette. Thinking one hit left, he took it. "Also, I paid in Canadian on account of I'd been fishing yonder in Windsor, what I had on me." Exhaling. "Why? You mean the DEA's here because I paid Tyler Gall in Canadian?"

"I'm here," Olin said, "because African Violet Mix is used to grow pot."

Mitchell dropped his butt, stepped on it, made a mental yellow sticky to collect it. "And, as I also told them, it's for 'other flowering plants.' Says so right on the bag. I have portulacas, as you can see, lots. Also, I have flowering herbs, like the nutmeg thyme lawn we're standing on. Needs help blooming more than twice, this far north."

"Okay." Olin took another half step back. "What I want to know is what happened here?"

Mitchell narrowed his eyes. "Keep my name out of it?"

"Depends."

"Depends, huh?" Mitchell locked eyes with the guy. "If it depends, maybe I should hire me a slicker lawyer, see if he thinks it depends. Also, didn't you say you was DEA?"

"Yeah, so?"

"So." Mitchell pointed at the paper. "Says here it's a FBI-Detroit Homicide investigation. You telling me the DEA's investigating itself? That's a conflict of interest right there."

"Look, the agents." Olin held his hands up, peace. "They were under my command."

Mitchell nodded, so he gathered. But, shaking The Freeps in his hand, he also gathered that bin Laden's cronies did it, evildoers, just like the government ads on 2, 4, and 7.

Now the farmer was hip to the narrative, enough. Olin said, "I'm just trying to find out how they got there, to the river, from here, your farm."

"I do remember them saying they weren't supposed to be here." Mitchell looked up at the blue sky, not a cloud. "Makes me think maybe you're not supposed to be here."

"I'm the one told them not to come. I just want to know what they were doing."

"Gave the barns, the property a good thrice over." Mitchell scratched the back of his neck. "Then they gave me a good thrice over. Checked me, a struggling farmer for—the lady called it keister stash. That what you teach 'em? To look in a 52-year-old farmer's tar-pit?"

Olin looked down, said no, he didn't teach 'em that.

"The young dude," Mitchell said, "I could see he was conflicted."

Olin covered his eyes, feeling himself wanting to tell the poor farmer, sorry, it shouldn't have been like that. Of course, the last thing Olin needed was someone else saying he didn't back his agents, especially now. But what this Hosowich said rang true, and did Enid have to pull that routine every time she interrogated someone?

Olin really wasn't supposed to be here, so he kept things polite and moving along, asking Mitchell what happened next.

"They left." Mitchell held an open hand to Unassumed Road. "Then they were gone."

"They didn't say anything? Mention where they were going next?"

"Like they're going to tell some poor shitkicker they just wrong-fully defiled with his own dish gloves?" Mitchell crossed his arms. "Guess you'd call that a debriefing."

Olin fought off a smile, said, "They were talking about a stripper, Italian descent, Gina the Ballerina, found a few joints in her coat after the fact. You were with her, they said."

Mitchell looked north on Unassumed Road in the direction of the Hoedown.

Yeah, he was sweating, hadn't figured how to handle this query, either.

"That's the reason I want my name out of it," he said, avoiding Olin. "Gets downright lonely out here on account of all the depopulation, no company."

Ah, Olin thought, this is how the cowboy got pulled in. "So you hired her?"

Mitchell looked in the distance, Hasty Kiss running. "You know how many times men outnumbered women on the lone prairie?"

"No, how many?"

"Ten to one, some estimates. Out here, it's just me and Mickey Joseph."

Olin allowed himself a frustrated chuckle, looking down at the nutmeg thyme lawn, clover-like formations, tiny yellow flowers. When he looked up, seeing the cow and horse in the pasture, chickens squawking, he said, "You mean to tell me you make a living out here?"

Mitchell puffed his chest, said, "Live pretty spartan on craft tomato and corn proceeds. Plus I do drywalling, painting, interior work in the off-season. But I'm aiming to go full-time in the spring, turn this farm into a tourist trap proper. That's the kernel of the plan anyway."

Olin looked around. The guy had remarkable gardens, lavender so purple it had to be hopped up on that African shit everyone was on about. Okay, that explained that, but who would drive out here to see it? The farmer didn't have a hook. Yet there he was, holding the *Free Press* like his numbers came in, pointing to an article in the bottom right corner. Olin took the paper, scanning the pink parts. "What makes you think you can get some of this?"

"Why officer," Mitchell said, big smile. "What came first? Grants or farmers?"

"I get it," Olin said. "I just don't see a Detroit farmer qualifying. I don't think your situation matches what they're talking about."

"Could be a U-pick-it." Mitchell chin-nodded to his field, Hasty

Kiss. "A petting zoo." Nodding to the southeast corner now. "Plus, I have stone formations yonder supposed to be part of history, our war with Canada." Looking back at Olin, smiling nice. "Folks coming back to the city need wholesome activities asides from losing their groceries at the casinos. And just think what I could do with that expired Joshua Doore billboard on the I-94."

"Back it up." Olin turned sideways, holding eye contact. "You say you have stone formations?" Mitchell pointed over the guy's shoulder. Olin looked, said, "All I see is barns."

"Behind the barns," Mitchell said. "Yonder southeast corner."

Passive, polite, Olin said, "May I ask you to take me yonder?"

Mitchell led the way, thinking he'd already been out there this morning. Rains had patted down the soil where he buried Wolfie, re-establishing the portulacas, so it should be fine. Right away, as soon as they made the turn around the first barn, Olin was pointing, almost shouting.

"I don't believe what I see." Olin turned to Mitchell. "Are you fucking kidding?"

Mitchell laughed nervously. "What?" Then he started grinning, because, by golly, this Olin appeared to know something.

Looking at the rounded corners, still pretty much the same as in his books, exquisite like mini-ruins, Olin stammered. Saying official records stated that the structure had been demolished in the '50s—academic work had been published, peer-reviewed—but the fort was still here, some of it anyway. Pretty good shape, too, considering, and did Mitchell know what he had?

"Partially." Mitchell pointed at his house. "Have some records from the last farmer, name of Fryer." Squinting at Olin. "Tell me your story. See if we jive."

"That." Olin pointed, breathless. "That's a . . ." He couldn't get it out, looking at the *Free Press* in Mitchell's hand. Shit, if the guy had had something to do with killing DEAs, would he be highlighting news items about farming grants? Plus, he didn't seem uptight about Olin walking the grounds, so he wasn't hiding a big-ass dope op. And Olin really wasn't supposed to be here, so why was he bothering? In seven short months, he'd be on a full pension, dedicated to historical pursuits 24/7, 365, so why was he doing something bound to piss off Jerome's boss?

All Olin wanted was to follow procedure, to cross these last contacts off the list. That's just the way he was taught. And sure, Olin could spend his last months chasing down people Enid abused. Yeah, Olin could do that, obsess over it, start bird-dogging. But even if he found something, it would run contrary to the narrative. By the end, he'd wind up testifying about expired Nytols under oath. Olin, he didn't see how that was going to make him very happy. Getting these rocks authenticated, however, would be a delight, and the notoriety that came with the discovery would provide him with a platform for all things historical Detroit.

Mitchell, still waiting, said, "Are you going to tell me what I have?"

"This was an enemy fort in a hostile territory," Olin said, "circa 1812-1813."

Olin looked at what was left, telling Mitchell that U.S. plans to take Canada in 1812, British owned, didn't pan. Plot was to beachhead Canadian real estate while operating from Detroit, other ports. Attacks backfired, because the Brits, pissed now, pushed William Hull's soldiers back, deep into Detroit. Message was, okay, now we're gonna take you over, see how you like that.

"And that's when the British built this fort by hand, others, establishing blockades." Olin pushed imaginary walls. "Trying to bugger trade, finances, like al-Qaeda today. Anyway, British held a bunch of ports through 1813, except." Pointing at the ground. "The Detroit frontier. We won it back when Oliver Hazard Perry sent ships, sank a whole Teabag fleet, forced them out. Until then, they had makeshift forts all over Detroit, this being the first, yours."

Mitchell said Olin's explanation, albeit more detailed, was consistent with Fryer's records. Only what happened to the British dudes set up this here fort?

"Long, drawn out deaths, terrible," Olin said. "Marksman Dick Medland, he'd pick 'em off at long range, send his men in to do biblical shit, stabby."

"Okay," Mitchell said. "I did not know that, but I guess we had to on account of Canadians are capable of meanness, no matter their PR." Looking at the formations, yes, Mitchell could see where they might've hung a roof, canvass. "As for the rest, that's good news, right? I mean, so far as the grant is concerned."

Olin reached into his pocket, giving Mitchell a business card, Olin Blue, Vice President of the Michigan Historical Society, Detroit Chapter. "It's not exactly Fort Wayne, but Fort Wayne was built in response to what happened here. You see the link, right?"

"Yeah, we built Fort Wayne on account of we better be ready to kill more Canadians."

"More or less." Olin rolled his hand. "You don't want to put it that way, political. You play it right, describe it in the grant materials as a predecessor of Fort Wayne, you'll have folks lined up from here to the I-94 for the first few years." Looking directly at Mitchell. "Now that you know what you have, you have to preserve it. That's what you're going to put in your application. You're going to get national landmark status and money to preserve it." Pulling back, calming himself. "I don't mean to tell you what to do, sir. I—"

Mitchell waved, told Olin to keep going. This was all very valuable tourist-trap information, affirmation that Mitchell could find a way to make the place support itself.

Olin said didn't Mitchell ever call someone, ask? No, Mitchell had no idea where to start, put it off, but Olin was some kind of expert, right? Olin said he was a learned layperson who knew enough to know what this was—a lost historical landmark.

"I have pictures of this back at the office in books," Olin said. "Once you file, this will get designation, no question." He leaned in again, closer. Not aggressive like before, no, this time the dude was seeking discretion. "May we speak off the record?"

Mitchell nodded, off the record.

Olin said, "I can get you in touch with the right people. They'll write support letters to get you grant money to maintain the thing, people to do the work for free."

"Free?" Mitchell looked confused. Was this a sting? "I'm not into exploitin'."

Olin smiled, tried to not be smug. "You can almost charge arch-eologists to maintain it. We're talking landmark status." Pointing at his business card. "I'll get you hooked up. Call me."

"I will at that." Mitchell flicked the card with his middle finger, slid it into his shirt behind his soft pack. "But why are you doing this?"

"It's my thing," Olin said. "What I want to do full-time when I'm retired, seven months."

Alright, Mitchell said thanks, then thank you, kindly.

"Regarding this other matter." Olin frowned, waving at every-thing and nothing. "If you see or hear anything, if anything comes to you, please get in touch with the officers quoted in the *Free Press*, Grier and Spungen."

Mitchell looked a bit hurt. "Don't want me to call you?"

"Not my investigation. You're right, I'm not supposed to be here. So, if someone asks, tell the truth. Just, you know, please don't advertise my visit."

Mitchell tipped his hat. "Agreed."

"Alright then." Olin shook Mitchell's hand and they walked back towards Olin's wagon. Passing the second barn, Olin kicked upon something in the nutmeg time. It was yellow, a duller shade than the tiny flowers. Bending, picking it up, Olin looked at it, handing it to Mitchell. "Dropped your lighter."

Mitchell held his breath, took the Bic and pocketed it, thanks.

Reaching the driveway, Olin stepped into his car, closing the door, hitting the ignition, and powering down his window. "I mean it, cowboy, you have something here." He briefly powered the window back up, stopping when something occurred to him, powering it down again. "May I ask, do you have deer around here?"

"Haven't seen any, no," Mitchell said. He wasn't telling, figuring, if he said something, slickers would be down here trying to tranquilize the poor thing, tag it. "My guess is someone's stringing someone a whizzer on that whole deal."

"Probably," Olin said. "I can see how a deer might live here, how it might survive, but I can't see how one might find its way here. You understand the difference?"

"I do, indeed."

"Call me, when you're ready."

Mitchell said he would, and soon. Olin powered up his window.

Watching him wave, driving past the gray-headed coneflowers, Mitchell reached for his soft pack, shaking it upside down until a roach fell into his open palm. He lit it, taking the smoke, thinking, yes sir, if a man was willing to wait long enough, something happened when he got up on a horse and rode into the wild blue yonder. Exhaling, he thought maybe Hasty Kiss craved to be mounted by no man, but Mitchell was thinking metaphorically. As for the talking, maybe this Olin was too sure about this history business. A fort in a hostile territory—suet, where did it say Mitchell would get a sniff at that grant kitty? It didn't. But Mitchell felt like he was out there anyway, riding into the next part of his life.

Yeah, maybe Mitchell was about to buy into a bunch of regulations, stipulations, and connotations. But, for now anyway, that seemed wholesome, for somewhere in his head, he was still riding, just riding along and hearing "Home on the Range." Not the campfire version. No, the voice was almost warbling, bringing new life to an old song with strung-out innocence. No backing instruments, nothing, just the voice of Neil Young. And for the first time in a good, long while, Mitchell didn't feel like crying when Neil got to the part about how the deer and the antelope play.

ABOUT THE AUTHOR

Windsor native Vern Smith grew up 20 minutes from the green ghetto—an actual Detroit phenomenon. His fiction has appeared in *Concrete Forest: The New Fiction of Urban Canada* (McClelland & Stewart), as well as the Insomniac Press anthologies, *Iced, Hard Boiled Love, and Revenge*. His novelette, "The Gimmick," was a finalist for Canada's highest crime-writing honor, the Arthur Ellis Award. A veteran of four newspapers and three magazines, Smith's non-fiction has appeared in *The Detroit Free Press*, *The Ottawa Citizen*, *The Vancouver Sun*, *Eye*, *Broken Pencil*, and *Quill & Quire*, among other publications. He most recently managed CJAM 99.1 FM, where he founded the 24-hour radio marathon Joe Strummer Day to Confront Poverty in Windsor-Detroit. He now lives on the edge of Chicago where urban Illinois meets the prairie.

ACKNOWLEDGEMENTS

Back around the turn of the century, I worked with author/editor Kerry Schooley (AKA John Swan) on three short stories. At the time, *The Green Ghetto* was this wisp of a thing. But even then, Kerry saw something that I couldn't. *The Green Ghetto* wasn't just the title and setting, Kerry told me. No, it was a living thing, a central character, I remember him saying, and to keep that in mind if I was going to make something of this. Well, the years flew by. I moved and lost touch with Kerry while radio ate my brain, then I ended up in quasi-rural America surrounded by animals I'd only seen on TV. One Monday, a blue-eyed beast woke me at five in the morning. That was the moment I decided to make something of this. Recalling Kerry's advice, I looked him up to see if he had a new book, only to learn that he had departed. When I got over the guilt of failing to stay in touch, I decided that the best tribute I could make was to simply let his sage advice forever inform the remaining 96,000 words, and so it did.